D1512123

THE FIVE

Gifts

OF

ILLNESS

ALSO BY JILL SKLAR

The First Year®: Crohn's Disease and Ulcerative Colitis
(2nd edition)

*Eating for Acid Reflux: A Handbook and Cookbook for Those
with Heartburn*
(with Annabel Cohen)

THE FIVE *Gifts* OF ILLNESS

A RECONSIDERATION

JILL SKLAR

Marlowe & Company
New York

For Joel and Jonah

THE FIVE GIFTS OF ILLNESS: *A Reconsideration*
Copyright ©2007 Jill Sklar

Published by
Marlowe & Company
An Imprint of Avalon Publishing Group, Inc.
245 West 17th Street, 11th Floor
New York, NY 10011

AVALON
publishing group incorporated

Library of Congress Cataloging-in-Publication Data

Sklar, Jill.
The five gifts of illness : a reconsideration / Jill Sklar.
p. cm.
Includes bibliographical references.

ISBN-13: 978-1-56924-299-5
ISBN-10: 1-56924-299-2
1. Catastrophic illness--Psychological aspects. 2. Catastrophic illness--Philosophy. I. Title.
R726.5.S555 2007
610--dc22

2007000775

9 8 7 6 5 4 3 2 1

Printed in the United States of America

CONTENTS

INTRODUCTION

Y EARS AGO, I NEVER would have written this. That's because years ago, I would have been dead.

Likely, if I had even been diagnosed with my illness a century or even half that time ago, there would be no effective treatment available to slow its progress. And just as likely, no doctor would have even known what he was looking at anyway, so I probably would have wasted away to nothing and died of an infection.

My great-aunt, Catherine Kiss, a young woman troubled by stomach pains, faced just this fate. Struck by what was then called intestinal tuberculosis, she suffered all of the manifestations of the disease I now have and one that is known to travel genetic lines, Crohn's disease. She had fevers. She lost weight. She had abscesses and fistulas that emptied their contents from her intestines through her back, clear markers of Crohn's. She had black, tarry stools. She had mouth sores. And then, at the age of twenty-four, delirious with fever and weighing just sixty pounds, she died.

I, too, have had Crohn's disease's hallmark signs—the fevers, the abscesses, the fistulas, the weight loss, the intestinal bleeding, the mouth sores, and more. I have lived through five major surgeries, swallowed buckets of pills, and undergone stacks of tests. But now I have lived fourteen years longer than she did and will likely continue to live and thrive, despite having an illness that has nearly killed me more than once. I have also joined a group of people who didn't exist back then, a group of which I am a proud member: survivors.

We are people who live in your neighborhood, shop in your grocery store, take our kids to your kids' school, work out next to you in the gym, toil in the next office or cubicle at your workplace. We share your hopes for a pleasant future and a life filled with dreams realized.

Because of the advancement of medical technology, there is an explosion in our numbers. While Great-aunt Catherine died before she ever married, I found a man I loved and married him, had a child, became a slave to my mortgage, developed a career—all well after diagnosis. I will likely see a few more decades, retire, and enjoy my grandchildren when they come, all while pumping medications into my system and undergoing further surgeries to arrest the very disease manifestations that Catherine could not.

And the same is true for people who most certainly would have died but for the most amazing scientific discoveries and inventions. Diabetes, heart disease, and cancer patients can, for the most part, look forward to the same things that I do as advances in early detection, diagnosis, and treatments have rendered even the scariest diseases into chronic states with possible acute phases. Autoimmune diseases have been identified and treatments developed for them, leaving less of a death toll in that area as well and allowing the individuals who have those diseases to pursue lives as fulfilling as the ones who are entirely well.

Still, while we share so many characteristics of individuals who have never faced diagnosis and treatment for grave diseases, we are different from them and we know it. It is as if diagnosis propelled us into a foreign land. Sure, we can come back and visit the land of the well, but there is permanent residency in the land of the ill. Once you have had the experience of having the length of your days threatened by a serious illness, you are never, ever the same.

Surprising to some, life after a diagnosis and treatment for a life-threatening illness can have unexpectedly positive attributes, as this generally is a life of greater strength, of newfound wisdom about what is really important. It can be a life in which there is a growing respect for nurturing relationships, where emotions and general tenderness are more easily felt and dealt with, where time takes on a new characteristic, and where there is a greater commitment to the well-being of the body. This is a life where trivial issues and relationships are recognized for what they are and dismissed. It is a life where helping others through rough times takes on a greater significance than it ever did.

But perhaps more obvious are the bad aspects of disease. Once touched by illness, individuals have a hard time accepting the loss of a life to which they simply felt entitled, a life that others have and don't seem to appreciate. This was a life we seemingly were promised at birth, one without scary tests and even more frightening periods of time until the results were rendered, an existence without taxing treatments that robbed us of our expectation of physical normality, whatever that meant. We weren't promised a life that still feels squeezed by fear, even after the treatments have ended and remission or cure was declared. No, we were assured of an existence in which the biggest worries included the safety of our children and our own prosperity, an existence that those not touched by illness seem to enjoy so effortlessly. Now, however, we are given a life marked by grief over the loss of what we thought *should have* happened and the impenetrable sadness over what *has* happened.

What we are dealing with now is not necessarily the physical mark of illness and the threat of imminent death. Instead, we struggle with a life that did not return to its normal and anticipated trajectory following the experience of diagnosis and treatment, yet will continue for a long, long time. We are blessed by our good fortune of having second or more chances and haunted by the experience of having stood at the abyss, knowing that someday we must return.

This new state of survivorship is something that has not been written about in the past. There is an expectation that continues to be held by the medical establishment and by those who have not experienced illness that once treatment is successful—no matter how scary and physically awful it was—the patient will no longer be a patient and that life will return to its prediagnosis state. Because of this prevailing wisdom, there are very few services available to people who survive diagnosis and treatment for most chronic or acute life-threatening illnesses. All of this depends upon the type of disease as well as where one lives, of course; however, beyond the support groups that are meant for those newly diagnosed and still shell-shocked by the change illness has thrust into their lives, there remains little in the way of programs to facilitate social and emotional well-being for long-term survivors.

What you are holding in your hands right now is one of the first books to examine this shared experience. It is a phenomenological exploration into the lives of survivors of chronic or acute life-threatening illness, a look into the positive and negative aspects of illness. It is also a diagram of sorts, one that concludes with different suggested paths and actions for improving the lives of survivors of serious illness.

The motivation for it began out of my own personal experiences, an idea that gelled as I was working on the introduction to my first book, *The First Year®: Crohn's Disease and Ulcerative Colitis.* I had written then that while I wouldn't wish the disease on my meanest sister, I wouldn't choose never to have experienced it, either: "Sure, the disease has had a profound impact in my life. But the impact has not been entirely bad. As a result of being ill, I developed a greater level of patience with others. I have had the opportunity to meet fantastically compassionate people—in person and on the Internet—I never would have met without the disease. I have learned more than I think I ever wanted to know about the human digestive system. I am more sensitive to the personal pain of those who are ill, no matter what their diagnosis. And I realize what is really, really important in my life, something that usually doesn't happen until late in life, if at all. For these things, I am extremely grateful."

I knew as I finished that paragraph that someday I would be writing *this* introduction. The truth is that the seed had been planted two years before, while I was spending time in isolation in the hospital for a very serious infection related to the treatment of my disease. It was during one of those sleepless nights at the hospital, tossing and turning to try to find a comfortable spot on the plastic-covered mattress, that I realized that the disease I had wasn't all bad, that there were wonderful things I had gained because I had suffered. I had known true misery from the illness, but that night I also discovered the proverbial other side of the coin.

I tried to find a book about the subject, but none existed. Sure, there were support groups to help the newly diagnosed and individual books on my disease that covered the finer points of treatment options, but there was nothing specifically for me, someone more than a decade out from initial diagnosis, someone who was still fumbling through this illness experience. As a journalist who specializes in medical writing, I started researching the topic, finding tons of scientific papers on the negative impact illness had on the quality of life of survivors of different diseases, but far, far less on the positive aspects. I devoured any book that had anything to do with any aspect of the illness experience. Then, I began interviewing over a hundred survivors of various chronic and acute life-threatening illnesses. That was when my eyes were opened to this huge community, their shared experiences, and their needs.

The Five Gifts of Illness: A Reconsideration is written by me, a writer who has authored two books on medical subjects as well as numerous health stories for many different publications. I am neither a psychologist nor a medical doctor, nor do I want to be one. Instead, I wanted to write a guide, based on extensive research, for those who are facing these illnesses and for their loved ones who want to understand the experience they cannot share.

The book is divded into three parts. The first, "Starting

at Point A," comprises the first three chapters, which provide an individual and global view of survivorship; it also lays the groundwork for understanding the five gifts of illness as they are presented in the next part. It opens with my experience, something I know best and something that was the impetus for the book. Believe me, if I could have written all of this without it, I would have. But one friend said, "You have to bear witness to it." And so I have. That chapter segues into the next, a more global view of survivorship in the past and as it is today. Here we begin to see that survivorship is really a relatively modern concept that is due to the vast changes in medicine. The first part concludes by detailing the process of grief as it applies to the illness experience, drawing parallels with Dr. Elisabeth Kübler-Ross's established work on the subject but expanding on it with the illustrative comments from the interview participants.

The second part, "Finding the Five Gifts of Illness," cuts a brand-new path in the understanding of illness. Tying in the idea of finding meaning in traumatic events as articulated by Dr. Viktor Frankl, the concept of illumination—the process of finding worth in suffering—is explored. The following five chapters in the second part highlight individually each of the five gifts of illness. Using excerpts from interviews of more than a hundred survivors of chronic or acute life-threatening illness surveyed for this book, as well as information from nearly three dozen published studies on the subject of survivorship, I show the positive transformative effects illness has on a person's life. In these chapters, I examine the impact the five gifts had on the survivors' lives, including how these individuals experienced their emotions differently, how they developed a new appreciation for time and being, how they reset their priorities, how they developed a different perspective on—and found enrichment in—personal relationships, and how they feel a need to help others through a new sense of activism.

The third and final part of the book not only establishes the value of the five gifts, it offers suggestions for individuals to attain the gifts and for the greater humanity to create a nurturing atmosphere for survivors. This part, "Moving Beyond Point B," starts with a chapter that proves what the patients saw as the value of illness in their lives. Each interviewee was asked, if the choice was offered, whether he or she would choose a different path and avoid illness while forgoing the gifts of illness, or whether he or she would relive the experience with the struggle and the gifts intact. Their overwhelming yet surprising answers attest to the worth of the gifts. The last chapter combines the suggestions of both the interviewees and experts working in the field of survivorship to create steps to help individuals who are newly diagnosed adjust to their new lives and to provide the rest of the world with suggestions on how to create a better climate in which survivors can flourish more easily.

As you can see from the above three paragraphs, this is not a medical book to help the reader navigate a particular disease. Books on cancer alone could fill a library, not to mention other common diseases such as diabetes or heart disease. Those who are sick absolutely should have those books to help make the best decisions regarding the course of treatment and to enable them to become the best advocates for their own health.

Because this isn't a medical book, there isn't a prescription in the following pages, nor is there a particular map to follow to get from point A to point B. Each person is different and each experience is unique. Some may experience one emotion or change more profoundly than the rest; others may even experience something that isn't written in these pages. What will be found are the most common changes those interviewed for the book went through following their diagnosis and treatment. Just because they didn't experience it en masse doesn't invalidate what another individual is going through.

Whether you are an ill individual grappling with a serious diagnosis or a loved one or medical professional caring for such a person, my hope for you, the reader, is that you discover something no less than revolutionary in the ideas discussed in the pages that follow. Just as Nicolaus Copernicus disabused the world of the idea that Earth was the center of the solar system, I hope to dismiss forever the received wisdom, passed down through generations before us, that illness is completely dreadful and entirely devoid of redeeming value. My hope is that the reader finishes this book learning and believing that there are attainable, positive transformative effects within the experience of serious illness—worthwhile and life-altering gifts for those who undergo the experience.

PART I

Starting at Point A

1

MY STORY: HOW THE HELL DID I GET HERE?

YOU KNOW THE FEELING. Just about everyone I have spoken with does. You start out at point A and hop in your car for point B. Somewhere along the way, perhaps even before you put the keys in the ignition, you are distracted by what is going on in your life. Maybe it is your significant other and thoughts of something that has happened between you. Maybe it is some sort of home repair or chore that you have been putting off. Maybe it is some facet of your work that intrigues you. Or maybe it is a memory, happy or sad, that wrests control of your thoughts and yanks your conscious mind away from the task at hand.

Whatever it is, you arrive at your destination, point B, and are somewhat befuddled as to how you got there. Sure, the car's hood is still warm or the engine is making soft cranking sounds that let you know it has indeed been driven. Yet while the keys are still in your hand, you can't remember a single turn, traffic light, or stop sign along the route. For some reason, the journey was erased by whatever it was that captured your attention.

That is how I felt when I stood in the stark October sunlight one afternoon in 2002, watching my son racing through a playground.

MY LIFE BEFORE ILLNESS

But before I get to that point B, I'll bring you with me to what it was like to be at point A. This was February, that time in a Michigan winter when it hurts to breathe as you stand in the bitterly cold air beneath a sunless sky. It was 1989 and I was technically a junior in college, having finished a semester of college while still in high school. I was barely twenty and attending Wayne State University in Detroit.

Life was fairly good. And really, how can't it be when you are young and the world is at your feet? School was my world then. I was a straight-A student, working toward a degree in journalism and English literature, two favorite subjects about which I am still passionate. My family—a big, loud group consisting then of my mom, my dad, six brothers and sisters, and a handful of nieces and nephews— were all pretty much supportive of my efforts. My professors were pleased with my work as well, giving me high marks and encouraging me to interview for the major internships. I couldn't get enough of the academic environment and thrived, so much so that I eventually captured a major award for my efforts upon graduation.

Outside of school, life was also ticking along beautifully. I had a great group of girlfriends, all pursuing university degrees, our dreams, and hot guys at the same time. To burn off energy, we would meet each Saturday night at one house or another and make each other up for a night of excess before heading into Canada—the land of the lower drinking age—to try on our budding adulthood in bars and dance clubs. On the way back across the border, we would laugh at our individual exploits, throwing phone numbers we had collected out the window and into the dark, cool night air while making plans for the next weekend.

In addition to having this group of friends, I spent part of my time at a job at a dry cleaner, where I had met a really sweet, handsome man. Joel was a customer, a young lawyer who brought his shirts in for cleaning but hung around for hours just to talk. We had started dating and things were going remarkably well, despite a ten-year age gap. We loved to laugh, to go to movies with subtitles, to try out new restaurants, to talk about culture or politics, or just to spend a quiet evening together.

Life was good.

MY LIFE WITH ILLNESS

So when the stomach pains started on the morning of February 1, I didn't really lend them much weight. My primary care physician at the time, not the greatest of diagnosticians despite his reputation for being so, had told me in the past that my recurring stomach pains, nausea, and diarrhea were related to stress. "Irritable bowel syndrome," he declared after patting my belly and asking my grade point average. "Eat more fiber and try to deal with the stress" were his instructions. Eating better wasn't terribly difficult, but cutting out stress was like cutting out breathing. Still, I vowed to make an effort.

That morning started with an hour-long Jane Fonda

workout tape and a bowl of oat bran cereal before a quick shower and a half-hour drive to school. The first pains caught my attention during Monsieur Renard's French class. The gripping pains made me catch my breath as they held for a few seconds before passing. I staggered across campus, attempting to make my classes but eventually giving in to the nausea and pain and driving home. It is incredible, sometimes, what you will put up with when you know something is really wrong but are so in denial about it. Still, something told me that this was nothing to mess with.

Persistent vomiting without any relief from the pain forced me to the emergency room at a local hospital. After spending nine hours in agony curled on an ER stretcher with no letup in symptoms, the doctors decided I had appendicitis and said surgery was required that night.

To say I was frightened would be an understatement. Up to that point in life, I had not suffered anything more serious than a couple of broken bones in elementary school and an ovarian cyst in high school. Now I not only had to have surgery, but because I was technically an adult, I also had to sign the papers granting permission for it to occur. In the two years since I had officially passed from childhood into adulthood, I had done nothing more momentous than open a checking account, vote in a presidential election, and get into a male strip club, none of which carried with it the risk of imminent death. But the doctor stressed that I really didn't have a choice, as time was of the essence. Through a veil of tears, I signed the forms with a shaky hand and went ahead with the surgery.

As I slept, the surgeon cut my belly open. He had been so sure when he told me what was wrong, so confident as to his diagnostic skills as to put me under the knife. Imagine his surprise when, after opening the right side of my abdomen, he found a large amount of yellow-tinged liquid—not a good thing. Further, after delving into the surgical wound, the appendix, and part of the intestine to which it is attached, he discovered not only that they appeared normal but that the intestine next to them was not. In his surgical notes, he said that the loop had the appearance of red, cracked leather instead of a smooth, pinkish-purple look and soft, pliable feel. "It became clear that this was a markedly inflamed terminal ileum consistent with inflammatory bowel disease which was limited to the terminal ileum," he later recorded in the medical records of that day. The pathology report later confirmed this rather delayed discovery of Crohn's disease.

The next morning, he very curtly rendered his diagnosis. He told me quickly how the disease was treated and that there was no known cause or cure for it. But what I am sure he didn't know was how much my life would change from that moment forward.

For many people, especially those looking for a reason for their symptoms, such a diagnosis would be a relief of sorts. But for me, the diagnosis really marked the beginning of the suffering. After I was finally able to eat again, I was forced to swallow handfuls of medication daily in an attempt to control the symptoms and fight infections. The medications, including the dreaded prednisone, gave me insomnia, mood swings, uncontrolled weight gain, and acne. Additionally, I wasn't used to taking medication for longer than two weeks at a time. My experience with illness in the past had taught me that things were usually resolved with a short course of medicine, but I wasn't getting better. I was still tired and still taking all of this medicine that didn't seem to help. I became obstructed again and was forced into another hospitalization, during which I was prepped for surgery for the second time as my intestines were on the verge of rupturing.

To top things off, I looked like a ghost then. Because Crohn's causes intestinal bleeding, my red blood cell count had dropped well into the anemic range, leaving my skin a sickly pale color and throwing off my balance. My hair was falling out due to the trauma of the surgery and to the malnourishment caused by the disease, which also left me extraordinarily skinny. One day during my second hospitalization, an orderly came to pick me up for some additional tests. As we were waiting for an elevator, he told me that his sister had what I had. "Oh, she has Crohn's disease, too?" I asked, hugging the thin hospital gown to my practically skeletal, 90-pound, 5-foot, 7-inch frame.

"No, she's anorexic. Aren't you?" he asked.

To say that my life truly sucked would be accurate. I was too sick to join my friends on what would have been my first spring break, a raucous time in any young person's life. When they returned tanned and filled with stories, I became further depressed. I didn't seem to fit in anymore; I lacked the energy for the late-night parties or for dancing in bars, couldn't digest the pizza and beer after classes, and couldn't stray far from bathrooms. As I look back on it now, I can see that the changes I went through were just too weighty for them to incorporate in their carefree lives. One by one, they stopped calling. It has been sixteen years since I have seen or heard from any of them.

My relationship with Joel suffered as well. Though his father—ironically—is a specialist in the disease, Joel backed off quickly. Two weeks after I left the hospital, he suggested that we take a break from the relationship for a while.

School was not much better. I nearly withdrew from my classes, having missed four weeks of the thirteen-week term. I was so far behind that I thought I would never catch up. One professor, a nasty woman with halitosis who never cleared foaming spit from the corners of her mouth as she talked, told me to drop her class or face a grade that would jeopardize my scholarship. But her uncaring attitude toward me and my intense dislike for her gave me the steel I needed to stick it out, earning my lowest grade point average ever but retaining my scholarship.

By the end of the term, I couldn't believe how much my life had changed. I had the worst report card ever, and my boyfriend was ready to bolt. Others were migrating away from me because a disease that they couldn't catch and that I didn't want had grabbed hold of me and wouldn't let go. I faced a future of four more surgeries, gallons of barium and other nasty preparations swallowed for painful tests, and countless days crying in the bathroom from the pain and fatigue.

I was depressed—and who could blame me? I grieved for the life I had before that moment in the hospital room when I had first heard of Crohn's disease and the fact that I had it. Even though my symptoms could be traced back for more than a decade, it seemed that I had crossed a line that very second, from being among the healthy to being among the sick. And I knew, as early as it was in my experience with illness at that point, that I would never be able to go back to being the person I was before the diagnosis was shared with me. I hated my new life. I hated being sick. I didn't want any of it, and I couldn't believe my great misfortune.

LIFE THROWS ANOTHER TWIST

Fast-forward thirteen years to that playground I mentioned earlier. The leaves that spent the summer clinging to tree branches were gold, and stirring in a light breeze at my feet as I watched Jonah, the son Joel and I share, race across the playground. While I watched him play, I usually struck up conversations with other parents, some of whom I knew, as this was one of Jonah's favorite haunts. Usually, we caught up on each other's lives or just bitched about a variety of subjects. One mother battled her weight through an ever-changing routine, about which she shared her trials and tribulations. Another talked seemingly ceaselessly about charity work she did. Still another frequently discoursed about home improvement projects—the good, the bad, and the downright ugly. Two parents complained about spouses they would soon divorce and how they were coping with it.

But this day was different. I was talking to someone I'd known for a month, someone I discovered had gone through a very serious disease and its treatment and was now in remission. I was struggling through a flare-up of my own disease. The topic was illness. We compared notes on prednisone and what it had done to us, sharing pictures of bloated faces and war stories of being awake at 4 a.m. while struggling through monster mood swings. We both agreed that the person who invented it should be shot, if he hadn't been already.

As we bitched about the effects of our respective diseases,

I broached a topic that I hadn't talked about with many others but had been thinking about for a few years. Taking what I considered a leap, since I didn't really know this person that well, I suggested that Crohn's disease, as awful and physically degrading as it was, had a really profound effect on my life in a positive sense. I was sure I would get only a quizzical stare, but that didn't happen. Instead, this person agreed. We started ticking off certain changes in our lives that happened to us because of our diseases—positive things. For example, we both met some incredible people we wouldn't have met but for our illnesses. We found that our sense of humor was sharpened because of what we endured. We experienced all kinds of emotions (joy, fear, disappointment, sadness) differently now than we did before we were diagnosed. Our definitions of success had changed. The direction and, to varying extents, the meaning of our lives altered because of the experience.

I walked away from that playground asking, "How the *hell* did I get here?" How had I gone from the devastation and grief I had felt when I was first diagnosed to actually believing with all my being that my disease had had such a profoundly positive effect on me? I was standing there with the keys of my life still in my hand, wondering how I had gotten from point A to point B without being cognizant of the twists and turns in the journey along the way. I'd spoken to others about my feelings since I realized these positive changes a few years back, and each had looked at me as if I were crazy or just plain Pollyannaish. Now it struck me that the individuals with whom I had spoken were all well and had never gone through the experience of illness.

Maybe, I reasoned, this was a mystery that occurred to those who had the same experiences I had. So I started by interviewing a number of people with acute or chronic potentially life-threatening illnesses, including diabetes type 1, an assortment of cancers, inflammatory bowel disease, and an exceedingly rare brain disease. I also put my hands on every conceivable research study on the subject, trying to find out what the experts had to say about it. The result is the book you are holding in your hands.

WHERE WE ARE GOING

I am not going to throw in a spoiler here, but I will tell you this: It seems that, no matter what the disease, we all suffered physically, mourned our misfortune, and at some point began to see how our lives had changed in a positive way. I am not saying that the diseases get the credit because, really, we all struggled in the wake of their physical devastation. Rather, it appears that in handling the diseases and their manifestations, in learning to cope with the circular aspects of grief, we became human beings who have grown in our compassion and understanding, who have a different perspective because of what we have experienced, and who have an appreciation of life that we might not have found otherwise but for the trials we went through. And in this process, we discovered gifts in the experience of illness, surprising and unexpected redemptive aspects that enriched our lives immeasurably.

I can't share with you a specific process of getting from point A to point B. Everyone is different, and I have learned that every journey is different. So many of us, when we are diagnosed with a potentially life-threatening acute or chronic illness, see so very much loss. That, and the grieving that follows, is expected. We have to meander through a new and uncharted course of learning to let go of what we felt we were entitled to while clinging tightly to our second chance, giving what we can to do it justice, and hoping it doesn't end too soon. But if I could go back to that twenty-year-old version of me, the one who was horrified and terrified by the diagnosis of Crohn's, and say what I have learned, I would tell her that it sure as hell hurt but that the disease brought me so much more than the physical pain. It bolstered my life and my experiences in ways I could never have imagined.

Now I am a medical writer, a career path very much influenced by my disease experience. I am not an expert in anything but my own experience, but it was valuable and I hope to share it and others' experiences with you, the reader.

2

SURVIVORSHIP: A GROWING COMMUNITY

Surviving chronic or acute life-threatening illness is a relatively new concept in the history of civilization. Looking back over the last millennium, most individuals were lucky to survive long enough to reach adulthood, leading most to see the age of thirty not as the beginning of life but rather as old age. The possibility of not only being diagnosed with a life-threatening illness but surviving one was rare, at best.

Just look at the situation in America in the past hundred years. If you were an American at the turn of the last century, you could expect to live about forty-seven years on average. If you lived to that advanced age, you most likely would have dodged a potentially deadly bout of a bacterial or viral illness like influenza, a gastrointestinal flu, pneumonia, or tuberculosis, largely because a third of all deaths in 1900 were attributed to those contagious conditions.

And if you developed a life-threatening acute or chronic condition at that time, you also could pretty much forget about planning your retirement. Back then, the medical establishment and all of their resources could do little to stop disease, as knowledge had not advanced enough to offer effective treatments. For example, people diagnosed with insulin-dependent diabetes generally died within months of a diagnosis. For cancer patients, it was nearly as bad: 20 percent of cancer patients in 1930 lived to see a five-year survival and beyond. If you survived a heart attack or developed heart disease, there wasn't a whole lot doctors could offer to you in the way of treatment, much less hope for a long life.

But as years went by, medical knowledge advanced and accumulated. Within the last century, the vast number of inventions—including the development of antibiotics, chemotherapy, steroids, and insulin, to name a few—have changed in dramatic fashion the way we live as well as the way we die.

A CURRENT VIEW OF SURVIVORSHIP

Today, an American has an average life expectancy of 77.6 years. That is three full decades longer than it was a century ago, an increase the length of which has never before occurred in a similar time span in the history of humankind. Americans now pretty much shrug off most viral and bacterial illnesses. While influenza and pneumonia still claim 2.6 percent of all deaths, neither tuberculosis nor gastrointestinal viral illness registered among the fifteen leading causes of death, as recorded by the National Center for Health Statistics (NCHS), one of the Centers for Disease Control and Prevention (CDC). Though there still is no cure for these common ailments, much of this improvement in survivability is attributed to the development of antibiotics and vaccines, as well as the increased knowledge about how our common daily activities such as basic hygiene, food safety, healthful diet, and exercise increase our chances of remaining healthy and living longer.

The same positive trend holds for those diagnosed with a chronic or acute life-threatening illness, as you are far less likely to die quickly of these causes now than you were a hundred years ago. Medical technology, including discoveries each day that further the knowledge about causation and treatment for most diseases, has made extraordinary advances, leaving a wider chasm between incidence rates and death rates than existed in 1900 and creating an ever larger pool of survivors. Here are a few examples of such changes:

- Heart disease is the leading killer in the United States, claiming 684,462 lives in 2002. But the percentage of deaths it represents has actually dropped in the last few decades. According to the American Heart Association (AHA), cardiovascular deaths, such as from strokes, declined 18 percent, while coronary heart disease death rates fell 26.5 percent between 1992 and 2002. An increasing knowledge of the importance of a healthful lifestyle, easier accessibility to heart defibrillator machines in public places, more awareness of the manifestations of heart disease in women, and a greater understanding of the role of genetics and other causative factors have led to the overall decrease, which is expected to continue in the coming years. In living with these diseases, patients can be sustained to a much greater degree with better medications such as thrombolytic, or "clot-busting," drugs and beta blockers, and cardiac events can be avoided with greater knowledge of predictors such as the presence of high levels of C-reactive protein in the blood, as well as consistent vigilant actions such as blood pressure monitoring. Even when heart transplant is the only option for treatment in cardiac disease, the survival rates and times have increased with the advent of immune-suppressing drugs such as azathioprine and cyclosporine.

- Cancer follows heart disease as the number two killer in the United States, accounting for 554,643 deaths in 2003. But whereas the survival rate in 1930 was one in five, nearly two-thirds of all people diagnosed with cancer today can expect to live five years or more after diagnosis. Improved early-detection techniques and advances in treatments in virtually every kind of cancer have led to this survival increase. In breast cancer alone, death rates dropped 2.3 percent per year between 1990 and 2000, the American Cancer Society (ACS) reports. The five-year relative survival rate in localized breast cancer climbed from 72 percent in the 1940s to 97 percent today. In leukemia in general, the five-year survival rate in the early 1960s was a dismal 14 percent, but by 2000, it had more than tripled to 46 percent. While not exactly a heartwarming statistic, it promises to climb with new drugs such as imatinib, nilotinib, and dasatinib for certain forms of leukemia and continued improved survival rates in stem cell transplantation.

- Diabetes as a whole contributed to more than two hundred thirteen thousand deaths in the United States in 2000 alone, according to the CDC. While the incidence of diabetes is climbing, the survival rates and times are increasing as a result of the introduction of insulin for type 1 patients and the accumulated knowledge about contributing lifestyle factors and the development of new medications like metformin in type 2 patients. Prior to these developments, survival for diabetic patients was measured in months, perhaps a few years. Now, the twenty-year survival rate for type 1 diabetes is 94 percent, and 84 percent at thirty years, according to *Diabetes in America, 2nd Edition* (National Institutes of Health Publication No. 95-1468); type 2 patients will likely see their life spans shortened by five to ten years, as opposed to several decades, as was the case in the past.

- Transplantation science was a mere dream at the turn of the last century, with scientists just beginning to experiment on farm animals. Kidneys were the first to be transplanted in humans in 1954, and the first heart transplant took place in 1967. Although the first transplanted patients did not survive for long, the advancement in antirejection medications, the increase in knowledge about the importance of tissue typing, and the growth in the awareness of the need for organ donation have led to greater availability of organs and longer survival times for hundreds of thousands of patients who would most certainly have died early deaths a hundred years ago; in 2006 alone, nearly ninety-five thousand people awaited a transplant of at least one organ and about twenty-three of those received their transplants. Further gains in this area are expected with the development of machines that act as organs, allowing the most gravely ill patients to live longer while they wait for organs to become available.

- Even diseases discovered in the last fifty years have seen significant treatment advances. One great example of this is in blood-borne viral diseases such as AIDS and hepatitis C. While the early patients with these diseases had bleak, shortened futures, some current patients are able to arrest disease progression or to erase the presence of the viruses from the blood with antiviral medications developed in the last decade. Even when damage is extensive in hepatitis C patients, there is usually the option of liver transplantation; in fact, hepatitis C has replaced alcoholic hepatitis as the number one reason for such a surgery.

- Chronic illnesses such as inflammatory bowel disease, multiple sclerosis, rheumatoid arthritis, lupus, and scleroderma have all benefited from the development of medications in other areas of disease treatments. Steroids and immune-suppressing medications, developed for cancer and transplant treatment, have allowed many individuals with these conditions to live longer, more comfortable lives. The development of biologic medications in the last decade alone promises to further this success, leaving the patients with fewer side effects and more targeted treatments.

What all of this means is that diseases that would most likely have killed a person quickly within the past century are now, to a large extent, highly treatable, if not curable. Because of this and other healthful lifestyle information, Americans are now living decades longer, even with acute or chronic life-threatening illnesses. In fact, it is estimated that 50 percent of individuals in North America alone have or have had such an acute or chronic condition, making us very much a culture of survivors.

SURVIVORS REFLECTED IN CULTURE

But while the medical and surgical science of survival has clearly accelerated, the art of navigating life beyond diagnosis and treatment lags woefully behind, as being diagnosed with a serious illness is still akin to receiving an automatic death sentence in most areas of our daily lives. Whereas years ago people wouldn't even discuss above the level of a whisper having an illness such as cancer, we are not much further evolved, as we are barely beginning to see a culture of survivors emerge, perhaps too slowly given the rapid change in survival rates of all diseases.

Nowhere is this slow pace more pronounced than in the most visible and omnipresent part of our daily lives: the popular media and entertainment sector. Major daily newspapers print multipart series chronicling the tragic death of a young person due to a major illness. In the Detroit area alone, the *Detroit Free Press* started out 2005 with a touching story about a young bride who died following her wish-fulfilling wedding after a long battle with cancer, while the *Detroit News* featured a four-part series the next year chronicling the colorectal cancer death of a mother of three young children; three days after the *News's* story appeared, the *Free Press* countered with a story about a boy's high school graduation pushed up so his mother, dying of cancer, could witness it. While the 2005 Pulitzer Prize for beat reporting was awarded to Amy Dockser Marcus of the *Wall Street*

Journal "for her masterful stories about patients, families and physicians that illuminated the often unseen world of cancer survivors," the prize committee declared, the subject of survival is not an otherwise popular one.

Nor is survival of a life-threatening illness a particularly popular subject of movies, on either the big or small screen. In fact, one would never know that cancer or other serious illnesses are survivable if information were received solely from major motion pictures. Any individual would be hard-pressed to find more than a handful of titles of films wherein the main character contracts a life-threatening illness and actually lives through the treatment and into a life of remission and beyond. In one, *The Doctor*, starring William Hurt, the main character is diagnosed with throat cancer, realizes what it is like to be a patient while undergoing treatment and meeting other cancer patients (one in particular, played by Elizabeth Perkins, dies in the end), changes the way he and other physicians practice by humanizing the way patients are treated—and lives. In another, *Something's Gotta Give*, an older man played by Jack Nicholson has a heart attack while attempting intercourse with the latest in a string of much younger babes. He changes his life, falls in love with a woman closer to his age, and commits to a relationship for the first time in his life.

But these are rarities in a slew of Hollywood productions that follow the same plot scenario: Young person in prime of life is struck by illness, struggles through treatment while discovering how to live a better life, and dies. Here is just a brief list of such movies in recent memory:

Life as a House—A man with a lovely family buys a piece of property overlooking the ocean and decides to build a dream house, all while struggling with painful and terminal metastatic cancer. The family rallies around him, building a strong relationship with him as he finishes the house. Man dies.

Brian's Song—A white football player befriends a black teammate, enjoys young family and success on the field, gets cancer, fights to live. Football player dies.

One True Thing—A mother builds life of traditional values and household perfection but is struck with cancer. Progressive, college-educated daughter returns home to care for the mother, learns that the traditional values carry meaning, rebuilds relationship with mother. Mother dies.

Big Fish—Father and son are estranged for years, as son thinks father never told a true tale in his life. Son returns home for dad's final days of a struggle with cancer and learns that dad was not all bad, that the stories not only held some truth but served a purpose. Father dies.

My Life—Husband flits through life with superficial goals, is diagnosed with lung cancer while wife discovers she is pregnant. He records touching videos for unborn child that show he has had a change of heart on what is important in life. Husband dies.

Love Story—Girl from wrong side of tracks and Harvard student fall madly in love, despite his wealthy parents' objections. Pair marries, tries to conceive but fail. Leukemia is discovered. Girl dies.

Beaches—Two girls, one wealthy but from a restrictive background, the other a street performer from an eclectic family, become fast friends under a boardwalk in New Jersey, grow up together, and see each other through success in life and ruinous love relationships. Friend number one contracts rare heart condition and needs even rarer heart transplant to survive; through this, friend number two realizes what is important in life. Friend number one dies.

Finding Neverland—Woman with four boys meets playwright, friendship develops between mother and playwright, children and playwright. Tubercular illness develops in mother. Mother dies.

Meet Joe Black—Man meets death in the form of a near-fatal heart attack and agrees to give a very handsome personification of Death a guided tour of life while realizing what is really important in his own life—family love, not money. Man dies.

Terms of Endearment—Mother and daughter have very different views on life and love but come together finally when daughter's husband proves to be an incurable cheat at the same time that she is diagnosed with incurable cancer. Daughter dies.

Steel Magnolias—A traditional Southern mother learns

she can't control forever the life of her daughter, who struggles with type 1 diabetes. Daughter marries and, despite doctors' orders, decides to follow her dream to become a mother. Daughter ruins kidneys in the process, so mother donates kidney to her. Daughter dies.

Forrest Gump—Mentally challenged yet strangely gifted boy has two great loves in his life: his mother and the girl next door. Mother contracts cancer; girlfriend contracts AIDS. Mother and girlfriend die.

And the list goes on and on. A search of the Internet Movie Database (IMDB.com) found more than two hundred such films that mention cancer specifically in the plot—all but two involve the individual with the disease dying at some point. With different illnesses in general plot lines, the outcome is larger yet equally depressing.

Some strides have been made outside culture's popular media and entertainment sector, however, largely in the last ten to fifteen years. There have been a number of interesting memoirs, biographies, and autobiographies of celebrities who have survived serious bouts of illness. Many of these books have become best sellers, if only for a brief time. The tennis champion Arthur Ashe and the comedian Gilda Radner wrote incredibly touching stories of their lives and their battles with illness, even if they didn't survive to see the eventual successes of the books, and both of their lives were featured in televised biopics. The film critic Joel Siegel's *Lessons for Dylan: From Father to Son* describes his battle with colon cancer and his relationship with his then four-year-old son, which he fears will be all too brief. In *Lucky*

Man: A Memoir, the actor Michael J. Fox illustrates how his struggle with the effects of Parkinson's disease changed his life for the better. While these books have not made great fodder for major motion pictures or even televised movies, they have helped to raise awareness of the individual diseases as well as of the fact that people can and do survive them while thriving, at times under the great physical burden that illness thrusts upon them.

One autobiography in particular has most caught the public's attention as a survivor in recent years. Lance Armstrong, a champion bicyclist, burst onto the scene when he became not only the second American to win the revered Tour de France but also the first cancer survivor to do so. Armstrong later detailed his struggle with advanced-stage testicular cancer and survivorship in his first memoir, *It's Not about the Bike: My Journey Back to Life*, and again in his follow-up book, *Every Second Counts*.

Beyond the books' popularity, Armstrong's eponymous foundation has made its mission advancing the case of cancer survivorship, partnering with other organizations to provide survivorship services to those living "with, beyond, and through" cancer. That phrase appears over and over in a joint effort between the Lance Armstrong Foundation (LAF) and the CDC to address the variety of issues faced by survivors of cancer. Called *A National Action Plan for Cancer Survivorship: Advancing Public Health Strategies*, the seventy-seven-page report issued in 2004 articulates the various needs of such survivors and sets forth a strategy to address them through education and support services.

The LAF, through its education component known as LiveStrong, also pierced the American psyche by adopting a symbol of survivorship: the yellow LiveStrong rubber bracelet. Introduced in 2004, more than 40 million of the bracelets were sold by the foundation in one year. Other organizations quickly adopted the format, changing the colors of and messages on the bracelets for their own purposes, nearly all of which illuminated the plight of those living with chronic and acute illnesses.

The bracelets followed the idea of the ribbon campaigns started in 1991, when the red ribbon came to symbolize AIDS and was similarly adopted with different colors denoting different illnesses (blue for colon cancer, pink for breast cancer, etc.). The major difference, of course, was that the ribbons symbolized awareness of body counts and tragedies, not specifically survivorship.

A GROWING FIELD OF STUDY

Though individual and cultural awareness on the topic of survivorship hasn't quite caught fire, in the past thirty years social scientists have been slowly but steadily gaining ground on certain aspects of the experience of illness and life after illness. They have looked into the unique experiences of heart attack survivors, of diabetes patients, of those affected by multiple sclerosis for months and years after diagnosis. Even in cancer, where there is inarguably the largest pool of data and studies available, the researchers have looked at everything from the experience of the moment of diagnosis to the lingering impact of the disease on life five or more years after treatment ends, from general emotional themes affecting survivors of various forms of the disease to the impact on spirituality from site-specific cancers such as breast, ovarian, colon, and hematological.

Taken as a whole, what these studies tell us is that although surviving a life-threatening acute or chronic illness is an experience unique to each individual, certain themes and ideas appear to recur more generally. For example, the financial, emotional, spiritual, and physical side effects of illness have been examined. The findings, however, are not entirely balanced, and they almost exclusively focus on the obvious negative impact on a person's quality of life. This may be because the negative impact is so easy to see, so visible to the patient as well as to the unbiased, trained researcher. The stump of the amputee suffering from diabetes, the scar on the deflated chest of the breast cancer patient, the oxygen tubing hugging the nose of the heart patient, the shaking limbs of a Parkinson's patient, the colostomy bag attached to the belly of the colitis patient, the bald head of the patient undergoing chemotherapy—these are all patently visible signs of a struggle with an illness and its less-than-positive physical effects. One need look no further than the stack of hospital bills not covered even under the most permissive health plans or the careers threatened with extinction to see the financial burden of illness. Emotional and spiritual distress are not hard to recognize in the patient who asks why something as terrible as a life-threatening illness happened to him or her, or in the survivor who agonizes over recurrence during a regular visit to the doctor. These negative tolls can easily seem overwhelming and insurmountable, more so in the eyes of those who have never gone through such trials.

Harder to see but no less valid, however, are the positive

transformative effects of illness on an individual's life, the gifts of illness. And yet this one area not extensively or exclusively studied by these experts includes the beneficial effects of the illness experience, all seemingly equally as common as the negative aspects. In fact, only a small number of such papers have focused solely on the positive transformative effects of illness and survival, despite the fact that some significant research has shown that finding positive aspects in the illness experience can ease the transition to long-term survival.

Instead of seeking the positive as a focus of the research, typically researchers studying the more damaging aspects of illness seem to have stumbled on this area, leaving notes in their discussion portions of the paper urging more study on this subject or briefly mentioning it elsewhere. Here is a brief sampling of such notes:

- In a study regarding the quality of life in long-term cancer survivors, the researchers examined completed questionnaires from 687 cancer survivors and then detailed their fear of recurrence, the distress that was characterized by loneliness and grief over the loss of a perceived future, and other damaging aspects of the experience. But the researchers concede in the very first paragraph of the paper the following: "What has received less attention is the positive aspects of surviving cancer that potentially may improve adjustment and adaptation in the long term."

- In another paper about the experience of gynecologic cancer survivors, the authors theorize about the grueling physical aftereffects of treatment, the depressing institutional and societal prejudices that block the survivors' path to enjoying full employment opportunities, the psychological and emotional wear of the entire experience. After this exhaustive review of the negative impact illness has had on the body of their patients, the authors—a physician and a doctor of psychology—concede to the reader that little is known about the positive effects illness has had on these women. "Another question that needs more attention is that of the positive gains of having been treated for cancer and having survived. In addition to survival, appreciation of life and reorientation of priorities may greatly add to quality of life." In fact, the authors express that better understanding through studies that incorporate the whole experience "will force [medical professionals] to come out from the comfort of technological medicine into a world that is less concrete and less controllable, but more human. Out of it we will be better physicians, more sensitive to the vigor, complexity and adaptability of the human soul."

• In an early landmark paper on cognitive adaptation to threatening events, one noteworthy researcher followed 78 women through their experience of survivorship from breast cancer. She reveals the general lack of knowledge about the positive attributes of the life-threatening illness experience in her observations in the discussion portion of the lengthy and otherwise thorough paper on the topic. "Not only did patients see themselves as generally well adjusted at the time of the interview and as better adjusted than they were during the cancer bout, they also saw themselves as better adjusted than before they had any signs of cancer!" To have a respected researcher use an exclamation point in a sentence like that is truly unusual. She goes on, "When you consider that these women usually had disfiguring surgery, had often had painful follow up care, and had been seriously frightened and lived under the shadow of possible recurrence, this is a remarkable ability to construe personal benefits from potential tragedy."

• In another exclamatory reference, the authors of a paper on long-term ovarian cancer survivorship were struck by the fact that these survivors "felt that their illness had had an extremely positive effect on their lives" in many important areas. "Although over half of all women in our study had some symptoms, they saw the disease impact in positive terms and felt that their lives had been enriched by the experience. Their ability to adapt and transcend the challenges of cancer was impressive and inspiring!"

• In a rare paper that focused on the topic of positive aspects of survivorship, an Australian researcher studying twelve survivors of hematological cancers found that "there are few studies highlighting positive outcomes from the illness experience, particularly from a spiritual perspective. This is despite the fact that early work indicated that researchers rarely focus on positive outcomes of chronic disease and, when they do, they view the findings with suspicion." This led to her further research in that area of survival. At the end of the paper, she concludes that "the experience of diagnosis and treatment for such serious, life-threatening conditions can have positive consequences."

UNDERSTANDING THE WHOLE PICTURE

Interestingly, one of the social scientists' favorite articles to quote in their research about survival remains a relatively unanswered rallying cry for survivors and for the creation of services to support survivors, now more than twenty years after it first appeared. Dr. Fitzhugh Mullan, a physician who was diagnosed with cancer early in his career, published the article in the *New England Journal of Medicine* in 1985. In it he described three emotional and social phases that cancer survivors go through from the point of diagnosis onward through the rest of their lives. He articulated the phases as follows:

1. The acute survival phase, in which symptoms are experienced, a diagnosis is rendered, and treatment takes place.
2. An extended survival phase, which occurs when treatment has ended and the person returns to regular daily activity but is still in fear of the illness and of the potential for its return.
3. The permanent survival phase, in which the individual may experience less uncertainty but is no less changed by the experience of having lived with and through an illness.

It is true that services for those in phase 1 of survival are abundant, for those with cancer or just about any major illness. Once diagnosed, patients and their family are often referred to support groups or educational programs. And that makes a ton of sense. People who are in the throes of diagnosis and treatment have been found to have high stress levels. The time of diagnosis is often tinged with confusion and fear as the patient enters a formerly unknown struggle and frankly frightening time in their life. Support groups help individuals see that they are a part of a larger community of sufferers who understand what they are going through with their new diagnosis and what upheaval the task of surviving can bring into a life. Education programs help foster a sense of comfort and control with what is happening in their treatment.

In just my spot in America, the Detroit metropolitan area, there exist a staggering number of programs for people newly diagnosed with a wide variety of illnesses. Here is a brief list, culled from the Internet in less than ten minutes:

- For those with Parkinson's disease, there are twelve support groups in the three metro counties, as well as regional educational events.
- For heart disease, every hospital in the area offers at least one support program, with some hosting regular educational meetings as well. Offerings include Helping Hearts, a support group for recently diagnosed heart patients and their family members; a Heart Walking Club, complete with monthly blood pressure checks and weight screening; multiple smoking cessation programs; and a wide-reaching nutrition program with cooking classes, grocery store education, and locally produced cookbooks aimed at heart health.
- For diabetes, literally every hospital in the area offers diabetes education programs for the newly diag-

nosed gestational, juvenile, and adult patients and their families. This was in part due to an aggressive statewide campaign cosponsored by the Michigan Department of Community Health and the CDC. Other local activities include support groups as well as cooking and exercise classes.

- For cancer, there is an abundance of programs to serve just about every need, in part because the Barbara Ann Karmanos Cancer Institute, a nationally recognized cancer treatment and research center, is located in Detroit. There, patients can choose from support and education programs for several different forms of cancer. Gilda's Club, the American Cancer Society, local hospitals, and private secular and religious organizations also offer support and educational events to people with many different forms of cancer.

- For those with autoimmune conditions such as inflammatory bowel disease, lupus, and multiple sclerosis, education events are available through local chapters of national disease-based, nonprofit organizations as well as through local hospitals. All organizations supply the area with support programs as well.

Clearly, how much initial support patients receive generally depends upon a number of factors, including the type of disease they have, the amount of money they possess, and the geographic location in which they live. A poor cancer patient in a highly populated area within reach of a cancer center will have access to a number of free or subsidized in-person support and education programs, while a heart disease patient of moderate wealth in a rural area will likely have to rely on Internet message boards and Web sites for education and, if he or she can afford it and if one is available, a grief counseling specialist for support. Even within certain types of cancer, there is a disparity among programs offered that is dependent upon the location of the cancer, with many programs catering to breast cancer or leukemia patients, for example, while fewer are available for esophageal cancer patients or those with sarcomas.

But while it isn't hard to find a support or education program for the newly diagnosed, far, far fewer programs are available to those in Dr. Mullan's second and third phases of survivorship who have completed treatment for an acute illness or have gone into remission for symptoms of a chronic illness. Dr. Mullan wrote in the same article about this very circumstance following his treatment. "It is as if we have invented sophisticated techniques to save people from drowning, but once they have been pulled from the water, we leave them on the dock to cough and splutter on their own in the belief that we have done all that we can," he wrote, further suggesting that survivorship be studied on its own and not as a by-product of cancer research. He also recommended the creation of an "alumni association" of cancer survivors, with "meetings, newsletters and periodicals."

Even in the most populated areas, the support programs that helped people accept the diagnosis and rallied them through the initial treatment are generally not designed to support the long-term patient. Education programs addressing these long-term issues are equally difficult to locate, even in highly populated areas. This deficit exists despite the fact that many researchers who delve into the subject of long-term survival acknowledge that these survivors need educational information on such things as late effects of treatment and need emotional support on issues such as calming a fear of recurrence.

To be fair, in the cancer community there has been a growing amount of progress on Dr. Mullan's suggestions. For example, Gilda's Club, a nonprofit, volunteer-based organization, has built facilities and added services for cancer survivors in larger communities across North America. There, long-term survival issues are addressed through various programs. But a wider dispersal of these services is needed as medical science progresses and the number of survivors mushrooms.

As Dr. Mullan suggested, some study has happened, though probably not nearly enough. And while the LAF and CDC joint report is encouraging, the follow-up action on the survivorship issue is in its nascent stages. Further, survivorship developments outside the world of cancer are nearly nonexistent and need to be studied and developed further, since it has been shown that individuals with other acute or chronic life-threatening illnesses such as heart disease face the same issues as cancer survivors.

MOVING ON

While it is important to understand the larger picture of survivorship in the United States, it is equally important to understand what happens in the individual as he or she begins and continues the journey of surviving acute or chronic life-threatening illness. In the next chapter, I outline what is known about the grieving process that follows the diagnosis and treatment of a life-threatening illness. This will lay the groundwork for the introduction of the five gifts of illness in Part II.

3

GRIEF: FROM THE DIAGNOSIS AND BEYOND

Life is a series of experiences, each one of which makes us bigger, even though it is hard to realize this. For the world was built to develop character, and we must learn that the setbacks and griefs that we endure help us in marching forward.

—Henry Ford

THE ONSET OF undeniable symptoms. The incidental discovery of an anomaly. The ensuing tests. The wait for results. The rendering of a diagnosis. The search for appropriate care. The commencement of treatment.

Each disease is different. Each treatment protocol is different. Each person's experience is different. And yet the commonality for those diagnosed with a chronic or acute life-threatening illness seems to be that these times of physical trial are usually packed with a variety of intense emotions, none of which is really pleasant to experience.

However, it also stands to reason that sometimes a person must go through the ordeal of the physical illness and the wrenching emotional grief that follows in order to gain an appreciation for certain gifts that such hardship usually imparts. What the ill are left with after the struggle ends is an enhanced perspective on life and its many different aspects.

And the emotional suffering is as close to inevitable as anything can be because the onset of disease changes the ways in which we view our future. Our bodies, the very physical beings in which our intellects and our souls reside, usually have such predictable patterns that we unthinkingly go about our daily routines without as much as a hiccough. We unconsciously stand, walk, grasp, see, balance, breathe, blink, chew, taste, swallow, smell, feel, digest, defecate, salivate, bend, grow, and hear, so much so that we take these very actions for granted, moment to moment, day after day. And then illness comes into our lives and suddenly some of those ordinary functions are lost temporarily or permanently to the disease and/or its treatment. Grief over the loss of expected function is a normal development.

There is also an expectation that many of us develop as we are growing normally and performing daily functions that we will continue to do so without interruption until we die. Illness or accidents happen to other people, not us. This entitlement to body continuity and to ongoing health has been passed down as the prevailing wisdom in our world, so prevalent in the media and the mainstream that those who don't fit these definitions—those physically less than normal—tend to stand out. And then illness comes into our lives and suddenly our own entitlement to health and normality are insulted or robbed entirely. Grief over the loss of entitlement is a normal development.

There is also comfort and predictability in the way we spend our time. As students, we make ourselves available to attend the classes, to do the coursework, and to take the requisite tests, all for the grade that we want to achieve and the career we hope someday to have. As workers, we make ourselves available to be on the job on time, to perform the tasks that are expected of us, and to aspire to the promotions we feel we deserve, all while being compensated for the time spent and the task completed. In our personal lives, we make time for family and friends, for daily chores, and for weekend diversions. And then illness enters the picture and our ability to devote time to these worthy pursuits must be directed toward the efforts of diagnosis, treatment, and recovery. Grief over the loss of mastery of our time is a normal development.

All of these parts of our lives—our innate abilities, our sense of entitlement to health and well-being, and our mastery of how our time is spent—are dependent upon each other and work together to foster a sense of security in this world. And then illness comes and insecurity starts to rule our days, subjecting us to inevitable fear, panic, and anxiety. Grief over the loss of security is a normal development.

IT STARTS WITH A DIAGNOSIS

Most of those whom I interviewed for this work told me that the feelings of grief with regard to their illness began with the diagnostic period, a stretch of time that is as individual as the people who become ill. For some, the drama of diagnosis began in the weeks and months—sometimes years—prior to the time when symptoms could no longer be explained away. Usually, these individuals experienced a slow progression of symptoms, things that were slightly out of the ordinary but didn't call for drastic, immediate action.

Ellen, a young lawyer, gives a classic example of this with her illness history. When Ellen first experienced a loss of vision in her right eye, she immediately sought treatment. Her doctor diagnosed optic neuritis that very day and sent her to the hospital for an MRI (magnetic resonance imaging), as this condition can be a precursor of multiple sclerosis (MS). The test revealed three brain lesions that are usually the hallmark of this disease. But at the time, five such lesions and two or more events like the temporary loss of a bodily function were needed for a definitive MS diagnosis to be made. So when the doctor explained the results and suggested that she cut back on stress that could cause a second event, Ellen put her fears aside and continued with her life, feeling as if she had dodged a bullet.

"The doctors said that I had this one event and it did resolve itself, so they aren't going to diagnose me with MS. They had certain things they wanted me to do, like cut out stress, lead a healthy life, not to overwork myself. And all I heard was, 'You don't have MS,'" Ellen recalled. "Even though I still couldn't see at that point—it took another four or five months for that to return—I, in my mind, felt it was just a blip."

The blip soon became an explosion. After a sudden loss of sensation in her right arm and leg three years after the optic neuritis resolved, Ellen had another MRI, which turned up more lesions. She was officially diagnosed with MS, but the symptoms went away again. Because of this, she didn't start active treatment for three more years, when yet another episode occurred. This time, Ellen was carrying her infant son down the stairs in her home, and her legs were suddenly rendered useless. She and her son tumbled down the steps. Though neither was injured in the fall, the scary incident and months afterward of not being able to walk forced her to confront her diagnosis and begin treatment.

In some cases, a delayed diagnosis is the fault of either the patient or the doctor not recognizing the seriousness of the symptoms. The latter happened to Linda, an artist. Linda was about to leave her gynecologist's office following a routine annual checkup, when a nurse happened to glance at her chart and noticed an abnormally low hemoglobin count. The result was brought to the attention of the doctor, who assumed this dramatic dip was simply due to an inadequate amount of iron in Linda's diet. The doctor put Linda on six months' worth of daily iron pills.

At the end of that prescription, Linda tried giving at her church's annual blood drive. She watched as volunteers took her blood sample and tested it. "We can't take your blood," she was told. "You're anemic."

She called the doctor, who ordered another six months of iron therapy. Her next annual appointment showed that her blood counts had only risen 0.7, despite a year of heavy doses of iron supplements. At this point, Linda became concerned and sought the opinion of another doctor, who diagnosed her blood cancer, multiple myeloma, within the week of her first appointment with him.

For others, the diagnostic period was shorter but no less intense. These individuals usually discovered a lump or a bump or other troubling symptom that led them to schedule a doctor's visit relatively quickly and then go through the requisite testing, which, depending on the specific case, lasted a matter of days to more than a month.

Bill can relate to this set of circumstances. As the chief of cardiac surgery in a hospital system in the Midwest, he led an enormously active life. Plugging away at a growing case load that took up as much as eighty hours of his time each week, he stopped everything when he discovered a swelling on his face. He knew this could mean trouble, so he quickly scheduled a biopsy.

While many individuals are given the results in the doctor's office in the presence of a loved one after weeks of testing, Bill used his connections in the hospital to speed up the process. Shortly after the biopsy was taken, Bill made his way to the pathologist's office so he could be there at the moment the diagnosis was rendered. Standing behind the pathologist as he worked, Bill watched in horror as they both came to the same conclusion: non-Hodgkin's lymphoma.

"I felt the usual stepping-into-an-empty-elevator-shaft feeling that you get when you have that diagnosis. Very traumatic," he recalls.

Mary Lou had a slightly longer diagnostic period for her case of amyotrophic lateral sclerosis (ALS). Because ALS does not have a specific diagnostic test, Mary Lou started with testing one January with her first appointment with the neurologist. In June of that year, she went through the final test, a spinal tap to examine proteins in her spinal fluid. An earlier premonition of the diagnosis helped to prepare her for the time it was finally rendered. Two doctors who had been examining her entered a hospital room to deliver the news.

"I knew the minute they walked in because I saw how hard it was for them to think that I had it. And my husband and I just sat there speechless," Mary Lou said. "And when we went to the car, we both broke down—my husband, who never cries, more than me. I was consoling him. I was more prepared to handle this."

For some people who go through this scenario, there is a strange sense of knowing what the diagnosis is going to be even before the doctor opens his or her mouth. Jen, an executive at a major cable television station, had been diagnosed with melanoma after a wayward mole began to change. The mole was removed, she was declared cancer free, and thus she continued on with her life, ascending the corporate ladder while balancing life as a new wife and mother.

Three years later, a different mole on her upper leg brought her back to her doctors, who then insisted that it be biopsied along with surrounding lymph nodes. "I just knew. I had a sixth sense. Truly, I had a sixth sense," Jen remembered. "I just knew it was in my node. I just had this weighty, sinking feeling."

And she was right. Her melanoma had recurred and her cancer, now stage 3A, had progressed.

Then there are people like Neil who have an immediate presentation of life-threatening symptoms and a quickly ensuing diagnosis. Neil, a university professor, was giving final exams the week before Christmas when a strong and persistent feeling of nausea hit him. He made his way home, sweating profusely while trudging across the freezing campus to his car and then making frequent stops along the way to vomit. His wife immediately took him to the emergency room, where doctors frantically worked to save him from the massive heart attack that ruined his heart and nearly killed him.

For the most part, individuals like Neil had no real sign

of trouble just prior to their diagnosis. Serious medical trouble can and does present at any time, while teaching a class, preparing dinner, working out, or shopping. Usually this is followed by a quick trip to the emergency room, where diagnostic tests are ordered and performed immediately. Many patients are then admitted to the hospital—some for the first time since their birth—and plunged into treatment to control or to reverse their condition.

And then there are individuals who stumble across the diagnosis of their disease completely by accident. Called incidental discoveries, these diagnoses are often made during a routine physical or while symptoms present for something entirely different. For example, Macklin, a literature professor at a major university, was diagnosed with leukemia during a regular blood test that was a part of his annual physical.

Whatever the circumstances in the course of diagnosis, what follows in that moment of diagnosis is common. All of the individuals interviewed for the book agreed that the point of diagnosis represented a crucial moment in their lives to that date. At that moment, these people—the vast majority of whom had never experienced a medical condition greater than a minor bacterial or viral illness or a broken bone—faced the possibility of realizing their mortality for the first time.

There seems to be an overwhelming consensus among the interviewees that the moment of the diagnosis became a point of no return, a memory so permanently seared into their minds and so significant in the course of their lives that it is easily recalled not only for the news that was delivered but also for the drama of that significant and unwanted change. Every single participant—even those decades out from their initial diagnosis—told me that they were able to remember exactly where they were when they heard the news, to conjure the immediate feelings they felt, to recall their own reactions and those of others, to remember verbatim the dialogue that took place, even to summon physical sensations such as smells and sounds that were present at that significant time. It was as if, most agreed, the uttering of the diagnosis ushered them into a different life stage, a state from which they would never completely return.

"BETWIXT AND BETWEEN"

In the literature of social science, some experts have suggested that people who are just diagnosed with an illness enter a state of liminality. Since this isn't an everyday concept, a little explanation may be necessary. The base of the word *liminality* the Latin word *limen*, which means "threshold." The concept of being at a threshold in life was first elucidated at the turn of the last century by the ethnographer Arnold van Gennep and later expanded upon by the anthropologist Victor Turner. Van Gennep theorized that there were three periods of transition in rites of passage: preliminary, liminaire, and post-liminaire. Turner applied these theories to actual acts during a rite of passage in an African tribe. In this particular culture, those who were transitioning through a major life cycle event such as getting married or entering adulthood from adolescence were first exiled from their society, lived apart for a period of time, and later were brought back and reintegrated into the tribe, according to their new status.

The passage between the two differing status points,

spoken of time that was "betwixt and between," was considered a period of liminaire, a point at the threshold between being, say, an unmarried person and a married person, or an adolescent who then becomes an adult. The individual would literally and physically be separated from the tribe in the preliminary stage, live on his or her own during the liminaire stage, and then come back into the society in the post-liminaire stage.

The authors of the book *Surviving Survival*, a group of modern social scientists based in Australia, apply the concept of liminaire to the immediate experience of life after a cancer diagnosis. They further break the liminaire stage into two substages: acute and sustained. In the acute phase, the diagnosis is anticipated or rendered and the patient confronts for the first time his or her own mortality, a concept that is really always present in everyday life but rarely examined as directly as it is in the presentation of a life-threatening illness.

The acute phase separates the person from the normally healthy world and all of its expectations. There may be a period of adaptation in which the individual accommodates the changes the disease and its treatment demand. A work schedule may be scaled back to fit in time necessary for treatment, a reduction in physical abilities may require modifications for the person to resume regular daily functions, family life may be tempered by the insecurity the disease ushers in.

Also in the acute phase, people begin treatment, sometimes wrestling with uncertainty as to whether they will survive. The uncertainty persists through the treatment—and sometimes for years after—before a cure or sustained remission is achieved. The Australian scientists hypothesize that as cure or remission is declared, there comes a marginally greater sense of security about the future.

Once treatment is finished and remission or cure has been achieved, however, the patient can enter the second substage: sustained liminality. During this period, the immediate threat has passed. The chance that life will continue is clearly greater than it was before treatment began, even with either continuing physical effects of the illness or treatment for most of them.

While the end of treatment is a time for most people to rejoice, this is also a time of instability as patients give up or break away from the near-constant attention and support given to them by their medical team during the crisis. In a review of literature on surviving adult cancers published in 1989, researchers said that the time of the completion of therapy can cause great distress and unhealthy behavioral changes such as panic attacks, separation anxiety, and an initially persistent though gradually lessening fear of recurrence of the disease. "Elation that the treatment is over is coupled with the anxiety of losing contact and health status surveillance by the treatment team," the authors of that article wrote. "Health care providers need to be aware of these changes and support the patient during his or her transition in the well role."

Because of the emotional and psychological changes a person goes through while battling a life-threatening illness, the survivors of acute or chronic illness find it difficult—bordering on impossible—ever to go back to their previously "normal" lives. It is not a leap to say that the grief and grieving over some of the losses experienced will continue through this stage as life progresses beyond the diagnosis and treatment experience for any illness.

The authors of the above paper noted this, saying the psychological scar left by the disease experience is a "permanent one, characterized by easy recall of the initial feelings and emotions associated with illness and the recovery period, a continuing concern about one's mortality, along with an enduring sense of vulnerability."

Bill also articulated this thought in his interview. "When you get that information [that you are sick], you experience this loss of control, and then it takes a little while to realize that the cancer or whatever illness you have really didn't create that loss of control. It reveals a lack of it. And that's something that once you really truly realize, you can never go back to where you were before because you know too much."

Not being able to return to the life that was lived before the illness experience is something that the caregivers, friends, and relatives of the patient may not be able to understand or sympathize with. In a 2002 article published in the journal *Psycho-Oncology*, the authors described a woman who had nursed her husband through colon cancer years before. Her frustration with his inability to resume life as it was before the diagnosis is apparent in a sampling of her statements made during an interview: "He doesn't seem as though he can forget about it, and just lead a normal life . . . It's curtailing our life . . . Something I wish that he would get over it, but I don't think that he is going to . . . I just feel as though I am at the end of my tether, looking after him."

THE FEELINGS THAT ACCOMPANY THE GRIEF PERIOD

The emotional components of grief in the liminaire and

post-liminaire states are well studied and documented in social science literature, so much so that it would demand an entire book just to cover the differing theories and their supporting evidence. Best known of the more popular works, however, are those of Dr. Elisabeth Kübler-Ross, a psychiatrist who dedicated her life to studying the end of it. In her breakout book *On Death and Dying*, Kübler-Ross wrote about five emotional stages that terminally ill patients went through from the point of diagnosis to death.

There has been a lot of controversy regarding these stages since they were first published. Some in the world of social science say that she is wrongly given credit for developing the stages, as she was not the first one to identify them. Others point out that not everyone goes through all of the stages, nor do they always experience them in the same order. Still more say that some people never reach the final stage, acceptance, and that those mourning their losses due to illness can feel like failures if they can't identify with all five.

Kübler-Ross addressed these points in her last book, *On Grief and Grieving*, published posthumously. In the first two paragraphs of the first chapter, she says that her five stages were never meant as a defining road map of grief with specific emotional points to visit along the way to acceptance. Rather, they were intended to provide "tools" to help those grieving understand what they are going through.

With this in mind, I asked all of my interview participants for this book whether they had experienced any of Kübler-Ross's five emotional stages. All of the participants were able to identify with at least one emotional state she named, with a significant number saying they went through more than one. They also added other emotions they encountered during the time immediately following diagnosis and beyond. Here are the results of those questions:

1. Denial and isolation.

Social scientists say that denial in its many different forms is a relatively common phenomenon. It is a tactic that humans employ to temper or to delay the realization or integration of the unsettling information that an individual is, in fact, sick. Denial allows people receiving the bad news time to hold this information at bay until they are better able to incorporate it into their lives.

As defined by *Webster's New World Dictionary*, denial is said to be "a refusal to believe or accept." Using this strict and narrow meaning, few of the interviewees fit that definition. One of those who denied the diagnosis was Debbie, a mother and an employee of a major automotive corporation. After a blood test taken during a physical showed abnormal results, she was sent to an oncologist for further testing. A bone marrow biopsy was ordered, which revealed acute myelocytic leukemia.

Still, she told me that she couldn't believe the results. Debbie went through three more physicians and tests, all of which confirmed the diagnosis. Even when she was admitted to the hospital to go through chemotherapy for a lifesaving stem cell transplant and the medication was literally just beginning to flow through her veins, she asked the cancer center's chief to review the results one more time. Once more, her results were confirmed.

"I just couldn't believe it. I couldn't believe it was happening to me. It didn't seem real," Debbie said.

Less intensely than Debbie, a few people entertained

thoughts of a misdiagnosis as a form of denial, still going ahead with treatment and making changes in their lives to allow it but experiencing nagging thoughts that a mistake was made all the while. Linda, in particular, had an interesting experience with denial. While going through the diagnostic period, a hospital worker read her some information about another Linda with the same last name but with a different birthday and address. These two individuals were being treated at the same two hospitals and even ended up having stem cell transplants at the same time, on the same floor.

"I thought, 'See? This is not me. Someone screwed up on the computer.' And that stayed in my head for months later. [I was] thinking, 'Could that have been the diagnosis for that other person, that other Linda?' How bizarre is that?" she asked.

Nearly all other interviewees readily accepted the diagnosis and began treatment shortly thereafter. That isn't to say they didn't experience denial at all, just in different ways. Some denied the physical effects of a disease or its treatment, continuing life without acknowledging limitations or making allowances for the disease.

Shirley's denial manifested itself not in that she didn't have breast cancer but with regard to the seriousness of it. She called this "tunnel vision," in that she blocked out the gravity of the situation and selectively focused on other events. After receiving the news of the initial diagnosis, she diverted her attention by planning a fantasy baseball camp trip for her husband. She came through a lumpectomy and radiation treatments and was declared cancer free. But then there was a recurrence a few years later, right before Shirley and her husband were scheduled to visit Lisbon and Barcelona on vacation.

"I just thought something was very wrong, and we did a mammogram of it. There it was," Shirley, a retired office worker, said during her interview. "And again, with the tunnel vision, we had planned a trip, and, you know, that was important to me. We went on the trip. And I had radiation afterward."

Macklin denied the seriousness of his impending bone marrow transplant for chronic myelogenous leukemia by investing in his hobby of birding. In the days leading up to the hospitalization for the procedure, he splurged on extra trips to find exotic birds and purchased new equipment, all while knowing on some level that he had a 50 percent chance of dying during or immediately after the transplant.

"I am about to have a transplant, so I go and order an eight-hundred-and-fifty-dollar pair of binoculars. Now, you could call that denial. That was an interesting move," Macklin recalled, adding that he didn't save the receipt. "But I thought, 'I am going to make it, so I am going to buy these binoculars. I am going to get through this.'"

Some individuals denied the deleterious effects that the illnesses or the treatments had on their sense of physical strength or continuity. For them, there was a strong urge to continue to live life as it had been lived prior to diagnosis. Violet, an editor, is one who experienced this. Diagnosed with type 1 diabetes at age thirty-two, she was stringent initially about adopting proper eating and exercise habits to help control her disease.

"Then, I discovered that I can be able to get away with some things. And so I did, you know, I tried to push the envelope," she said, adding that she still can be lax at times with her necessary lifestyle modifications.

Others said denial was something that didn't occur following their diagnosis or during their treatment. In part, this seemed to happen more with individuals who had anticipated or simply knew what the diagnosis would be.

Isolation was another common theme among those interviewed. When the isolation happened was as important as how it occurred for the patients who experienced it. For some it came during treatment, while others experienced it right away with their diagnosis. Cardinal Joseph Bernardin, who died of pancreatic cancer, wrote about his experience with isolation in his book *The Gift of Peace*. "Initially, I felt as through the floodwaters were threatening to overwhelm me. . . . My initial experience was of disorientation, isolation, a feeling of not being 'at home' anymore," he wrote.

Some interviewees found that they isolated themselves shortly after diagnosis, as they were unable to speak to others about the news that was difficult to accept on the personal level. James, a professor at a New England college, said he eventually felt very open about speaking about his Crohn's disease but initially told very few people.

"At that time I still didn't like to talk about it. And so the only people who knew about it were Ann [his wife] and my family, really. I mean even our close friends. I either didn't say anything to them or I let Ann tell them or I didn't really know how much they knew about it," James recalled. "I didn't talk about it myself. You have this idea that no one else really understands what you are going through."

Others felt it later, if at all. Isolation comes easily from the effects of treatment, especially if physical changes occurred. Steroids make some people bloated and depressed, chemotherapy can cause hair loss, radiation can cause burns, and surgery leaves scars. Linda felt this. As she prepared for her stem cell transplant, she went through chemotherapy, which made her long blonde hair fall out. Her husband suggested that she buy a wig.

"I ordered one ahead of time, just to be prepared. It wasn't the same color blonde that I was. It was weird to put on. I thought, 'If it was going to be weird, I would just be a redhead.' In all, I got three: one I never wore, the redhead one, and one I wore once. It was very uncomfortable to me. And this is kind of isolation because it put me apart. I had something artificial on," Linda explained.

How it occurred to people varied as well. At times isolation was seen as abandonment. Interviewees frequently spoke of close friends or relatives who slowly or abruptly cut off all contact, in part because they could not bear to face the notion of their own mortality expressed through the perceived demise of a loved one. Mostly, however, this feeling of isolation or loneliness was felt while being completely surrounded by a sea of supportive family members, friends, and colleagues. Violet struggled with this right away. "I had a very strong sense of isolation about it because I didn't know anybody else at the time who had diabetes except for one person at my workplace who happened to be someone who I interpersonally could not connect with at all and mistrusted. So she wasn't a possible resource," she recalled. "Initially, I felt very alone."

Deb, the director of a support program for young breast cancer survivors, also felt isolation, mostly because she was the youngest patient in her oncologist's office, usually by about two to three decades. "I just didn't know anyone my age. I didn't know anyone else going through it. I'd go to the oncology office and felt like I was the youngest in the waiting room," she said.

Two other emotions that appeared to be related to this state are disbelief and numbness. While it may not have been denial in the classic sense, some people expressed a sense of disbelief at their bad fortune of being diagnosed with an acute or chronic disease. They know it can happen, but they just can't believe it is happening to *them*.

Despite being hooked up to machines in the emergency room and drifting in and out of consciousness, and despite being told he had all of the key signs of a heart attack, Neil told me that he was in a state of disbelief in those moments. "I said, 'I am not having a heart attack,'" Neil said, crying. "Then, I was out of it. Somehow, kind of semiconscious, I heard a doctor sort of telling some poor woman that her husband was dying. He said, 'You better summon the children.'"

"I realized it was my wife. I went unconscious again, although I dreamt that I was telling the doctor off, chewing him out that he was worrying my wife for nothing."

Though individuals tended to accept their diagnosis and move into treatment, many lost emotional sensation, akin to feelings of shock. Jen felt the same disbelief as Neil did, along with a sense of numbness, which persisted from the moment of her recurrence of melanoma throughout treatment. "I was numb, just numb. In fact, in the beginning, it felt totally surreal, like I was just watching someone else's life," she recalled.

2. Anger
From admitting to swearing and screaming about the great

misfortune of being diagnosed with a serious illness to expressing disgust with the health care system of choice, from claiming frustration with a below-normal-functioning body to assailing relatives who made bad choices in attempting to be supportive, many of the respondents during their interviews expressed a sense of anger following their diagnosis, through their treatment, and into life beyond.

Some interviewees who otherwise seemed very mild-mannered during our time together became quite animated when discussing their anger over their diagnosis and treatment. Macklin was one of these individuals. As we sat on his deck on a beautiful summer day, he told me how he felt the anger at the injustice of being diagnosed with leukemia almost right after getting the news from the doctor. Dramatically pounding his fists on a picnic table, he illustrated how the anger manifested itself through his language. "'Why me? Why should this be happening to me? What did I do to deserve this? Nothing! Fuck! Shit!' That sort of thing," Macklin said and then laughed at the memory. "To put it in more genteel terms, this was not a part of my plans. I didn't want it. I didn't need it. I didn't ask for it. It didn't seem fair."

His comments also bring up another point of anger: that it is directed at the seeming injustice of the situation. Nobody sets out in life with the hope of contracting a life-threatening illness. In fact, many people do things like eating right, taking vitamins, and exercising regularly in the hope of avoiding just that. So when a diagnosis is uttered, there is a crushing sense of unfairness to the situation, usually verbalized, as Macklin did with the question, "Why me?" Many, many of the respondents said those same words.

Violet, however, did not ask that question and was not

necessarily angry with the diagnosis but, rather, directed those feelings toward the callousness of medical personnel that she encountered during her initial hospitalization. At one point, a nurse made her guess what her blood sugar numbers were rather than simply telling her, while later a doctor treated her as if she was hysterical when she was reporting actual symptoms. She also was mortified that she had to call a nurse to report each and every time she urinated. "I would say that my anger was at my feelings of powerlessness, feelings of not being in control of my health and also not being in control of how I was perceived," she said.

Loss of control of normal functions or abilities of the body can bring about frustration, which leads to anger in some. Again, this leads back to the expectation that our bodies will always remain intact and working properly. Patty, a housewife we will learn more about in chapter 6, can attest to this. In the wake of two strokes caused by an exceedingly rare brain disease, Patty was in a coma for several months, from which she emerged to find that she not only had been moved to a new house but also was now a quadriplegic. Though she has regained some of her physical abilities, she is still angry.

"I felt angry and violated that someone would have the nerve to move me to this strange house," Patty said. "I was pissed off at the world because I loved my life the way it was. And then to have to wait for everything has driven me absolutely nuts. I had to wait for this wheelchair; then I have to wait to have people take me places. I am sick of waiting!"

Deb felt anger rising toward some people who said insensitive things to her following her diagnosis of breast cancer at age thirty-two. "I had a low tolerance for people who were very naïve and were saying things like my ex-mother-in-law. At the time, instead of being sympathetic and saying something appropriate, she'd say, 'Oh, you're so lucky. You never have to have another mammogram.' And I would get angry because people would say those kinds of things," she said.

3. *Bargaining.*

In the truest sense, bargaining is bartering for one thing in exchange for something of value. With regard to illness, the goal of this is to delay the inevitable loss of denial and thus realizing the impact of the diagnosis and its treatment on life and the plans for it. In Kübler-Ross's first work, she found that the dying wanted to exchange living in pain for more time or to enjoy specific moments. Many times, her subjects would strike deals with God. But in other instances, they would make specific requests with their physicians regarding changing their treatment schedules in order to accomplish a personal goal.

For those who would live through their initial diagnosis and treatment, few admitted to me that they bargained. But when they did it, their requests were not that different from Kübler-Ross's patients.

For some of the most gravely ill people interviewed, the bargain struck was for more time. Time to watch a child grow into an adult, time without pain, time pursuing one last pleasure as they felt their end was quite possibly imminent. Linda can attest to this. Her multiple myeloma, initially forced into remission with a stem cell transplant, relapsed recently. Her twin boys and her daughter were in high school during her initial diagnosis.

"At first, bargaining for me meant: let me get the boys

through high school. They are college age now," she said. "There is this sense that, okay, we made this deal. But my mother is ninety-three, so maybe we can wait now until she is gone."

A devout Catholic, Mary Lou started her bargaining with God on the way home from the hospital after she was given her diagnosis. "I just prayed all the way home, 'Help me get them through high school,'" she said. "And I wanted them to learn from it."

Now that the children are well on their way through college, Mary Lou continues to bargain, moving the deadline back as they grow. "I negotiate all the time. I got my kids through high school. They're happy. They're sensitive to others. I hear of other parents and all of the trouble they go through with their children, and mine treat me with love and tenderness. Neither of them went through a bad phase," she said. "And so now, at times, I say, 'Can I just see them married?'"

Another bargain struck less frequently was with the utilization of certain modes of treatment to secure future goals. In this case, a person will agree to faithfully take medication, to report for regular tests, or to submit to painful procedures in order to remain disease free well into the future, knowing all the while that the future promises nothing. Violet did this when she decided to have an insulin pump inserted. Her goal for the future is to have the option to bear a child. In order to have the best chance to do so, she must maintain average blood sugar levels from now on.

"It's an ongoing bargain, really, and I'm trying to strike a deal with the universe. If I do all these things, I'll have my numbers well enough, and I'll be able to have my baby and my baby will be safe," Violet said. "But it is just a story because, really, in the end, there are random factors. There are so many things that you can't control. The best you can do is to stack the cards in your own favor."

4. Depression

Okay, let's just consider this for a moment: You are used to living a life that is fairly unremarkable as far as health is concerned. Maybe there was a broken bone from a sporting mishap here, stitches from a childhood accident there, and a helping of bacterial or viral illness thrown in for good measure. Then, seemingly suddenly, you are told that you have something that could possibly shorten your life. Depressing?

One thing that I find interesting about the original theory of the five stages of grief is that fear and panic are not a part of them. Fear of diagnoses, fear of treatments, fear of physical side effects, fear of loss of function, fear of returning to a normal life after treatment ends, and fear of recurrence seemed to haunt the lives of those interviewed, either in small or large part, some for years after the treatment ended and cure was achieved. Panic, an emotion intimately connected to fear, usually appears during these times. And both of these feelings contributed to the depression of those interviewed for this work, I found.

The timing of the depression, fear, and anxiety was as individual as the patients themselves. A large portion of those who were interviewed for this book said the dark clouds of depression drifted into their vista shortly after diagnosis, either fleetingly or more permanently.

At the time she was diagnosed with breast cancer, Shirley had watched other relatives die of the disease and was witnessing the swift decline of her sister from an advanced case of breast cancer. Shirley had just married off her daughter and was caring for her elderly father, who was struggling with dementia. And though she had kept a close watch on her own health, she couldn't help but feel that an opportunity for diagnosis had been missed during an earlier mammogram.

"[Depression] was just there because there was so much to deal with. It was, like, 'Why did this happen now?' And then, 'How did they miss the diagnosis?'" Shirley recalled as she sat at her kitchen table during our interview. "The size [of the malignant tumor] was not the size one would want. It was larger than it should have been for someone who has annual mammograms."

The impact of the disease and its treatments on body image, body continuity, and body function can be negative for the individual, which can leave the person feeling less than whole and normal. Having surgery not only is traumatic but leaves a scar that wasn't there before. Being administered potentially toxic chemicals to shove a disease into remission can leave a person bald, bloated, vomiting, and thinking less than clearly. A chronic disease can slowly impair normal body functions, leaving individuals with a greater reliance on others than they had before they were diagnosed. As a result, depression is an expected response.

Violet struggled with depression after being diagnosed with diabetes, for the most part because of the permanent changes it dictated in her life. "For me, the worst period of depression probably was in those initial two months after I was diagnosed, when I had to make such radical changes in my lifestyle, not only the insulin and the shots but also the restrictions in eating. I love food. I still love food. I had a sweet tooth and I was eating just insane amounts of food before I was diagnosed," Violet said. "I had a lot of grief and depression about the food . . . and about the way [diabetes] changes your whole life. For always."

With degenerative diseases, the depression can and does recur often, usually as yet another body function is lost to the progress of the illness. For Mary Lou, depression related to her ALS has been an ongoing struggle and most often reared its head when her disease progressed and her abilities diminished. With ALS, there is a slow wasting of muscular coordination and physical abilities, forcing those with it to continually adapt as they lose normal functions. Mary Lou was keen to notice this. "Every time I had to move from a brace to a cane, from a cane to a walker, walker to a wheel-chair—every time I had a period [of transition] I would go through sort of being very emotional about it," she said.

For some individuals, the diagnosis of the chronic or acute life-threatening illness ushered in a change to the way they viewed the future, something that will be explored in depth in chapter 9. When we are young, we envision a future filled with all of the things that we want for our-selves—a long and happy marriage, wonderfully healthy and productive children, a home with a white picket fence and a golden retriever, retirement digs in Boca, grandchildren to spoil. But illness can force early retirement, can break up a marriage, can cause foreclosure on that house and the retire-ment digs, and can engender infertility. Any of those losses adds up to a loss of the future.

Jen claims she didn't fall into a state of depression after her melanoma returned but that she does feel it at certain times, "dark days," as she calls them, brought about by thoughts of the future. "I see an old person. I see an old couple. And I say, 'I hope it's me. I hope it's me.' You know, I see it every day. I think the way that I look at the future is completely different," she said, crying. "When I am talking to my son about how he will go to school and then he's going to go to college and, it's like, every conversation is about the future. And my second thought is, 'I hope I'm here. I hope I'm here.'"

Alicia, a young ovarian cancer survivor who underwent a hysterectomy at the age of twenty-two, thought about a future with children as something she wanted, with or without a husband in the picture. But when her medical and surgical treatment took away the option of bearing her own children at the same time that it forced her into menopause, she became depressed. She told me that she still feels profound sadness at times, sharp twinges of it especially when she sees her peers do things that she will never do.

"You know, I can't have kids. I'm sterile now. I'm twenty-five, so my friends are getting to that age where they're having babies or talking about it and I'm just not even a part of that. I can't have the same conversation they're having," Alicia said. Later, she added that it was difficult for her to plan anything in the future. "More than anything, I think it's not that cancer made my life uncertain. It's that it made me aware of the fact that life is uncertain."

The period directly after active initial treatment ends is a common time for yet another slug of depression for many survivors. It is during this transition that contact with medical personnel and support staff generally dwindles from daily exchanges to scheduling a cursory checkup every six months or so. There is usually a set pattern to treatments—

five days in a hospital after surgery, six months of a regular chemotherapy program, a standard physical therapy program for cardiac rehabilitation—that constitutes a routine; this certainty evaporates when the patient is cut loose at the end. As I wrote earlier in this chapter, there is an expectation for some that life will return to "normal," or as it was prior to diagnosis.

Deb felt this happen to her. After her double mastectomy with reconstruction and follow-up chemotherapy, she felt a strong surge of anxiety. "When you come off the chemo, it's emotional. You're flying on your own," she said.

During the time after treatment, the fear of relapse or recurrence would cause depression and anxiety to return for some. The fear of facing more painful or debilitating treatment and tests, the fear of not making it through another occurrence, the fear of dealing with the emotional component again is enough to make anyone depressed or anxious. Deb again illuminated this concept. "For the first year— maybe the first year and a half out—anytime I had back pain or shortness of breath, I would have severe anxiety," she recalled. "I knew. I would just think the worst. I would think, 'It's back. I'm going to die.'"

While some said they never really battled depression prior to illness, others were more familiar with it in their lives before illness and ascribed the depression following diagnosis to a familial predisposition to it, saying that the appearance of the illness was merely a prompt for them to explore these feelings. Ellen's family members battled depression in the years prior to her MS diagnosis. When she was diagnosed, her neurologist handed her tissues and a prescription for an antidepressant.

"Depression is something I grew up with. My mother fought it, as did an older sister of mine. It was always on the periphery when I was growing up," Ellen said, adding that it had never affected her directly prior to her diagnosis. "I believe it was in 1996 when my neurologist did a spinal and put me on an antidepressant. When I went back, I told him I was having trouble sort of muddling through what I was going through and how it was going to affect me."

Whatever the case, many people interviewed who said they were depressed following their diagnosis were pre-scribed antidepressants by their doctors as a prophylactic or as a treatment. Others found solace in support groups, either in person or online.

5. *Acceptance.*

In the earliest explanation of this stage, it was said that indi-viduals about to die would reach a state of acceptance, which included no further emotional struggle. It was described as a state that was devoid of negative feelings such as anger or depression about what was soon to happen.

For this book, interviewees described it to me a little differently, perhaps in part because my interview subjects were to live through their illness experience, whereas Kübler-Ross's patients did not. This particular stage meant different things to different people, but in very few cases did it mean an acceptance of an imminent death, despite the fact that many people had excruciatingly close calls in their experi-ence of illness. Instead, acceptance meant that they acknowl-edged the fact that they had a particular disease, learned about it, and underwent the appropriate treatments.

Some of the respondents said they reached acceptance

almost immediately, in part because they expected the diagnosis and wanted to start treatment as soon as possible. Others had either suffered for a long time prior to the final diagnosis or had recently whittled down a list of possible diagnoses through tests and were awaiting the last word from their physician.

After a year of feeling tired and worn out by the anemia she suffered, Linda found that she accepted the fact that she had multiple myeloma shortly after the delayed diagnosis was made. "It was really early on," she said. "How can you not when you are physically having a hard time? You accept it. You have to."

Some interviewees told me that when they could talk about the disease with others, either after diagnosis, during treatment, or thereafter, the acceptance of the disease came more easily. This was especially true of those who had a difficult time speaking to others about their illness after diagnosis. For them, discussing the disease with others was a sign of acceptance.

From the beginning, Deb had a hard time calling herself a cancer survivor, a common term that the cancer community applies to anyone from their moment of diagnosis; even the individual with the most advanced case of cancer with the gloomiest outlook is given the label of survivor, as they are seen as surviving cancer for the time being. Deb didn't feel that term applied to her as she was struggling to get past the effects of surgery and chemotherapy. But once she found a more comfortable way of addressing her experience, she was able to discuss the disease and became more accepting of its place in her life.

"I had a really hard time saying, 'I'm a survivor.' But

I could say, 'I have breast cancer.' And I would. I would tell people in Target or you know, wherever I was," she said. "I would tell anybody. If I thought somebody else was going through it or something, I'd talk to them and share it with anybody. Or if somebody asked me, 'Are you wearing a wig?' I would stop and I would educate them about it," she said.

A few interviewees found that they reached acceptance after they could no longer deny the impact of the disease on their lives. Ellen's third episode of MS was the harbinger of acceptance for her. Months passed after her tumble down the stairs before she regained the use of her legs. In the meantime, a nanny cared for her son while her parents flew in from their home in the south to take care of her. She was forced then to accept the fact that her disease was incurable. "That was the one [episode] that in terms of realizing that this was not going to go away, that was it," Ellen said. "[I was] thinking, 'I am not going to escape it anymore.'"

Another element that completed acceptance for some was the immersion into learning about their disease and its treatments. This remains a powerful way to combat fears about illness and instill a bit of certainty into an otherwise uncertain situation. By knowing what the disease can do, learning about treatment options, and advocating on behalf of themselves, patients can discover some measure of control over decisions that are made regarding their care.

Again, Ellen is one who did this. A patent attorney by training, she was encouraged by her neurologist to learn as much as she could about emerging therapies for her disease. She eventually made a trip to Israel to visit the lab of a pioneering scientist in the field and created a fund-raiser to support this woman's work. It was a step in her ongoing process of accepting the disease and its impact on her life, she said, as well as a way of fighting back.

Bill also strongly believes in education. Shortly after being diagnosed, he retired from the active practice of surgery and devoted himself to advocating on behalf of lymphoma patients, serving as president of the Lymphoma Research Foundation for a number of years. He continues to help individuals who are newly diagnosed learn about their shared disease and its treatments.

"From my own experience and what I've now seen with dozens of other people is that when you have the feeling that your life is out of control and you're falling through the darkness, that anything you can do—whether it's learning about macrobiotics or learning about your disease or learning about religion or spirituality—tends to give you back a bit of a sense of control that you think you lost," he said.

But knowing that acceptance doesn't always come quickly or completely can be comforting to those who are not far out from their diagnosis and have yet to achieve it. Violet, who was diagnosed just over a year before our interview, had counseled people through grief in a past job and knew that acceptance could be a far-reaching goal for her.

"I feel like [acceptance] is an ongoing, probably never-to-be-finished process. I feel grief almost every day, and yet there are also periods where I feel like I have a handle. If not on the disease itself, I have a handle on a way of living with it that works for me," she said. "So it comes and goes."

THE GRIEVING PROCESS: SPIRAL RATHER THAN LINEAR

And, really, that leads to the next piece: the process of grief. In the past, in Kübler-Ross's work and others from that period, grief was seen as an adaptive yet very linear and pre-dictable process. Individuals mourning everything from their own deaths to the death of a beloved pet, from the loss of a job to the loss of a limb, could be expected to move through certain stages, reach a sense of acceptance, and be done with it.

Because her work related to individuals who were studied through their stages and then fairly quickly died, the findings may not relate directly to patients who now live through or at least for considerably longer periods with diseases and condi-tions that in the past were almost always fatal. Now, as I pointed out in the last chapter, better detection methods and advances in treatments for most diseases leave individuals to cycle through some of these emotions long after treatment has ended and a remission or cure has been achieved. As Violet said, emotions related to grief come and go.

Shirley is discovering this. Now undergoing treatment for yet another relapse of her breast cancer, she found herself approaching a double mastectomy and cycling through feel-ings of depression and fear, emotions with which she thought she was finished. This time she sought professional help in coping with them.

Many, many others also reported feeling denial, isola-tion, disbelief, numbness, anger, frustration, bargaining, depression, fear, panic, and anxiety alternating with accept-ance when faced with regular appointments following the end of initial treatments, when scheduling and following through with tests even years after diagnosis, and when confronted with the news that the disease had reappeared. Certain incidental contact with the medical world or their past treatment experience—the smell of rubbing alcohol, driving by the hospital in which they were treated, hearing the name of their doctor—caused some to experience flashbacks to their earlier trauma. Even when the news is good and the all clear is given once again, individuals said it took them a while to readjust to living their lives as a well person again.

Because of this, it is perhaps more accurate to say that those who live through diagnosis and beyond treatment experience grief in a more circular or spiral fashion than a linear one. For them, these are emotions that may lessen with time but will likely be felt repeatedly in relation to the disease for years to come.

One other aspect of grief to remember during this time is that it cannot be rushed through or avoided altogether. Grief takes as long as it needs to work its way through a person, and the length of time it takes is as individual as the person experiencing it. Some seek to avoid the pain of grief by numbing themselves through addictions. One study on long-term breast cancer survivors, for example, found that thirty-eight percent of these survivors used alcohol or prescription medication to soothe fears years after treatment ended.

Others either rush themselves through it or are rushed by well-meaning loved ones who force those who have completed treatment into positive thoughts and a return to living a normal life in order to avoid the negative aspects of grieving. One Australian study published in 2004 found that the survivors of blood cancers felt it was important to face the grief rather than feel frightened of negative emotions. "Allow them to digest it all and allow them to be upset about it," one participant said. "Allow yourself to feel unlucky."

REAL STORY—TONDA

To understand the myriad feelings that Tonda experienced with regard to her diagnosis of Parkinson's disease, it is important to understand her life before she ever heard those words or suspected she had it.

Tonda

It was 1997 and Tonda fit the definition of supermom with her very full life. She and her husband raised their children in a suburban home where the value of helping others was central to their lives. Tonda often spent four to five hours a day with her kids, taking them to their after-school activities and helping them with homework. On weekends, she also took them with her to volunteer at a local children's museum and somehow squeezed in time for friends and social life around her sixty-hour workweeks spent teaching social studies at the middle-school level.

Life was good.

"I had your sort of 'death really hasn't touched me' kind of thing. I'd never been sick. All my kids were healthy. My husband was robust and my parents were raging. Everything was great," Tonda said during her interview, adding that one of her friends had died but she had recovered from that experience. "Other than that, it was just sort of this thing happened somewhere else."

This "thing" is an incurable, degenerative illness, Parkinson's disease. It first showed up in her life in that year as a vague but present muscular heaviness and weakness. She went through a few tests, but doctors diagnosed her as having rheumatoid arthritis (RA). Despite the lack of a positive test for the condition, they began to treat her for it.

Tonda somehow knew this wasn't exactly right when one of her hands occasionally began to shake uncontrollably—something that worried her. But what worried her more was the thought that it could be much more serious than RA. So she went along with the doctor's program of losing weight to reduce stress on joints, all the while hiding her shaking limb in her pocket and making alterations to the way that she lived her daily life.

"I was making a lot of drastic behaviors in my lifestyle, you know, changing what I did and hiding the tremors that had come. I had no idea what it was from. I didn't even complain about it," she said.

Looking back on it, she realizes that she was in denial over the severity of the symptoms and afraid to press for answers she didn't really want. "It was very important for me to deny any serious physical condition, especially if it might be chronic or terminal," Tonda said. "I was hiding it in every possible way, while inside I knew that there was something that was really wrong with me. I knew that there was something really wrong with me to the point where it got to be almost on a daily basis. I would actually get a physical reaction of fear because I knew that something was terribly wrong, but at the same time, I would take that moment and shove it down and pick up my work and put on my shoes and get ready and go and take care of my kids and laugh.

"And if I did that long enough, then maybe these things would pass. But they didn't," Tonda continued. "I spent so much time with my hands in my pockets and under my arms and everywhere else to keep people from seeing my tremors that my hands became paler than the rest of my arms. You know what I mean?"

But she didn't fool her family doctor. While having her blood pressure checked during a regular physical exam in 2003, Tonda's arm began its familiar dance. It did not escape the doctor's notice. He put her through a series of neurological tests and told her he suspected Parkinson's disease. That was followed by a series of CT (computerized tomography) scans, MRIs, and further tests, all of which confirmed his suspicions.

Though she was stoic when she heard the final diagnosis and the fact the disease had progressed fairly far already, Tonda began to feel isolated. She desperately wanted to talk to others about the diagnosis but found there were few who understood. "I can tell you that when you have those moments of fear and you say, 'Gosh, there's something really wrong with me,' you don't feel like there's anyone you can talk to about it. That's an extremely isolating situation, don't you think?"

Her grieving progressed from that point. She felt anger over the fact that she had put off things she wanted to pursue and enjoy in order to raise her kids and set up her lifestyle and now felt limited by the disease in accomplishing those pursuits. Her frustration comes and goes with each progression of the symptoms. In the week before she was interviewed, Tonda realized it was becoming too difficult to handwrite anything anymore.

"Now, that doesn't seem like a big thing, but I was a teacher. I was a big communicator. I used to love to hand-write. I prided myself in it. It's a small private thing, you know," she said. "I've never complained about this to anyone either. But a week or so ago, I kept struggling to try to write. I put my pen down and said, 'I won't be writing anymore.' It's just too difficult and I can't read it. It's a little, small thing that was private because it happened to me and it made me sad."

While she didn't bargain in the traditional sense, Tonda did feel the crushing sense of depression. Changes in the brain due to Parkinson's can cause depression, a known symptom of the disease. With the help of antidepressants and patient support, she has been able to manage this aspect of grieving thus far.

In fact, she finds the depression to be somewhat cathartic in that it has helped her becoming more accepting of her diagnosis and move past it. "With the depression, you kind of realize the fact that, okay, here you are standing in a room all by yourself and you have this thing with you. It's not going to go away. It has affected your life and it's going to continue to affect your life so that's what the depression kind of comes from," Tonda explained. "But that's like a threshold of acceptance. You're not going to be able to bar-gain your way out of it or be good enough to get out of it or find a doctor who can cure it. It just is not going to be there for you right now.

"And then one day, I started having some days where I

actually thought I was living again, you know. I found something that was enjoyable in spite of everything. It wasn't just all about the disease every minute of the day," she said, adding that she still experiences grieving, especially when she finds she has lost abilities due to the progression of the disease.

But Tonda also learned to cherish some of the changes that the disease has brought into her life, including an increased closeness with family and friends and greater inner strength. It continues to teach her a better way of dealing with the curve balls that life has thrown to her with Parkinson's.

"Life is always good. Even when bad things happen, it can be a good day. Experience it. Deal with it. Incorporate it. Live it. And go on. Because every day is another opportunity and change is what life is about," Tonda said. "Life isn't about becoming so intelligent, wealthy, and powerful that you can control all the aspects of it. Sometimes, life is about letting go and just riding the wave and appreciating it for what it is and not being afraid just because you don't know what's coming next."

PART II

Finding the Five Gifts of Illness

4

ILLUMINATION: FINDING MEANING AND WORTH IN SUFFERING

That which does not kill me makes me stronger.
—Friedrich Nietzsche, philosopher

GOING THROUGH THE experience of diagnosis of and treatment for a life-threatening illness easily highlights the worst parts of life. The fear for one's life, the mourning for the different losses, the treatments that are physically excruciating, the worry that one may have to do it all over again—all of this can take an emotional and spiritual toll and leave those who experience these illnesses morose and bereft of hope, as we learned in the last chapter.

And yet there appears to be much to gain from the experience of surviving a chronic or acute serious illness. All of those whom I interviewed for this book could attest to at least one area of positive change in their lives that came as a result of having the illness with which they were diagnosed. For them the experience is not an entirely negative one but rather one with some redemption, sometimes significantly so.

Before seeing these gifts of illness, which are individually highlighted in the next five chapters, many of the individuals went through what I call illumination. For the purposes of this book, illumination is a term given to the process of finding the positive transformative effects of illness. It can occur in a moment when the bleak, dark, initial experience of illness dramatically gives way to the luminous discovery of the positive gains and gifts from the experience, or it can be a more gradual dawning, a collection of small moments accumulated and realized through the various trials that these illnesses present along the way.

It is also important to note that this illumination is different from the grieving process, though it can and usually does occur at the same time. Grieving is a more reactive process, while illumination is a more proactive process, as you will see.

FIGHT OR FLIGHT

It's not whether you get knocked down. It's whether you get up.
—Vince Lombardi, professional football coach

Amy was certainly knocked down when, at thirty-seven, she was diagnosed with type 1 diabetes, usually considered a pediatric-onset disease. Though the signs had been there for months, she explained them away. A mother who had just given birth to a third child five months earlier, Amy was thrilled that the pregnancy weight loss continued despite the fact that she had weaned her daughter from the breast to the bottle, usually a time when the mother's weight stabilizes. She also was exhausted, something she knew from prior experience came with the territory of having a newborn. Her unquenchable thirst was attributable to using allergy medicine, she was sure.

Nearly in a diabetic coma with sky-high blood sugar levels, Amy sought help at the insistence of her husband after he pointed out that she'd withered away to almost skeletal proportions. Her primary care physician diagnosed her within moments, and she was sent to the hospital for a week's stay.

Upon her return, she fell into a funk. "We got home and I got on the couch. I cried and stayed there all day. Then I got up in the late evening, you know, off the couch and said, 'Okay, screw this. I'm not going to lie around and feel sorry for myself. I'm going to do something about this,'" Amy said. "I told that to my husband. I said, 'You know, I'm really bummed and this sucks. But don't worry. This is the last day that I'll be sitting on the couch crying.'"

"I got up and I got on the Internet. I started looking for medical IDs," Amy said, adding that she then ordered her first medical alert bracelet that day. "Then I started researching [the disease] and I basically haven't stopped since.

"I'm telling you: It's fight or flight. I was like, 'I'm going to fight this. I'm just not going to lie down and let this misery wash over me, you know. I choose not to do that.'"

When met with the possibility of mortal peril due to a life-threatening disease, none of those interviewed for this book decided to lie down and take the consequences. When faced with the attacker that their diagnosis represented, they decided to fight back, most with tooth-and-nail ferocity. This was often their first proactive step following the diagnosis.

Even those who had a history of depression and who had considered suicide in the past told me that they decided to undergo rigorous treatments rather than immediately dial the nearest hospice. Marilyn is a good example of this.

A while before she was diagnosed with colon cancer that had metastasized to her liver, Marilyn's father committed suicide. Deep depression also dogged her, making her feel that she, too, would follow his path and take her own life. But when confronted with the diagnosis, she decided to undergo not only having a third of her colon surgically removed but also entering a rigorous medical treatment program that included several rounds of chemotherapy to kill the cancer in her liver.

Marilyn moved from her house in a big city to her sister's more rural home to be closer to the treating hospital. Her hair gone from the chemo, her body bloated from steroids, her surgical scars still an angry red, Marilyn relaxed on the back porch one afternoon between treatments and began to love her life.

"The first time I remember it happening, I was just on the back porch and the sunlight was so bright and pretty. I just felt this exquisite joy, just joy at being able to draw breath. It was like joy for no reason other than just being alive," she said. "My cancer taught me that I want to live so much. I love being alive. That suicide is not going to happen for me."

Another proactive step in fighting back, aside from entering into and enduring treatment, is using the weapons that education provides. Learning about the causes of a disease as well as treatment options gives a person a feeling of some control over a traditionally uncontrollable situation. By researching the medical and surgical choices, an individual can make an informed decision over which treatment path to take, rather than blindly groping for solutions or letting others dictate the direction. A diabetic, for example, can learn about different food choices and how they affect how much insulin is needed, how exercise can help with weight loss and blood sugar maintenance, how an insulin pump can help achieve optimum blood sugar levels, and how to prolong life and avoid serious complications. A person with Inflammatory bowel disease (IBD) can figure out which medications can control certain immunological responses, which surgery will best deal with a complication that medication cannot help, how the disease can manifest itself in other areas of the body, and how to slow its progression. A heart attack survivor can learn about safe sodium and fat counts in his or her daily diet, how exercise can strengthen his or her heart, which medications can ease symptoms and prevent others, and when transplant is the only option. The effect in all of these situations and more is to calm a person's fear by giving that person the confidence that comes from taking an active role in fighting one's illness.

And this education helps to foster acceptance, a key part of the grieving process. Why would a person learn about a disease he or she still deeply denied having? Why would medical and surgical options be weighed if the disease demanding his or her consideration was a fallacy? An individual learning about and considering all of his or her medical and surgical options may still bargain or be angry or be depressed. But the action of gaining the weapon of education and using it forces an individual out of some parts of denial and into acceptance, a necessary and healthy process for moving the grieving process forward.

According to a literature review published in 2001 on the topic of adjusting to cancer, Dr. James Brennan found that reaching acceptance was an important part of the grieving process, one that if not achieved could have lasting drastic consequences. He compared two papers, one on cancer adaptation and another on bereavement literature, saying, "The authors speculated that acceptance of the situation is important for adjusting to it when the situation, like cancer, has to be endured. This view is consistent with bereavement literature, which indicates that denial is a 'temporary situation' or defense which, if it persists, can lead to later maladaptive adjustment."

FINDING A REASON FOR THE ILLNESS

To survive is to learn to live, because the skills and attributes of survivorship are not innate, they are learned.

—Ellen Bushkin, cancer advocate

At the same time that they were looking into ways to treat their disease, the respondents also reported seeking the answer to the question, "Why me?" And while there are seemingly a million replies, two particular themes arose in the searches: finding the medical cause for the disease and discovering purpose in its journey.

The first of these themes seeks to locate or pinpoint the set of circumstances or specific predisposition that caused the occurrence of the disease. Researchers, like the psychologist Dr. Shelley Taylor, believe that this is an attempt to make sense of the diagnosis and the disease. Taylor published a landmark paper in 1983 on the theory of cognitive adaptation with regard to adjusting to threatening events. To understand this thought process, she interviewed seventy-eight female breast cancer survivors. Taylor found that 95 percent of her study subjects spoke of a reason for their diagnosis, including stress, which was usually attributed to a problem relationship, exposure to a carcinogen, hereditary factors, diet, or a blow to the breast.

"People will make attributions so as to understand, predict, and control their environment," Taylor wrote.

For some diseases, the cause is obvious. To the woman born into a family in which breast cancer kills most of the females before they reach their sixth decade, such a diagnosis is not hard to fathom. To the smoker who consumed three packs a day for three decades, chronic obstructive pulmonary disease is almost expected. To the sedentary, overweight, and overstressed individual, a heart attack is not out of the ordinary.

But some diseases require more imagination, more digging to find reasons for their existence. Sean is a vegetarian who ate only organically grown fruits and vegetables. Sure, she had a high-powered job, but she also sought balance through her daily exercise routine of rigorous mountain biking or climbing for hours on end. At forty-five, she was as fit as a person her age could be.

And then she was diagnosed with ovarian cancer, a disease that generally strikes women in the sixth and seventh decade of life. With no family history, Sean told me that the first question in her mind was, "Why?" At the time of her diagnosis, she asked doctors to remove a contraceptive intrauterine device (IUD), only to find that a previously inserted one was still in place.

"It was a shock about being betrayed by my body," Sean said. "But they think that there's a high likelihood that the two IUDs and the ongoing inflammatory infections was a contributing factor. So I had an explanation as to why. This wasn't just some random act."

For some individuals, the cause may never be known. Why, for example, did the fit, athletic, young woman have a stroke when there was no family history of cardiovascular disease and no other risk factors? Why did the active artist develop lung cancer when he never smoked a day in his life? Why did the healthy, young white woman develop a disease found almost exclusively in older black men? For these people, there may be a prolonged and sometimes unending quest to make sense of the senseless.

FINDING DEEPER MEANING IN ILLNESS, IN LIFE, IN SURVIVING

He who has a why to live for can bear with almost any how.

—Nietzsche

But there is also a deeper search for meaning involved in survival, in particular the assigning of meaning to the challenges illness presents as well as to the remainder of one's life, no matter how long or short that time will be. This second theme emerged quite often and led to illumination of the five gifts of illness.

One predominant piece of literature that explores this quest for meaning in the extreme experience comes from Dr. Viktor Frankl in his 1946 book *Man's Search for Meaning*. In the book, Frankl, an Austrian psychiatrist, details his experience as an inmate in several Nazi concentration camps during World War II. On page after page he tells of the nearly constant assaults on his very being that he was made to endure:

the loss of his freedom for the "crime" of being born a Jew, the murder of his family and friends, the confiscation of a manuscript to which he had devoted his professional life, the exposure to constant cruel and inhumane treatment, the forced job of having to choose who would live and who would die while serving as a slave in the camp infirmary.

And yet he found meaning in the struggle. Frankl wrote eloquently of the elements of life that helped to sustain him during that time, things that he took for granted in the past that now became greatly appreciated: love, humor, art. He focused on images of his beloved wife and parents, all of whom had died shortly after arriving in the camps, though he was not aware of this at the time. He revived his spirit in the sparks of humor he found in camp life. He cherished the sound of a violin mournfully playing one night. In other words, Frankl believed that he survived the nearly unsurvivable conditions and experiences by finding meaning in his suffering, something he believed was an active choice.

"If there is any meaning in life at all, then there must be a meaning in suffering. Suffering is an ineradicable part of life, even as fate and death. Without suffering and death, human life cannot be complete," he wrote.

Also, Frankl believed that *how* a person handled the inevitable suffering very much influenced the meaning conveyed in the experience. "The way in which a man accepts his fate and all the suffering it entails, the way in which he takes up his cross, gives him ample opportunity—even under the most difficult circumstances—to add deeper meaning to his life. It may remain brave, dignified and unselfish. Or in the bitter fight for self-preservation he may forget his human dignity and become no more than an animal. Here lies the chance for a man either to make use of or to forgo the opportunities of attaining the moral values that a difficult situation may afford him. And this decides whether he is worthy of his sufferings or not."

Frankl believed that sometimes just finding a reason to go on gives people the gumption to continue, at the same time imbuing the lives of the sufferers with greater depth. Even in the face of unavoidable pain and loss, meaning can be attained, he said. "When we are no longer able to change a situation—just think of an incurable disease such as inoperable cancer—we are challenged to change ourselves," Frankl wrote. "In accepting this challenge to suffer bravely, life has a meaning up to the last moment, and it retains this meaning literally to the end."

Obviously, Frankl's work is applicable in the understanding of life-threatening illness. Many, many research papers on the topic quote directly from his work or list it in the citations. In one such paper published in 2001, Susan and Peter Strang, a Swedish nurse and professor, respectively, studied twenty people with brain tumors and sixteen of their spouses. They found that while some patients fared well and reported a good quality of life, others with the same external circumstances did not. The researchers theorized that, in addition to developing good coping skills and an understanding of the situation, this positive transformation was in part due to a patient's ability to construe personal meaning from the situation.

"Everyone wrestles at times with existential and spiritual issues, but these questions are accentuated when a person is diagnosed with a serious disease," the Strangs wrote. "The component of meaningfulness creates motivation and is therefore central. Frankl supports this by stating, 'There is nothing in the world that would so effectively help one to survive even the worst conditions as the knowledge that there is a meaning in one's life.'"

In a 1999 paper on the subject of the meaning of quality of life in cancer survivorship, the authors also quote Frankl's work, adding, "He believed that making meaning is a basic human need necessary for human fulfillment. Deriving meaning from one's life may not be an easy task. It is a journey that people often postpone until such time that they must face their own mortality, experience suffering or undergo a life-changing experience."

In the nearly three dozen papers reviewed for this book, nine cite Frankl as a source, if not quote from his work directly in the text, while most of the others cite the papers as sources, clearly indicating the importance of meaningfulness in survival.

MEANING, ILLUMINATION, AND THE GIFTS OF ILLNESS

For the individuals interviewed for this book, finding meaning in their illness, in their survival, and in their lives in general was also linked with illumination of the five gifts of illness. In many ways, finding the meaning in a life marked by the suffering from illness is a necessary struggle involved in sustained survival. Without meaning, there is no purpose in getting through the treatments or weathering the worries of relapse or recurrence. The gifts of illness were the meanings assigned to particular areas of life that the interviewees discovered or the greater value they found through illumination.

While finding the gifts of illness seemed to be inevitable, there appeared to be neither a prescribed path nor a time frame involved in their discovery. Meaning and the gifts for those interviewed for this book were uncovered either all at once or as part of a process, something I referred to in interviews as either a point or a process of illumination. Nearly everyone who spoke about illumination in their interviews had a different experience, though they arrived at very similar emotional and spiritual destinations.

For some, illumination came at a singular point in time, a sort of "Aha!" moment. Like a bolt of lightning out of a clear blue sky, the realization that there are affirming elements in illness or that a diagnosis and treatment can lead to a positive transformation suddenly dawned on these individuals.

These points in time happened in places as varied as in a hospital room or in a church, in a car while driving, or on the phone while talking to a friend. And they happened at various points in their illness, anywhere from shortly after diagnosis to years after a remission was achieved. Usually, the positive benefits or effects were always there, but something, somewhere, at some time made these individuals suddenly take notice.

Jim is one individual who experienced the point-of-illumination phenomenon. He told me that one day not long after experiencing some trouble with his body functions due to his early-onset Parkinson's disease, he found himself inside a church. He stayed up all night, praying, reading from Scripture, and meditating on his fate, hoping to find answers as to why he was suffering.

"When I was finished, I remember I felt really just hopeless, as if my life was never going to get any better. I turned off the light and sat there for a long time," Jim recalled. "And when the sun came up, I remember thinking, 'You know, this isn't the worst thing that could happen to me. Whatever is going on is not—there are worse things in life.'"

That moment occurred to him again later when he and his father went duck hunting. "We were talking and he said, 'You know, it really sucks that this is going on with you.' I looked at him and almost automatically said, 'No. You know, it's not.' By that point, I had realized that even though it was having effects on my life that I didn't want, it was also rapidly becoming a very powerful method of change for me," Jim said.

But most interviewees said that illumination came to them as the gifts were realized, in a slow but rewarding process. One such individual is Brenda. After receiving a diagnosis of sarcoidosis of the lungs, she essentially put the disease out of her mind, not really comprehending the serious threat it posed to her existence. She got married and focused on raising her son.

When a particular exacerbation of her disease landed her in the hospital for three months and brought her to death's door, Brenda began to see all of the little things in her life for which she was grateful. At first she saw new value in relationships. Though she was forced to quit her job, she replaced that work by spending her time creating a national support network for others with her rare condition; in doing so, she began to value her new role in helping others.

"I call the sarcoidosis the gift of enlightenment. It's done a lot of positive things in my life. Before the disease, I took my life for granted. I thought I was sort of invincible, I guess. I just thought, you know, I'll be here forever,"

Brenda said. "I don't think that way anymore because I don't take life for granted. I don't take people for granted."

And like the process of grieving, the process of illumination cannot be rushed. Rather, it unfurls either slowly or quickly, but only at the pace of the individual experiencing it and likely not until some grieving has been experienced. Nor can the negative parts of the illness experience be swept under the rug, to be entirely forgotten or dismissed. Commonly, either the patient or his or her friends or family members want to put the episode behind them as soon as remission or cure is attained, prodding themselves or the individual with the illness to pick up with life as it was before the illness was diagnosed, seen as a "return to normal." But when the body has undergone the assault of disease and treatment, it is not the only part of the person that changes. A newer depth and understanding of life and its meaning alters everything from relationships to emotional reactions, from living in the now to resetting goals for the future.

One researcher who addressed this topic is Karen Hassey Dow. In 1992, in the journal *Cancer*, Hassey Dow, then a doctoral candidate in nursing, wrote, "Getting well does not mean getting back to normal. Return to normalcy does not mean a return to the same place, but a re-entry into a different place after treatment."

Another researcher, Dr. Pam McGrath of Australia, in studying the spiritual and emotional effects of serious illness for a paper published in 2004, reported that the hematological cancer patients she interviewed were pushed by well-meaning friends and relatives to get back to their pre-illness selves as well as to develop a positive attitude toward survival and life in general. She found that this process of finding the positive in the experience, if it was discovered at all, could not be forced upon the patient.

"The outcome of allowing a positive orientation to unfold over time with despair acknowledged and integrated is an authentic, rather than artificially forced, positive orientation. The findings affirm . . . that a positive or hopeful outlook is a power that comes from within. It cannot be imposed or given, only fostered," she wrote.

The 2001 paper published by the Strangs further backs up this notion of self-discovery by saying, "An individual struggling with the questions of life has to find his or her own answers to the challenging life questions and thus find meaning by himself or herself."

REVEALING THE FIVE GIFTS OF ILLNESS

However and whenever it happened, the interviewees said they found the gifts of illness in this point or process of illumination. We will get further into the five gifts in the following chapters, but for now they are briefly summarized below by a handful of participants as they were revealed during their point or process of illumination:

- For some of the interviewees, relationships and their newly assigned values were seen in a positive light. These were relationships with family members, with old friends, or with new friends made during the diagnostic and treatment experiences. While there was a general weeding-out process and some accompanying loss with older relationships, many told me that they found that they placed deeper value on the remaining relationships at the same time that they found a reward in discovering new relationships.

Violet is one who can attest to the latter. Diagnosed with type 1 diabetes as an adult, she found solace and more in a support group for diabetics. "A big moment was when I first went to the support group because I had a sense of camaraderie that I hadn't expected to feel, and I had a sense of support and goodwill with a type of understanding that comes from living the experience," she said. "I felt a kinship with those individuals and I realized, too, [that] I felt very quickly feelings of caring for several of them. I realized that I would have been sorry not to have had the chance of encountering them. But I never would have had that experience had I not gotten [the disease]."

Later in her interview with me, she said she continued to find friends through publishing online written works about her experiences with diabetes. "I'm an introvert, so I naturally have a small circle of close friends rather than a larger circle, and so for me to make a friend is a life-changing event. You know, it doesn't happen that easily," Violet said. "So, when I say that I've made some important acquaintances and one good friend in the year that I've been blogging [about diabetes], for me, that's remarkable."

• Still more interviewees saw a new value in the experience of helping others through similarly difficult times. The vast majority of those I interviewed reported little or no volunteer activity prior to their diagnosis, with some saying that they did a little charity work but nothing with regard to their specific illness. Following diagnosis and entering treatment, most said they took on new volunteer roles, with some devoting the rest of their lives to helping others survive a similar experience.

Marianne is one of those individuals. Diagnosed with type 1 diabetes at the age of twenty-two, she was then working for a large Internet company. After initially denying her illness or hiding it from others, she soon decided to embrace the diagnosis when she saw that others were learning from her experience. She dropped her job and entered a master's program, in the hope of becoming a diabetes educator. "What really started this whole gradual awakening to where I really saw all the positive things about it is that I've become a resource person," Marianne said. "So many people have come to me with questions about diabetes, and so that motivated me to learn more not just about the condition but living with it.

"Everybody started coming to me and it was a really great feeling. I could be a resource," she said.

- Some felt a new or greater appreciation of the sense of time and being. For so many people when they are enjoying good health, time passes without notice and the sense of well-being is taken for granted. But when serious illness entered the picture, the existential threat to time and being became a motivational force for many of the interviewees to find meaning in these elements.

Graham is one who understands this concept

deeply. At twenty-seven, he had just moved in with his girlfriend and was discovering joy and fulfillment in his job as a Web site designer. He had thoughts of enjoying travel in the future and maybe someday getting married and having children. Then Graham was diagnosed with a grade 4 cancerous brain tumor and had to undergo surgery to remove the tumor, plus radiation and chemotherapy to prevent it from coming back. The experience left him with an inability to plan far into the future, as he feels the amount of time that remains for him is uncertain, at best.

Because of this, Graham shortened the time line on his existing plans and sought to make new ones at the same time. He took motorbike lessons, something he had always wanted to try but for which he lacked real motivation or courage. Now thirty, he also married the woman who was his girlfriend at the time of his diagnosis and is considering starting a family with her, the timing of which has increased in urgency. "We are seriously thinking about having a child, which I probably would never have considered at my age," Graham said. "It was always, you know, five years ahead."

"I feel like I have to [have a child now] because, you know, with all the research I've done, there is a strong chance that I could have a recurrence," he said, adding that the likelihood of his continued survival would diminish considerably if that were to occur.

- Some of those interviewed became more committed to having a more emotionally fulfilling life. After facing a threat to their very existence, most reported having less fear in their daily lives, freeing them up to experience greater joy, a decreased intensity of sadness, more sentimentality, and fewer negative emotions such as anger and jealousy.

Emily used to be somewhat fearful of what others thought of her and often placed their happiness above her own. She also felt disappointment in others and in her own actions at times. But after doctors discovered a seventeen-inch-long tumor in her belly, she began to lose that fear, replacing it with a more predominant and present fear for her own life. After treatment for lymphoma, she found a significant and welcome shift in the way she experienced these and other emotions.

"I've started to see more clearly over the years because cancer has changed my perspective on things. It changed the way I act toward people. It changed because I just decided life's too short," Emily said. "I used to be really submissive and deferential and, you know, I'd do things to make people happy even if it took away from my happiness. And now I do things to help people but I don't do things anymore that are going to make me sad. I don't say, you know, 'Sure, let's go do that thing' even if I don't want to."

• All of these changes led to strong shifts in the life goals of many of the interviewees. Professional goals, family goals, retirement goals, and spiritual goals all changed as the life they lived before diagnosis at times bore no resemblance to the life they lived after.

Dave was a high school art teacher when he was

first diagnosed with early-onset Parkinson's disease. It was a job he loved, but he always had a secret ambition to live solely for his own art. When the disease progressed to the point where he could no longer teach, he left his job and devoted his time to his art. He developed a greater level of concentration for his work and honed his skills considerably in the process, eventually leading him to national shows and greater recognition for this passion.

"I feel like I've done more with this since I've had Parkinson's than I did before, and I don't mean just the time I spend on it. But I feel like I've made great advances in the level of my work," he said.

When illness strikes, it is natural to react to the losses that follow and to grieve for them. It is also natural to learn about the disease, to use the knowledge to fight it, to seek answers as to why it happened in the first place, and to find meaning in the experience as well as the time remaining in life. We are different people as a result of having survived a challenge to our very existence. Because of this, it is normal to pay attention to the lessons of the experience and to integrate the negative changes that illness brings. At the same time, many actively seek the positive elements in the experience, with the result being illumination.

In the following chapters, I discuss the separate gifts of illness, using some of the interviewees' comments as well as research on the topics to broaden the understanding of the five gifts of illness.

REAL STORY—MY ILLUMINATION

My moment of illumination, a turning point in my life when I began to seen a disease that ravages my intestines as a gift, happened in the first half of September 1999 in a darkened hospital room in Royal Oak, Michigan.

Really, the trouble started earlier in the summer when I had developed a rather large intestinal abscess along with severe Crohn's symptoms. I had dropped weight, alternately sweated and shook through fevers that registered greater than 104 degrees, and found myself in the bathroom an average of twenty times a day with bloody diarrhea and unrelenting abdominal pain. My doctor and I had exhausted all of the other remedies that had worked in the past, so he sent me to a renowned specialist in another city for a consultation on a new drug, Remicade. I had initially taken a single dose of the drug once just four months earlier, but the specialist suggested that this time we try a course of three doses of the drug, then a new biologic weapon that short-circuited the inflammatory cascade of events that was causing all of this trouble.

I had my first dose of the three-dose cycle at the end of August, infused over a four-hour stay in the hospital. The drug carries with it some wicked side effects, including anaphylactic shock and severely suppressed white counts, possible events my doctor had warned me about. He also said to call in case anything else out of the ordinary happened.

Ten days later, I called my doctor. Though my intestinal pain and the trips to the bathroom had decreased dramatically, my elbow was killing me. And while joint pain is an expected part of my disease, this was extreme. I couldn't straighten my arm without feeling as if I had broken the joint. I called his office that evening and was directed to the doctor on call, not my usual gastroenterologist but a great one nevertheless. He didn't share my concern, so two Tylenol 3s later, I was in bed, struggling for sleep.

I awoke three hours later, now with pain in both knees, both elbows, both hips, and both shoulders, and a strange surging feeling in my head. On the way to the bathroom, I fainted twice and then twice more after that on the way to the living room couch. My mother came to watch my son and my husband took me to the emergency room.

On the way to the hospital, I recognized that I was seriously sick and in no position to be fighting whatever it was that was attacking me. A very recent blood test had shown that a different immune-suppressing drug plus the Remicade had lowered my white blood cell level to dangerously low levels, a condition known as leucopenia. Forcing back vomit, losing consciousness, head hanging out the car window as it moved briskly through the crisp morning air, I silently pleaded with God to let me live through whatever was happening.

Then just thirty, I had a lot to live for. My family was young and my death would destroy it. Well, maybe not my husband, who had hinted that he would hire a hot young au pair to take my place in the event of my death, but my son would not fare as well, as he and I had developed a tight bond. I also felt in that moment that I hadn't accomplished all I could as a writer, a career that is more of a vocation for me. "I'm not done yet," I prayed.

Once in the emergency room, I was ushered into a private area that is designated to protect people with little immunity from all the germs that otherwise reside in the

ER. Copious vials of blood were taken and tested, the results of which adjusted the on-call doctor's view of the situation, as it showed no immune system and a septic infection. To rule out another abscess, he ordered a CT scan, a test for which a large amount of nasty-tasting contrast liquid must be swallowed first. I knew this wouldn't work the normal way, as I was nauseous to begin with, and after I projectile vomited the liquid a few times across the room, the nurses agreed as well. Two of them held my arms while a third shoved a tube up my nose and down my throat. The liquid stayed down, the scan was taken, and the results were negative for another abscess.

My doctor, a saint of a man in my experience, came to the hospital early that morning, his day off, to follow what was happening to me. He tried to reach some of the researchers who had worked on the development of the medication to see if they had experience with my unusual reaction to it. As I waited for the admitting staff to find me a room, he sat with me, soothing my fears and his own, as he appeared a bit shaken by this drastic turn of events.

Shortly after I was moved to a room, herds of specialists descended on me. Teams of people in white coats— gastroenterologists, gynecologists, infectious disease specialists, internists, and surgeons—came in, checked my test results, pushed on various parts of my body, scratched their heads, and left. Medical and nursing students poured into my room, none having any regard for my pain or my exhaustion. They probed me, their special septic-patient/sideshow-freak-of-the-day, posed the same queries over and over, and wouldn't leave until I finally refused to answer any more of their questions. I regret to say that I was pleasant only to one of the nursing students, who was particularly gentle with me, since all of my major joints were now seizing in incredible pain with the slightest movement. He helped me clean myself, taking great care in the process to preserve my dignity. I appreciated the way he also found a different method of weighing me as he wrapped my body in a thick rubber sheet and dangled me from the device, something he confessed that he had just done to a feeble 92-year-old woman. *This just gets better*, I thought.

During the next few days, I was pumped full of the strongest antibiotics available, along with several other medications, to attempt to arrest the infection and to increase my blood counts. Though blood was drawn seemingly every hour, the results remained the same. It didn't matter what they did, what cocktail of chemicals they delivered into my veins, my white blood cell levels refused to budge; all of my vital blood levels—hemoglobin, hematocrit, platelets, everything—stayed in the basement of blood results. At this point, my immune system was depleted, leaving me with very few white cells to fight the infection that pushed my fever to 103 and 104 degree for hours a day.

Without a functioning immune system, I was ordered to stay in my room for fear that I would catch yet another infection that I would be even less equipped to fight. Except for close family members, all visitors were dissuaded from coming and were told to call instead; my husband was the only one to visit after that proclamation, coming in for five minutes and wearing a surgical mask, as he had the beginnings of a cold.

As the tests continued, my spirits sank. The effect of these restrictions, the daily disappointment with the blood test results, and the suddenness of the illness sent me into a spiral of sadness and loneliness, feelings that recalled my original diagnosis but the depths of which were new to me. It is hard not to feel lonely when you are sick, even if the hospital isn't choking off support systems like friends and family members. Being ill is an inherently isolating experience, as you rarely, if ever, can share an illness with someone. And being alone can lead to a desperate sense of sadness, even in the strongest of souls. During the days I spent in this form of isolation, I wept often, unable to find relief even from the soothingly sweet Nigerian-born nurse, who watched over me daily and hugged me often. The end seemed nowhere in sight, as my blood tests returned worse, not better.

Since I had nothing but time to myself during those days, I began to think about all that had happened in the ten years since my diagnosis. Since that cold February day in 1989, my life had gone on as if nothing had happened. I finished college, graduating a semester early with honors in December 1990. I started writing for local newspapers and then as an assistant to a bureau chief of a national newspaper. Joel and I married in April 1994, bought a house six months later, and had our son a little over a year after that. This constant motion to the rhythms of young-adult life helped to keep my mind from integrating the disease fully into my life.

But in reality, my disease kept creeping into my life, despite my best efforts to shove it out. I was well when I graduated at twenty-one, but then I went through several bowel obstructions over the next two years, which resulted in my second surgery, at twenty-three. I was well when I married at twenty-five but was sick by the time we bought the house; my disease went into remission while I was pregnant at twenty-six but returned with a vengeance following the birth of Jonah. I had my third surgery at twenty-nine, but the disease returned again four months after that, when my father died of colon cancer. Through all of this, I suffered but then pushed myself to get back to "normal" life, despite having to take handfuls of pills each day to combat the symptoms, endure countless colonoscopies and other painful tests and procedures, and struggle daily through fevers, abdominal pain, joint pain, and bloody diarrhea.

While it would have been logical and easy at this point of pain and abject misery to simply wish my life away, that didn't happen. In fact, the opposite did. And it all started on my last night in the hospital.

Finding the Meaning and the Gifts

A hematologist was called in to consult on my condition. As he sat on the edge of my bed, he explained that he was brought in on my case because my blood counts were not budging from way below acceptable levels and I really needed for that to happen if I was to head home anytime soon. He said a medication he ordered would help to push the new white cells from the bone marrow, thus boosting my counts. A nurse gave me the first shot, taking care to teach me how to do it, as I would have to continue this at home.

For many reasons, sleep did not come to me that night. Gazing out the window at the darkening autumn sky, I began to acknowledge just how serious the disease had been. I realized then that, yes, my disease was grave enough and I could—despite what some of the experts had written about it—die of it or a related complication; in fact, I was able to count at least five people I had known or read about, ranging in age from twenty-two to sixty-six, who had died from infections or cancers related to the disease. Though I had been hospitalized numerous times for surgeries, intestinal obstructions, abscesses, and all sorts of other lovely, potentially life-threatening, disease-related conditions, it never really sank in that this could be deadly serious.

As the streetlights blazed in the relative stillness of that weekday evening, I figured that there had to be a flip side to all of this and, for the first time since I was diagnosed, I focused on all that the disease had *given* me.

I realized that there were a great number of people who came into my life for the very reason that I had the disease. My doctors and nurses who cared for me and the individuals with the disease whom I knew in person or through an online bulletin board were all people with whom I never would have crossed paths but for Crohn's. These were individuals of great character and compassion, and my life was immeasurably richer for knowing them and having them with me through my physical struggles.

My relationships with my own family and friends had metamorphosed as well, leaving me with a greater appreciation not only of them but also of the good times we had shared. I had relied heavily on those good memories and those relationships to sustain me at times when I was sickest. I leaned on these friends and family members to help pick up the slack that I could not handle when I was fatigued or hospitalized. I truly grew to treasure these people much more than I would have had I been entirely healthy, not for what they did for me but rather for what they meant to me.

As the darkness faded and the first rays of light slid across the landscape, I realized that the illness ironically had a positive effect on the way I treated my body. Being sick forced me to pay greater attention to my body and the way it worked. I took twenty-five pills in four increments during the day, a ritual that made me stop and recall my illness and note how I was feeling—whether I wanted to or not. Those simple acts gave me a greater awareness not only of my body and its feelings but also of the way time moved and how much I had accomplished in the hours between doses. My usual frenetic energy became much more focused as a result, for there is little room for throwaway days in a life measured like that. I also began to appreciate and strive for the quality of my time as opposed to the quantity. As clichéd as it sounds, I lived in the moment more than ever and was sure it was due to the awareness of the fragility of life, something brought to light because of the disease.

The awareness of my physical being had changed as well in the years since the diagnosis. In the process of caring for myself, I accumulated a ton of information about the digestive system and the body in general. I was an English literature and journalism major in college, and medical science, honestly, was something I couldn't have cared less about. In fact, I took Astronomy 101 and Geology 101 (aka "Rocks for Jocks") to fulfill my science course work in college. This avoidance of all things scientific was largely owing to a high school biology teacher who was limited in her ability to teach and who not so gently suggested that the language arts were really my strength. But now that it clearly mattered in the most personal way, medical science became a healthy fascination for me as I struggled to teach myself the how, what, and why of my disease. While I never would have cared about the latest medical studies in the past, I now could not get enough of them, frankly. As a result of this fascination, I became a freelance writer specializing in medical and health-related stories.

As the rose- and golden-colored morning light erupted before me, I realized that even my reaction to feelings and situations had changed during the course of my illness. Sure, I had been sad, bewildered, and angry with this latest situation, but on the whole, I handled such events much differently than I would have if I never had this illness. Confronted with regular health crises, I no longer reacted with great fear or worry when unexpected things happened. Instead, I gained an inner peace and confidence that this, too, would pass or, if not, I would most certainly be able to deal with whatever came from it. I found myself being able to keep my wits about me when I was in a serious car accident, for example, or when my father had a stroke. I was rarely frantic any longer.

No, even sad events didn't seem to shake my bearings as much as they did before I was ill. During the night that my father died, I sat about his bed with my six siblings and my mother, unmistakably sad but still able to right myself in grief. Again, during the national crisis that was September 11, 2001, I found myself initially horrified. Who wasn't? However, in the days and weeks that followed, I became prepared for further events but didn't find myself terribly depressed or consumed by the events as I am sure I would have before the illness happened.

Joy, on the other hand, seemed to be a heightened emotion for me. While the lows I felt weren't nearly as low, the highs were higher than ever. I cried more easily from joy and general sappiness than I ever did in the past and looked forward to finding it in the smallest moments. Along these lines, my sense of humor also sharpened and darkened at the same time. I found that this change had happened when I was able to laugh at the absurdity of the idea of a colonoscopy, something I now scheduled annually for colon cancer surveillance.

The changes even reached as far as my profession. My goal was to make it to a major newspaper or magazine, a far cry from my initial job out of college as a reporter at a small newspaper chain in the southern suburbs of Detroit. But when later working in a bureau of perhaps the best paper in the nation, I was surprised when I found I no longer wanted that lifestyle. My personal and professional goals had shifted as a result of my illness. Creating my own family and being there to raise my son became a priority, not writing a story that would soon be forgotten. If I was to work in the traditional sense, I didn't want to waste my time on the mundane; I wanted what I did to make a difference in the lives of others.

This feeling of purpose led to a growing sense of altruism in the form of volunteering, something I had never really done before. I helped create and moderate message boards for people with my disease, became a fund-raiser and supporter of a charity for people with inflammatory bowel diseases, and advocated for others who faced the same obstacles I did by creating legislation that fostered greater access to bathrooms in public places. I was transformed into a happy, hardworking, unpaid volunteer.

Living in the Light
With the sun fully risen, activity on the street below and in

the hallways of the hospital began to pick up pace as it finally dawned on me that I had to listen to what my illness was teaching me in all of these small lessons, to fight it as passionately as I had in the past but to live each day a little more cognizant of its gifts. That long night and the blossoming morning before me brought me greater peace and strength than I had ever known.

So when my doctor came in, I felt confident enough to tell him that I wanted to be released immediately, whether or not the blood results were up to par. He surprised me by saying that not only had they crept up out of the basement of blood results but that now they were fully within the normal range and that I wasn't required to give myself shots or to take extensive germ precautions such as wearing a mask when I returned home. Then he apologized for what had happened.

I was stunned as much by what he said as by my own reaction to it. "Please don't apologize," I said. "Neither of us knew that this would happen and it hasn't been entirely bad."

It was true. It hadn't been entirely bad, for in that moment I realized there was another side to illness, something beyond grieving. At least for me, that side was an appreciation for all of the gifts that come from the illness, all of the things that were in my life and wouldn't be there but for having experienced and at least momentarily having survived the illness. I also had a newer and better perspective on my life in general that had not existed prior to the pain and the torture that the disease brought with it.

It is easy to see what a disease has taken from us but harder—much harder at times—to quantify the positive things that happen as a result of having to live life through some of the worst it has to offer. The changes can be profound but difficult to articulate—much more so to realize—at times. But like a coin, illness has two sides to it, the bad and the good, as I found that night in the hospital. Though it is less obvious to see the good, that doesn't mean it doesn't exist. On the contrary, these gifts that illness brings may improve life immeasurably in unexpected ways.

5

GIFT 1: RELATIONSHIPS: PERSPECTIVE THROUGH ADVERSITY

No man is an island, entire of itself; every man is a piece of the continent, a part of the main. If a clod be washed away by the sea, Europe is the less, as well as if promontory were, as well as if a manor of thy friend's or of thine own were. Any man's death diminishes me, because I am involved in mankind; and therefore never send to know for whom the bell tolls; it tolls for thee.

—John Donne, from *Meditation XVII*

LIFE-THREATENING ILLNESS strikes each person differently, from the time of diagnosis and into years of remission. The symptoms may be different, the treatment different, the outcome different. But two people who have the exact same disease, strikingly similar symptoms, and the same treatment still may not fare equally. For whatever reasons, one may thrive while the other may die.

As Donne wrote in his meditation, we are all so interconnected through relationships with others that what happens to one has an effect on those around him or her. Then it makes sense when one person becomes ill that the illness itself will make an impression on those who have a relationship with the sick person. For example, if a husband is diagnosed with cancer, he may be the one to undergo treatment, but his wife, children, other relatives, and friends will go through some emotional and spiritual trials as well.

And just as the disease can strike its victim in any number of ways, the diagnosis and treatment of the disease has varied effects on those who love the patient. For example, after receiving a diagnosis of Parkinson's disease, heart disease, cancer, or any potentially life-threatening illness, the ill individual may find that one friend seemingly drops off the face of the earth, as he or she is not able to face the concept of mortality; another friend who is unsure of how to react or what to say may step back during the illness and resume the friendship after the danger has passed; and still another friend may soldier on, continuing the relationship while strengthening the bond with the ill person throughout the ordeal. Some marriages break up under the stress of the illness, while others cement themselves together through the trial. Children may be forever scarred emotionally by the experience. Others may change in big or small ways, even if they try to ignore that the illness ever occurred. It is impossible to tell who will be there when sickness happens and who will not, as an illness impacts everyone—the sick as well as the healthy loved ones—differently. A sick person could have a hundred friends or relatives and a hundred different reactions. Some will leave, some will back off, and some will stay.

Looking from the outside in, it would be easy to say that there is just too much stress and too much hardship on relationships to consider illness a gift. But most of those whom I interviewed for the book felt differently. For them, the real gift of illness in relationships was that, though there were big challenges and some losses along the way, their remaining relationships were strengthened and perhaps cherished a bit more due to the illness experience. Even where losses occurred, those interviewed found that they were better off leaving those relationships behind. Further, illness offered them opportunities for new relationships—some with deep, lasting impact—among those met along the path of treatment.

AS ALWAYS, IT BEGINS WITH A DIAGNOSIS

The many tests of a relationship regarding life-threatening illness begin not long after diagnosis, continue through treatment, and at times stretch into life beyond remission or cure. Perhaps the most obvious effect illness has on a relationship is that it reminds the patient and his or her loved ones of the subject of mortality, an equally uncomfortable notion for the sick and the healthy. Knowing that we all share the same fate—death—is disconcerting at best, and at worst provokes paralyzing fear, especially when a known threat exists.

But for the patient, the proximity of death is closer and the potential for a bad outcome is far more real, far more present than it is for their friends and relatives. The Australian researchers Dr. Miles Little and Emma-Jane Sayers wrote about this in a 2004 study on the topic of surviving cancer. "There is inevitably a difference between those who observe and those who participated in *mortal* extreme experience, the experience which threatens a life," the article said, including the emphasis. "Participants are aware that *their* lives are actually at risk. Observers know that a life is at risk, but not their life."

Shelley, a colon cancer survivor, had been best friends with another woman since their school days. When Shelley was diagnosed at age thirty-three, the calls and the visits from the other woman went from a deluge to a trickle and then stopped almost entirely. Only after remission was declared did the friendship resume. "She pulled away from me at the time because she just couldn't handle it. And, I mean, I recognized that about her," Shelley said during her interview with me. "I knew. Like with the death of, you know, members of her family, I mean, she couldn't even get through the funerals. She just can't deal with it. We've since reconnected, you know. But I think when I was sick, it was very difficult for her to talk to me."

Sherrell had the same experience. When she was diagnosed with congestive heart failure on her thirty-eighth birthday, she began to see changes in some of her closest friends, alterations she could only explain by what was happening to her medically and how they were reacting to it. "I didn't necessarily drop anyone myself. I had several friends who could not handle my illness," Sherrell recalled. "I think that it made them realize life was short and they did not want to watch me go downhill. And so they quit calling. They would ask others about me, but they didn't make contact with me.

"So I didn't fault them for that. I just understood and some of them have gone on and our relationship will never be the same. You know, they've not tried to renew it," she said.

Another area of discord can arise from the fact that the experience of the illness is not easily shared by those who are well, leading to a sense of isolation in some of the sick. Many of the interviewees spoke of how, though they were surrounded by a sea of supportive friends and relatives, they still felt isolated following their diagnosis, through the treatment, and after a cure or remission was achieved because it was impossible to truly convey the experience of being sick. Sometimes there just is no language to describe how treatments feel, what thoughts race through the mind, and how difficult it is to face the losses that come with illness, especially with those who have no basis for which to understand the experience. And usually there are no family members or friends who have gone through the same illness and treatments, increasing the feeling of loneliness.

One journal article that validated this finding was presented in 1995 by Dr. Sarah Auchincloss. Regarding the psychosocial aspects of gynecologic cancer survivorship, the article states, "Almost every woman who has had gynecologic cancer must grapple with tremendous feelings of loneliness and isolation, and these feelings recur constantly. . . . She may struggle to talk over her feelings with friends and family and may find that they are uncomfortable or require a lot of education to be able to understand even a little of what she is feeling."

Dana can especially attest to that notion. Though her diagnosis was not gynecologic cancer but breast cancer, she was twenty-two at the time it occurred and had tons of friends her age, but none could honestly connect with her on this subject.

"I have lots and lots and lots of good friends. And you know, my husband is my very best friend. But he himself can never understand what it's like to have your own body turn against you and try to kill you," Dana said.

For the most part, a patient's isolation can be compounded because his or her social scene shrinks considerably when treatment commences for the illness. In the extreme, some therapies require patients to be physically separated from others, usually because their immune systems are too weak to fend off even common, otherwise harmless infections. This means cutting off all one-on-one contact with others while being confined either to home or in a hospital's isolation room. When treatment is less confining or more convenient, such as portable chemo delivered through a fanny pack, some treatments still are arduous or time-consuming enough to require time away from work or social commitments, separating the patient from his or her usual surroundings and support systems.

Even within close, personal relationships, distance is created by disease. Being in treatment may mean being physically separated from others, as hospitalization may be required. Having a compromised immune system can make touching or kissing taboo. Exhausting treatments can make sexual intimacy a chore, if not off-limits. And sometimes survival is so perilous that initiating any kind of contact becomes superfluous.

While her findings could easily apply to any life-threatening disease, Auchincloss's article again bears out these circumstances in the gynecologic cancer survivors she studied when she wrote, "Most women who have undergone treatment also find that some of the people who they thought would be most helpful are instead anxious, withdrawn, absent, or hostile in response to the cancer. These revelations may be hard to bear: close friends may disappear for good, partners may be angry or unavailable, and colleagues may be thoughtless, dismissive or intrusive."

RELATIONSHIPS THAT WEATHER THE STORM

The brain may take advice, but not the heart, and love, having no geography, knows no boundaries: weight and sink it deep, no matter, it will rise and find the surface.

—Truman Capote, *Other Voices, Other Rooms*

And, still, this can be a time of renewal and rejuvenation of relationships. Despite all of the barriers to relationships during diagnosis and treatment of a serious illness, most patients are fortunate to have family members and friends rally around them during their diagnosis and treatment. Even if they can't understand what the patient is going through medically and emotionally, loved ones are often regular visitors in the hospital and supportive helpers during the recovery period, the interviewees told me.

Beth was twenty-six when she was diagnosed with a bone tumor at the top of her spinal column. Due to the location of the tumor and the way it pressed against her brain stem, it had to be removed surgically, a procedure that carried with it potentially grave complications such as the loss of her ability to move her facial muscles and some cognitive deficits. Prior to her surgery, Beth planned a party and asked her loved ones to come up with physical, humorous things that could replace the space the tumor occupied once it was removed.

"My friends came up and my family came up with such creative and funny and kind and sensitive and sweet things that they would put in my head," she told me, laughing at the memory. "And it was such an outpouring of love and caring for me, and I think on that day I really realized that everything was going to be all right.

"Even if the surgery went horribly wrong, and I ended up not being able to smile and not being able to smell anything and with double vision and—you know, even if the worst happened and I didn't make it through the surgery, I had tons of people who love me and my life was good," Beth said.

Sometimes it is the people in the periphery of life, those acquaintances who have never made the leap to becoming friends, who become more valued for the actions they take during this time of great stress. September can speak to that. Before she was diagnosed with metastatic melanoma, she met a woman whose children attended the same preschool as September's children. They exchanged friendly greetings but little else in the course of their daily comings and goings.

After the diagnosis was made, someone gave September, a Methodist, a Catholic saint's medallion to wear. One morning at preschool drop-off, the woman, a devout Catholic, spotted the pendant, knew its purpose, and commented on it. "Then in the afternoon at pickup at preschool, she said, 'You know, maybe we should get our kids together for a play date.' From then on, we've been good friends and she's just such a wonderful woman. She has me on a prayer chain and she made me a rosary. But otherwise, we'd never have had anything to do with each other," September said.

Others told me they found their very reasons to survive in the feelings of love they have for others. These people may divert their attention to pain as they focus on the subject of their "happy" thoughts during a particularly grueling therapy; For example, one man, while reeling from the effects of chemotherapy, would picture his toddler son playing on a hill near their home. Or thoughts of spending another day with that special person may give some the gumption to hang in there when surrender would otherwise be so much more appealing.

Viktor Frankl acutely understood this idea. After being separated from his wife during the selection process at a concentration camp and losing track of a treasured manuscript, Frankl despaired. But at a particular low point during a forced march, he began to think of his wife, thoughts of whom thereafter sustained him during even the worst times in the camps and led him to write the following in *Man's Search for Meaning*:

> *I saw the truth as it is set into song by so many poets, proclaimed as the final wisdom by so many thinkers. The truth—that love is the ultimate and highest goal to which man can aspire. Then I grasped the meaning of the greatest secret that human poetry and human thought and belief have to impart: THE SALVATION OF MAN IS THROUGH LOVE AND IN LOVE. I understood how a man who has nothing left in this world still may know bliss, be it only for a brief moment, in the contemplation of his beloved. In a position of utter desolation, when his only achievement may consist in enduring his sufferings in the right way—an honorable way—in such a position man can, through loving contemplation of the image he carries of his beloved, achieve fulfillment.*

Many, many of the people interviewed admitted to using loved ones as a motivation to survive and then bargaining with a divine presence to ensure that outcome. Sherrell found that focusing on staying alive to watch her three children—ages ten, fourteen, and fifteen at the time of her diagnosis—grow into adulthood gave her the strength to withstand the trials of her slowly dying heart and subsequent transplant.

"I know you're not supposed to, but I told God, 'If you would just let me live longer to see my children grown, I'd be happy.' And then, after they were grown, I'd say, 'God, I need to live a little bit longer. I need to make sure they get married, you know,'" Sherrell said. "So, now they're all out. My baby daughter's a senior in college. The other two have their homes and live away, but none of them are married. So now my bargain is, 'God, please let me live long enough to see them get married and have those grandbabies.'"

THE SHIFT IN THE RELATIONSHIP TO SELF

Adversity introduces a man to himself.

—Seneca, Roman philosopher

Time is something we seemingly have more of when we are going through treatment. It moves more slowly as we visit doctors and tend to the treatments we have to endure to be well once more. Because we have more time and less with which to occupy it (jobs on hold, social scene at a standstill, etc.), we can focus more on ourselves.

This can be both a blessing and a curse for the patient. The blessing comes in the lives of those who were so focused on the other aspects of their lives, such as a demanding career or a growing family, that they forgot to spend time on themselves. Hobbies are put away, exercise becomes a thing of the past, and reading a book is a rare luxury, while other aspects of time spent on themselves, such as getting a haircut or even brushing their teeth, are hastily done so as to save that precious resource. But when a life-threatening condition is made known, the focus becomes survival and all of the trivial—and even some important aspects of life—are put on hold, giving many of the respondents time to spend on themselves.

During his interview, Bobby told me he was grateful for the time that treatment of his testicular cancer gave him. Prior to diagnosis, he had pushed himself first through college, then through graduate school, and finally into a doctoral program in psychology, with very little time off in between.

"I was ready to be done with schoolwork and that whole life. And that burnout was causing me to sometimes skip class or not do all the reading, not do the things, and it was frustrating because it's the stuff I do enjoy. It was becoming overwhelming, I think," Bobby recalled.

He dropped out for a semester to have surgery and go through chemotherapy. But the break also gave Bobby a chance to take a step back from his studies and his field of choice and evaluate what he loved about it and what he didn't. He was then eager to return to school.

"Since then, I also found one part that I really like about school. When I was taken out of it, I missed parts of it and parts of it I didn't," he said. "I think I found a new appreciation for the things I am doing now."

At the same time, this extra pause for reflection was a curse for some people, as they were forced to see what they had become throughout the course of their lives. Undesirable behaviors like short tempers or selfishness became impossible to ignore. Superficial priorities were examined and recognized for what they were.

Jim is one who saw this in himself as well. Prior to his diagnosis of Parkinson's, he spent much of his time away from his family, either at work or following his admittedly materialistic and self-promoting behaviors. His first marriage crumbled, as did his relationship with his daughter from that union; she eventually asked him to terminate his parental rights so her stepfather could adopt her. Jim married again and had a son, a child with whom he also spent little time.

But following the diagnosis, he took a disability leave from his high-powered job in the technology industry. The dozens of hours that had been spent each week focused on climbing corporate ladders and schmoozing with higher-ups shifted to being spent on self-examination. He quickly found that he did not entirely like the man he had become. As a result, Jim devoted more energy to raising his young son, slowly increasing the time he spent with him per day from an hour prior to diagnosis to three to seven hours now. He also spends up to five hours a day on activities he enjoys, such as writing.

"I was kind of a bastard for a long time in life, and it wasn't until I got sick that I made any change," Jim said. "The person I am today is nothing like the person I was a couple of years ago."

RELATIONSHIPS THAT ARE LOST

It is almost inevitable that some relationships will not survive the test of illness. Some friends and relatives make hasty exits, others more gradual ones. Some leave until remission is declared and a cure is achieved, while others stay away forever. The lesson is rarely lost on the student—in this case, the patient.

In a 1989 literature review by five experts on the subject of the psychosocial implications of surviving adult cancers, the process of relationships either dying or blooming under the glare of an illness was found to be a significant aspect of survival. While some families were strengthened by the illness experience, other relationships in the patient's life did not fare as well. "A sorting out process transpires between those friends and acquaintances with less personal investment avoided or abandoned the person with cancer," the authors observed.

Sandee can attest to that. A beautiful and vivacious woman, she always had a lot of friends. She made friends with her children's friends' parents, friends through people who worked out at her gym, friends she went out with on more than the occasional girls' night out. But during her experience with metastatic breast cancer, Sandee found she has fewer but deeper relationships. "My friendships are more intense now. The friends I had before, many of them haven't stuck. Because I had training buddies and I had, you know, girls that I would go out for dinner with every now and then, and you know, basically I'm not the same person for them anymore," Sandee said. "Lots of friends just continued their lives. Basically, they don't see me as part of their life because I can't keep up with them.

"My good friends now I can count on one hand—on one hand," she said, adding that she also avoids those who are "negative."

But more times than not, the interviewee reported to me that he or she was the one who severed the relationship.

And time after time, the reason given was that the relation-ship was too difficult, too meaningless, or too toxic to con-tinue while fighting for one's own life.

In an article published in a 1996 nursing journal, Dr. Elizabeth Lindsey extensively interviewed eight individuals about the phenomenon of feeling healthy while living with a chronic condition. One of her findings was that the illness led to a sense of deeper self-awareness, which was then reflected in their relationships. "If previous relationships could change to connect at this deeper, more authentic level, then those relationships remained," Lindsey wrote. "For other relationships, there was a falling away."

As one of her interview subjects stated, "I put out a cer-tain kind of energy and meeting people more that think the way I think, and those are the people who are more impor-tant to me. So rather than the plastic connections, I had a falling away and I'm finding there are deeper connections with people who are important to me. I am seeing those connections more. . . . I am learning that people are more important to me than anything else."

Tonda has some experience with this phenomenon. Before she was diagnosed with early-onset Parkinson's dis-ease, trips to the salon were a big part of her life, not only for a fresh coat of polish and a blow-out but also for the social scene that it afforded her. Secretly, however, she hated going, even though she did it for years.

"The ladies were so boring. All they did was talk about the salon, blah, blah, blah. It wasn't really me and I didn't like it. And I always felt like I was wearing someone else's hair or somebody else's nails, you know, because it just didn't seem like me," she said, adding that she used the disease as an excuse to drop the ritual. "I said to them, 'I'm not going anymore.' And believe it or not, a couple of those people got weeded out."

She told me that that experience prepared her for the future when her illness forced her to give up a political career and many of the friendships that went along with that part of her life. "These were the ones where you say to yourself at the end of the day, 'Oh, my God! That person just sucks the life out of me.' And you say, 'Oh, but I have to keep up with them because of appearances or they're friends with so-and-so or they're related to me or, you know, something like that. It just was really simple. I didn't have to do anything," she said. "These were people that, once I lost what they thought was my power and my position, they weren't as anxious to be friends with me anyway. I knew that was going to happen so I didn't bother to pursue the relationship."

Sometimes the relationships were dropped by the patient because the patient went through a profound personality change as a result of having the illness. This shift caused them to no longer be attracted to the people with whom they used to be friends.

Jim also understands this. When he left his profession in the technology industry, he left behind those in his life who were attracted to his power and prestige, as he no longer possessed these things. "There were people in my life who had been, how do I say nicely? I can't. They had been users of some sort of another, you know. Whether it was the fact that I had money or whether it was the fact that I couldn't provide things for them or I was a coattail to somewhere else," Jim said. "I was pretty successful at what I had done professionally. And as I started to go through a sort of transformation, a metamorphosis into something much better, I realized that these people for whatever reason were people that I would not choose to be around.

"As I grew up and as the illness allowed me to see a whole new side of myself and a whole new side of people, I realized that I no longer wanted to be that way," he said.

RELATIONSHIPS THAT ENDURE

Those who stay will be champions.

—Bo Schembechler, former University of Michigan coach

When the late Bo Schembechler first took over as head coach for the University of Michigan football team, he and his team members faced a brutally hot Michigan summer. The players began to drop out of the program in droves, forcing the young coach to place a sign with the above phrase over the entrance of the locker room, both as a challenge and as a promise to his players. What Schembechler meant in those six words was that toughness, dedication, and hard work led to great things. Those who made it through the grueling heat and humidity, those who fought to make the required grade point average, those who sacrificed to become great players would prevail in the end. He wasn't necessarily blowing smoke, so to speak: Schembechler and the teams he coached went on to win thirteen Big Ten titles and ten Rose Bowl championships in the next twenty years.

The same quote could apply to most of the relationships that survived the illnesses suffered by those who were interviewed for the book. The friends and relatives who stood by their sick loved ones even if they didn't grasp what was happening, those who remained steadfast in their commitment and love for the patient, those who looked past the physical effects of the illness and saw that the person's true spirit remained intact were most times rewarded with more durable relationships, often deeper emotionally and spiritually than had existed before the illness.

Commonly, the interviewees expressed this to me by telling of examples with more intimate family relationships, such as those with a spouse or children. Again, the literature bears this out. In a 2004 study of hematologic cancer patients, Dr. Pam McGrath wrote, "Sharing the journey with intimate family members affirmed relationships, solidified bonds, and reinforced the importance of the family."

Despite what one of her study subjects called the "ups and downs" during treatments, families experienced increased closeness, spousal relationships were examined and cherished, and there was improved communication all around. As one of her interview subjects said, "I think it was a good year in the fact that we were all together as a family for a change. It made me realize that life is too short and family life is very important to me."

Pat found this to be true as well. She and her husband had a fairly typical long-term relationship. In their suburban home, they raised two kids while both holding down blue-collar jobs. Even when she was diagnosed with hepatitis C, life went on as usual. She went through with treatment and continued to work. But when a lump on the back of her leg was diagnosed as advanced melanoma, the couple realized that their remaining time together might be shortened, something that cemented their devotion to one another.

"I think it made us closer because he realizes that, you know, I'm just not going to be here ten years or whatever so we have to do things now, not put it off," she said, adding that they splurged in a season-ticket package to professional hockey, something they both enjoy watching and something they would not have done but for her bout with melanoma. Her children also have made a point to spend more time with her. "[The illness] just makes us closer in that, you know, we're all thinking more along the same lines."

When Lynda was diagnosed with breast cancer at the age of twenty-eight nearly thirty years ago, she saw how differently other people going through the experience were treated. One woman who had a similar diagnosis and treatment and who also had two children came to chemotherapy alone or with her mother; her husband was never present, even on the last day. But Lynda's husband, who had just buried his mother after her fatal bout with breast cancer, rearranged his work schedule so he could take his young wife to her chemotherapy appointments. When they would return home, he would make her comfortable on the couch while he and their two young children went shopping for dinner ingredients. He would feed the children and make dinners for the days when she was recovering and was too weak to cook. And he remained supportive in the decades after, soothing her when she became anxious before regular tests and examinations.

"My husband was so wonderful during the whole thing. It was very hard on him," she said. "But, you know, I value him more now."

RELATIONSHIPS THAT ARE FOUND

And then there were many new relationships that individuals reported finding during their journey through illness, almost always involving people who had something medically in common with them. These often were people who were fellow patients or former patients, a doctor or a nurse, a participant on a Web board or in a more traditional support group.

Usually, the first new relationship came in the form of someone directly involved in their care. While doctors, nurses, and therapists may have made brief appearances in the past, they become semipermanent fixtures in life after diagnosis, during treatment, and into the years after treatment ends. Many of the interviewees recalled specific medical professionals who helped them through difficult times or were just there to listen.

Fear struck Bobby during his treatment for testicular cancer, starting almost from the time that he noticed his testicle was enlarged. He was ordered first to undergo surgery, something he knew he could handle with the help of pain medication. But the prospect of chemotherapy shook him, as he didn't know what to expect, and all of the side effects were unpleasant.

What changed his perspective was the kindness and caring shown to him in part by his oncologist and surgeon but mostly by his oncology nurses, the ones who administered the chemo drugs to him for several months. "Chemo nurses, oh, they're the best in the world! I would go to see them and make sure that they were taken care of," Bobby said.

Relationships also formed frequently between the interviewees and others who suffered similarly through the same diagnosis. The notion of "misery loves company" took on a new meaning, as these people shared the challenges that illnesses present with others who knew exactly what they were talking about, usually using a certain shorthand form of language they instinctively knew.

Dana felt isolated after her breast cancer diagnosis at twenty-two. None of her contemporaries had gone through it, and her husband had no basis for comparison. Instead, she turned to a support group for cancer survivors. There she immediately felt the sympathy and shared knowledge she had been groping for. "My fellow survivors understand what that's like," Dana said. "There are things you don't—I mean we can go and talk and there are things that you never have to explain. You just know."

Sometimes these new friendships also serve as a source of inspiration for each other, as well as a source of comfort. Knowing that others have bravely made it through the same trials makes it easier for anyone to face the challenges of illness. September serves as such a role model for Jen and vice versa. The pair met through the Internet while they were both going through treatment for melanoma.

"Jen is very inspirational to me. She thinks of me as a strong woman and that I'm so brave and inspirational to her," September said. "Jen is one of my closest friends, and I know she'd do anything for me, and I would do anything for her. That is one of the biggest gifts in life, in cancer, is having her as a friend."

Interestingly, many of those who said they formed such relationships said they did so on Internet Web boards or in chat rooms designated for those who shared their diagnosis. Here, these people connected with others who understood what they were going through, who had been through some of the same treatments they were facing, who were willing to walk them over the rough spots even if they weren't physically present to hold their hand. For most, the friendship occurred and endured without the pair ever meeting face-to-face.

Again, Bobby jumped online almost right after receiving his diagnosis. In addition to researching his different treatment options and potential outcomes, he also connected with an online support group for testicular cancer survivors. In particular, he soon spoke on the phone with one survivor who helped calm him prior to surgery. The effect of these relationships from the virtual support group was to lessen the sense of isolation he initially felt with the diagnosis.

"With the testicular cancer Web site, I got support from people who have actually been through it," he said, adding that he didn't know of anyone who had been through the experience prior to his diagnosis. "It helped me quite a bit. I mean, honestly, I think I felt a new connection that I didn't have."

Whichever way they evolve, in person or in cyberspace, the relationships created among those with a common bond of illness are a gift to both the mentor and the mentee, the interviewees told me. Sherrell's whole outlook on her then impending heart transplant was changed by Missy, a heart transplant survivor who came to visit Sherrell during her hospital stay.

"She was the first transplant survivor I ever met in person. Healthy-as-a-horse-looking person. Just so pretty. And she handed me the pictures. She said, 'This was me before I got my heart,'" Sherrell recalled. "I would not have recognized her. She looked like I looked. She was sick. And so, I said, 'If Missy can do it, Sherrell can do it, too.' That gave me the hope to know that I could live normally after a transplant."

Now Sherrell mentors others who are waiting for hearts or have gone through transplant, a process she began while she was still in the hospital. "I met people in clinic, and as I met people in the hospital, where there were several of us waiting, we became family. That's the way I feel now," she said. "I've already been through that; I can offer them hope and encouragement and get to know them. So, I've got, like, eighty family members of heart."

THE GIFT THAT RENEWS ITSELF

In the end, life-threatening illness helps to sort out relationships in a way that likely would not happen but for the illness. Dead and dying relationships, time- and spirit-consuming friendships are left along the way, leaving more room for those who now share a similar pain and path. Those relationships that remain from the time prior to diagnosis are likely deeper and stronger from having faced the challenges that illness presents.

Beth agreed. "Going through an experience like this really helps you understand where you stand with different people you have relationships with. I really learned who I could count on and who I couldn't necessarily count on," she said.

The Heavenly Relationship Does Not Go Untouched

For those who were interviewed, the relationships between themselves and other people were not the only relationships affected by illness. Some individuals reported a shake-up, either positive or negative, in the way they viewed their relationship with God or with their sense of spirituality.

And it makes total sense. Everything else has changed.

Why not religious and spiritual relationships as well? In his 2001 literature review on the experience of adjusting to cancer, Dr. James Brennan, a British psychologist, stated, "Rarely does a cancer patient describe a sense of continuity with their lives before cancer—there is inevitably a shift in the individual's sense of themselves and the world."

For some, the shift in the relationship was immediate and not entirely positive. Just as anger was manifested in other human relationships, it was manifested in some individuals' relationships with God.

This happened to Shelley. Raised a Catholic, she was at a stage in her life when she was beginning to question some of her beliefs anyway. When she was diagnosed with colon cancer at the age of thirty-three, the testing of her faith accelerated.

"I went through being sick, this whole thing, and I was pretty angry," Shelley said, adding that the target of her anger was God. "I mean, I felt like he picked the worst cancer in the book, and gave it to me, you know, to teach me a lesson, I guess. I don't know. You know, I kind of went through that feeling and sometimes still struggle with that, though, I would say."

Brennan explains in his paper that illness poses a threat to the usual assumptions that there is justice and fairness in the world. Most people are taught that if they take care of themselves and others in the world, then goodness will come their way. If they take a misstep and commit immoral or unjust acts, then they will be punished. The Bible is full of cautionary tales to support this contention. Miriam is struck with a skin condition when she gossips, Samson loses his strength due in part to his lust for Delilah, the slaves of Egypt must wander the desert when they worship false idols. For goodness' sake, Lot's wife is turned into a pillar of salt for just looking.

So when illness befalls us, those who were taught the certitude of fairness and justice wonder why the disease occurred in them and what they did to deserve the great misfortune. Brennan explains: "A sense of injustice and spiritual doubt is sometimes felt by people who have attempted to adhere to a doctrine of religious principles; but similarly, those with more atheistic beliefs may feel a sudden need to re-examine preciously held assumptions about the nature of existence, even though this may lead them to question their implicit and explicit beliefs (e.g., in a rational or fair universe). In either case, loss of spiritual meaning and a sense of existential isolation can result."

On the other hand, some people find meaning in the event and ascribe a certain quest to fulfill, a special assignment or duty given to them by a heavenly creator. Eight authors of a 2000 study of sixteen people with brain or spinal cord injuries found that there were frequently changes in spiritual beliefs after a traumatic disability, especially in the area of newly assigned sense of purpose. This feeling of purpose, the authors said, can lead to a closer relationship with God or with spirituality.

Dana admitted to me that she feels that way. She had become much more involved with her Christian beliefs just before her diagnosis and then used those beliefs to sustain her and find meaning in her breast cancer. "It caused me to come far more dependent upon God, I think, just to make it through every day," Dana said. "And at some point in time, I felt like part of the reason for my sickness was so that God would be glorified through it, so that I would be used for greater things."

Many others interviewed felt that they were "given" their diseases so that they could help others through similarly trying times; often, as we will see in chapter 7, this sense led them to increase their activism and altruism. In the paper on changes in spiritual beliefs, the researchers found that this purpose could be specific, such as living to help their own family, or more general in nature. One of their study subjects stated, "I just believe I was saved for a purpose—to help somebody or to do something. There is actually a reason for me to be here. I'm not just a statistic—another brain injury file. I'm here for a purpose."

Some of those interviewed for this book said that they found a renewed comfort from their early religious beliefs. Beth is one of those. Prior to her brain surgery to remove her bony tumor, she really relied on her Jewish roots, especially when she was confronted with creating a power of attorney and advance directives right before the surgery date.

"I mean, it was scary. It presented its own set of crying fits," Beth recalled, saying she first thought of going to relatives to discuss certain aspects of her fears. "How do you call your mom and go, 'Mom, I'm trying to write my advance directives, and if I become a vegetable, do you think that I should have them leave me on life support?' How do you talk to your mother about that? No mom wants to talk about that with her daughter, I don't think. And you can't talk to your boyfriend about it because he hasn't thought about it, either."

So she went to her rabbi to discuss the directives, as well as organ donation. He assured her that it did not go against her religion to be an organ donor.

"I think I kind of surprised myself when I turned to the

rabbi when I was facing those questions of life and death. I never thought of myself as needing spiritual guidance, but I think the fact that I did turn to the rabbi kind of taught me something about myself," she said, adding that it led to a higher and deeper level of observance of her religion, something she continues today.

September found comfort more in the sense of community that her new "church family" gave her. Raised a Protestant, she previously saw her religion as an obligation, a duty she followed without great, driving passion. "Before, we went to church because I thought we had to," she said.

But during her treatment for melanoma, she was touched by how many in her church stepped forward and cared for her and her family. "They came to the hospital. They call every month to see, you know, how it's going. They put my name on the prayer list every Sunday. Everybody knows who I am and asks how I'm doing when they see me," September said. "Now it's comfortable, like a family."

While some respondents found the challenge to their spirituality too great and turned away from religion, others eventually returned. Shelley did just that. When her sister asked Shelley if she could officiate at her wedding, Shelley decided to become a pastor. She skipped the option of signing up for a quicky Internet course and instead decided to study more, in part to explore her readjusted relationship with God and religion.

"I really felt like it was an opportunity for me to learn something and to try to gain a more positive relationship with God. And so, you know, it allowed me to do some studying of the Bible and reading the Bible and so the relationship with

God definitely is a bigger part of my life. And I mean every-single-night-type-thing and even during the day."

REAL STORY—HEIDI AND NELDA

Heidi jokes that her family should change their last name to the Chernobyls. In a weird way, the name seems to fit: four of five members of her immediate family are cancer survivors.

The Schultz family

The first to be diagnosed was Heidi, the daughter of Ken and Nelda. At the age of twenty-six, Heidi had returned home, as so many twentysomethings do in the time between the end of college and the beginning of the rest of their lives. While home was a comfortable solution, she still was not sleeping well. Pain in Heidi's lower left leg was keeping her awake at night, nearly every night.

Doctor after doctor came up with different diagnoses. One said it was a sports injury, not entirely implausible, as Heidi played soccer and ran. Another said it was a bone bruise; another thought it was phlebitis. On and on it went until finally an MRI was ordered and Heidi was diagnosed with Ewing's sarcoma, generally a pediatric cancer. Chemotherapy soon followed, with radiation thrown in for good measure when Heidi turned down amputation. For fourteen months, she underwent treatment that eventually forced her cancer into remission.

During that time, Heidi wasn't the only one to change. Some friends rallied around her, making time to visit or to call. But other friends, frightened that she was facing mortality at such a young age, tiptoed around the subject. In particular, she recalled that one friend called and talked to her for forty-five minutes, not once mentioning the cancer or its treatment. She promised the caller a short conversation if they couldn't discuss what was happening to her medically.

"I think a lot of times that happens because people don't know what to say. They don't know how to react," she said. "I was kind of merciless in that way. People are afraid to say the wrong thing, so I just said the wrong thing first."

Heidi also made friends with a number of people whom she otherwise would not have met but for her cancer. But it wasn't always easy to find them, as few services exist for young adult cancer patients. While sitting in her hospital room, she heard the strains of the rock band U2's music wafting through the halls. She grabbed her IV pole and went on a room-by-room search for the person playing the music, in the hope of locating friendship as well as understanding of what it means to be young and sick. This young man was the first of many, many relationships she has formed with other young cancer survivors.

"They are my partners in crime. They are my colleagues.

They are my compadres," she says of these fellow survivors. "Some of my best friends are cancer survivors. They understand without my having to explain."

Heidi's family, perhaps more than her friends, was deeply affected by her illness. Her parents, Ken and Nelda, were in the room at the time of the diagnosis, an event that touched off a period of mourning for Nelda. She immediately felt shock, which evolved into anger at the injustice of her daughter's illness. She felt depressed and helpless to protect her child from this unwanted yet inescapable diagnosis. And, boy, did she bargain with God.

"It was sort of, like, you know, you may want her but we do, too. And we're going to have to do battle with you. There are things that she can do that would be helpful to you and to her and to us. And, you know, if you really, really need somebody, why not me? Why not me, you know? I mean, any of us who are older, but not this young lady," Nelda said. "We've never raised the question, 'Why us?' It was just more the parent wanting always to protect the child.

"I felt particularly with Heidi that she could die of her disease, and that was really traumatic," Nelda said, adding that she began to cherish the special times when the family was together, as well as everyday interactions.

As Heidi approached the time for treatment, her family—including Heidi's twin brother, Chad, and her younger brother, Chris—came together to help her through it. Chris went shopping with Heidi for a wig it turned out she never wore and spent time in her hospital room, at times sleeping on a couch there as she endured rounds of chemotherapy. He also returned home from college to spend Thanksgiving as well as the following summer with her.

"I remember being impressed by that. When you are in college, it's fun to spend the holidays with your friends, hanging out. But here he was, home with me. I remember saying, 'That's giving up your holiday for me.' It was something, really nice of him," Heidi said.

Heidi felt that support from the beginning and thrived on it throughout her treatment. "My family has always been close, but everyone kind of rallied. We circled the wagons," Heidi said.

Unfortunately, the lessons from Heidi's cancer did not stop with her treatment, as other members of the family began, one by one save for Chris, to be diagnosed with other forms of cancer. When Nelda went through an incidental diagnosis of chronic lymphocytic leukemia in 2002, Heidi used what she learned from her experience to help her find the right practitioner to manage her care. Though Nelda does not yet need treatment for her disease, she also employed what she learned from Heidi's experience to make changes in her life, such as leaving her job and professional ambitions to spend more time with her family.

"Success to me was always to make a contribution in the field of education and that, in turn . . . would impact the lives of students, of children. So that cycle or that circle is still there," Nelda said. "It's just that instead of thinking of the world at large and those children, the focus is now more on my immediate family and their immediate children. My scope, the lens I have looked through, is just more focused."

As for friendships, Nelda found a falling away among a few friends, saying she would rather "read a book" than interact with them. She also made new friends, mostly when Heidi was in the hospital and later when Chad was diagnosed with and underwent treatment for a carcinoid tumor in 2004.

The family's cancer experiences have led them to become activists and advocates for better cancer care, research, and support. Based on her experiences as a cancer patient in her twenties, Heidi founded Planet Cancer, a nonprofit organization that provides supportive services such as young adult retreats for survivors and advocates for better supportive services and research for young adults who have been diagnosed with cancer. Chad has become involved with fund-raising efforts for St. Jude Children's Research Hospital, a pediatric cancer facility in Memphis. Nelda and Ken, who was diagnosed with prostate cancer in 2003, regularly help out at events and are proud of their children's efforts. Chris has had magazine articles published about his experiences watching his family suffer.

But the biggest gain has been in the valuing of familial relationships and the closeness that has ensued.

"My dreams now are to live long enough to really see my little grandchildren grow up; see my son, Chad, get married; and then to see Christopher, my other son, get married and each to have their children. Just to have bundles of fun with their kids. Not to become dependent on medical kinds of care. All that stuff," Nelda said. "Just to have fun with my own family and with my siblings and grandchildren. You know, walk out in the sunshine with them."

6

GIFT 2: TIME AND BEING: A NEW APPRECIATION

⌒

TWO ELEMENTS OF human life, time and being, are easy to ignore when we are well. Time is measured by the passage of birthdays, holidays, and anniversaries, happy occasions for most. During other times, it moves with such fluidity that its passage is hard to detect, if noticed at all. Our sense of well-being is taken for granted in much the same way. When we are born into this world, we begin to hit certain milestones—rolling over and then sitting up, crawling and then walking, running and then climbing— that give our parents and us a superficial feeling of well-being about our physical selves.

Assuming that we duck the bullets of childhood and adolescent illnesses and accidents, we develop a sense of entitlement to our health and our time. We are told that if we refrain from smoking, eat and drink in moderation, and exercise regularly we will live a long, healthy life. And why shouldn't we believe it? We are inundated with stories about the growing number of people who are living well into their nineties, about burgeoning retirement developments, about the strain on Social Security because of the large amount of people living longer and better than ever; we believe that we, too, will face these issues in our eighth and ninth decades of life. In our culture that celebrates youth and vigor, we are assured that we will have health, and because of that, we will have plenty of time to achieve what we want to achieve and to experience what we want to experience before we die.

As a result, these elements of time and being become most cherished when we face a life-threatening illness. That is because when we are faced with personal annihilation, the continuation of both our time and our physical being is exactly what is at stake.

A SHIFT IN THE EXPERIENCE OF TIME

To get all there is out of living, we must employ our time wisely, never being in too much of a hurry to stop and sip life, but never losing our sense of the enormous value of a minute.
—Robert Updegraff, *All the Time You Need*

Time is like the wind: We can't see it, but we know it exists because we can feel it as it passes. Those feelings are never truer than when illness enters the picture. Time becomes almost personified, somehow far more noticeable in the sluggish pace in which it passes while we are sick and in the value of it as it speeds by when we are well once again.

There are a few inherent elements of time within illness. On a daily basis, time is easily marked by how we now care for our bodies. Medication and our use of it dictate the passage of a day. We count the hours between those pills and shots that must be taken two, three, four times a day, watching the sun rise and set in the sky but becoming aware of the day's passing more by the number of doses taken and how many we have still to take.

Monthly and yearly doctor's appointments and tests are another way of marking time's passage for those who have faced grave diseases. For cancer patients, as an example, regular doctor's appointments in the first five years following a diagnosis often are met with feelings of trepidation, as the prevailing wisdom dictates that recurrence is most common within this period. Some of these patients feel as if their life is on hold during this time, their illness making it pass more slowly and more significantly as a result. For people with chronic illnesses, exacerbations or acute phases of the illnesses require more monitoring, necessitating appointments that are closer together. As the disease and its symptoms become more controllable, time between appointments grows and thus moves faster.

Daily, monthly, or yearly examinations also mark the passage of time. For people with normal health, mammograms are scheduled at thirty-five for a baseline and every year thereafter; the first colonoscopy happens at fifty and every five years thereafter; blood sugar is measured at regular physicals; cardiac stress tests happen as needed; and a bone marrow biopsy may never happen in their lives. But for those who have faced certain medical conditions, the examinations to survey for problems or recurrence—which often produce anxiety in the days leading up to the exam as well as in the days following until the results are rendered—are more significant than a regular exam and are usually scheduled more often; in the end, these exams are really just another way to measure the time spent since diagnosis.

For those who have lived with illness for a while, time within a year is marked with newer, sadder anniversaries of certain events related to our illness. The beginning or end of a therapy or the date when normal activity such as work resumes are significant in ways that birthdays and anniversaries are for those who are healthy. For me, February 1, December 26, October 6, February 24, and May 30 were days when I underwent major operations for my condition, and they pop into my mind as easily as do my son's birth date and my wedding anniversary.

In particular, the date of diagnosis seems permanently etched onto our life's calendar. The events of that day can easily be recalled on its following anniversaries for each remaining year left in that person's life. The individual may or may not remember when treatment wrapped up or when other significant illness-related complications arose, but the date of diagnosis is as important to them, in an inversely sad way, as is a happy occasion such as the date of a college graduation.

A literature review article published in 1989 in the *Annals of Internal Medicine* found that this annual distress regarding certain dates was common. "Many other patients in other studies suggested that the time around their anniversaries of diagnosis or completion of therapy were also times for distress, as they were often linked with doctor's visits and memories of the ordeal," the authors wrote.

Kathy, a breast cancer survivor and an author of a book on the subject, recalls the date as the day "the line in the sand was drawn." She had had a difficult year; after taking a leave from her job as a professor in a southern university, she gave birth prematurely to her only child, a daughter. In the sleepless months that followed, she was irritated by a persistent itching in her breast. Tests were done but, at thirty-seven, Kathy didn't really think it would be cancer.

"It never occurred to me. It wasn't in the family. It just wasn't on the radar," she told me during our interview.

But at the moment she was given her diagnosis, Kathy clearly remembers standing in her kitchen on that October 1986 morning, watching her then one-year-old daughter clutching a chair and struggling to stand. Then the phone rang. Just as Kathy's doctor told her that her mammogram indicated that there probably was cancer in her breast, her daughter let go of the chair and took her first steps. Twenty years later, Kathy easily recalled that moment, now frozen in time.

"I was looking at my one-year-old, who is balancing and grinning at me and looking at me like, 'Mom, I am getting ready to walk.' And I am going, 'Oh, shit, I am going to die and she is not going to remember me.' It was really awful," she said.

Receiving a diagnosis of a life-threatening illness is much like any other major trauma in that time seems to stop or slow considerably as the person swims in disbelief at the events unfolding. This slow tempo can continue during the next weeks and months, even years, as treatment plans are developed, put into place, and, in some cases, completed.

Stewart, a musician and writer, was first diagnosed with chronic myelogenous leukemia on June 10, 1998, a date he will remember forever. After going through a successful stem cell transplant in early October of that year to treat the condition, he returned home in mid-December with a full septic infection. Though he was happy finally to be home to celebrate Christmas after more than two months in the hospital, time seemed to inch by.

"I was on that super antibiotic, vancomycin. Twice a day, they'd hang a bag. It was such a big infection. They said, 'We think you will respond better at home. You can take the bag home.' We would hang it on a bag tree and they would just put it into my line. At that point, every hour was like a day, every day was like a month. Time just dragged," Stewart said.

Ernest, a musician and event planner who was diagnosed with stage 4 throat cancer in November 2002, began chemotherapy and radiation treatments for his disease in January 2003. He was scheduled to go through three rounds of intense chemotherapy and daily radiation. The idea of being ill was so foreign and frightening to Ernest that he can recall watching the medication first enter his body through an intravenous line.

"I remember the very first drop of the chemical going in me and being terrified about what this was going to do to my body," he said. Though he had ended a smoking habit the year before, he religiously took care of his muscular, 190-pound body, running five miles a day, biking, and swimming. "I knew [the treatment] was going to destroy me. I could feel it after the second day. I knew then that this was going to be much more difficult than I had planned."

And it was, whittling his body to 110 pounds in two months. The chemo made Ernest nauseated and caused sores in his gastrointestinal tract, while the radiation burned the back of his throat, a new kind of torture that led him often to pray to pass out so time could pass a little more effortlessly.

"Time changed a lot while I was ill. It went so slow that I didn't think I would live twenty-four hours down the road.

If I had known that this illness would end at a certain date, I would have dealt with it better. But you don't know and you think that it is going to just go on forever," Ernest said.

To those who have survived the threat of serious illness, time takes on very different qualities than it possessed prior to illness. It becomes important in the simple fact that there is more of it when its very existence was so threatened, seemingly so imminently perishable. It becomes more of a precious commodity, a currency of sorts that must be spent wisely or it will be thought to be lost forever.

And, really, again, it is impossible for this not to happen. The worst seems to be over, a reprieve granted, the imminent threat of death put off to face another day. The result is that the tempo picks up considerably at the same time that it is realized that the length of one's life may be shorter than ever. This means that each minute having greater significance. In the 2004 paper mentioned in the previous chapter, Dr. Miles Little and Emma-Jane Sayers verified this change, saying that survivors "recognize, whether they want to or not, that they have confronted their own annihilation, and that they will at some stage have to do so again. We all know that we will die, but there is a greater vividness and proximity in that knowledge for someone who has been through mortal extreme experience."

Because of this knowledge, those I interviewed for the book agreed that time became far more precious and seemed to move more rapidly following the conclusion of treatment when it appeared they would most likely live. Most of the individuals felt that time became a prized commodity and vowed to spend it doing things that "mattered" or pursuing dreams previously unfulfilled.

Heidi, a Ewing's sarcoma survivor mentioned in the previous chapter and author of a book on cancer survival, returned to her regular daily routine following successful treatment with chemotherapy and radiation. In a short time, her work in an advertising agency no longer suited her, as her illness had changed her priorities.

"Immediately afterward, I had this sense of 'you gotta beat the clock.' I wanted to go out and do everything. Right now. I need to do everything right now," she said. "It was a sense that time is precious and I don't want to waste time doing something that wasn't meaningful to me."

In her spare time, Heidi started (www.planetcancer.org) and a related charity to connect with other young adult cancer patients, a group to which she belonged and for which she discovered there was a lack of psychosocial services. The Web site and charity grew, eventually consuming all of her spare time as well as her vacation time from her "real" job. Eventually, she gave up her advertising job and shifted her focus entirely to her charity and its now popular Web site.

Passions outside of work also changed in importance for some. These individuals took trips that they had always wanted to take prediagnosis. Others pursued interests they had in the past but which they had always felt they had plenty of time to do, such as one man with a severe chronic illness who learned to play the piano or a brain cancer survivor who took up motorbiking. It was as if the experience of having the life-threatening illness gave them permission to pursue their bliss.

Macklin, mentioned in an earlier chapter, a literature professor at a top university, a leukemia survivor, and the author of a book of poetry about transplants, was an active amateur ornithologist prior to his diagnosis, a passion that picked up steam following a successful stem cell transplant. He made more trips to different areas to see new and different birds that he had never seen before.

"I really feel on the one hand you go through this experience and you go back to life and become more normal. But you don't really go back to normal or I didn't and I assume others don't, too, unless you forget about the experience, which I think is impossible," Macklin said. "I came out of it on the other end like, 'Wow, life is pretty sweet. Life is more precious than I felt it was before.' There is more living in the moment than I did before.

"I don't say that you can't feel that way without experiencing this process, all of these ideas of living in the present moment. It is one thing to say it and to do it on spiritual factors and so on, but it is another thing to have this life-threatening situation, which basically intensified that feeling."

And the existing literature on the subject supports what Heidi, Macklin, and others expressed. The Australian researcher Dr. Pam McGrath found that patients who had survived the rigorous treatments had a "heightened appreciation of the present and new insights on life that translated to an improved QOL [quality of life]. Sometimes these insights were found in transitory moments, such as watching the sunrise.

"There were just times you'd wake up. The sun was coming up and I'd go, 'Oh, geez, this is great!" said one participant in her 2004 study. "'Geez, drink this in! Absorb this!' Not necessarily enjoying the moment but recognizing it and sort of take the snapshot in your memory."

The participants in her study found that facing the very real possibility of an early demise was directly connected to this newfound importance of time and what remains of it. "The threat of death focuses you on your life, on my life, on our lives," one participant told Dr. McGrath, making them interested in "living our lives now." Another participant who talked about going whale watching—something he wouldn't have done in the past—said the inclination to do so was a part of the realization that "in the end, your life becomes another year."

Ellyn Bushkin, a nurse and three-time survivor of breast cancer and sarcoma, perhaps best elucidated this perspective shift in time in a paper that was delivered posthumously in 1993 at an oncology nursing forum. Realizing that she was dying from metastatic disease, Bushkin wrote in part about the common experiences of survivors in relation to the passing of time, wisely postulating that the feelings were shared by people who had any life-threatening illness.

"There is a new awareness of time, or more to the point, of the uncertainty of just how much time is left," Bushkin wrote. "'Will I have enough time?' With this heightened awareness, you come to value time as a precious and limited resource that must be used with economy and wisdom."

TIME SPENT IN A DAY

To see how this emphasis on time changed for those I interviewed, I asked each person to detail how he or she spent a typical twenty-four-hour period. The idea for the question originated with Dr. Viktor Frankl, the concentration camp survivor, psychiatrist, and author of *Man's Search for Meaning*. Again, Frankl's emphasis on finding meaning in life as a means to move through trauma has been widely adapted in the world of psychology.

Frankl wrote about the ways of looking at life, as measured by a traditional paper desk calendar where a small page represents a day. In this exercise, the pessimist becomes anxious as he sees the stack of days growing shorter and frets over the time when no pages will remain. The optimist, he writes, assiduously keeps a diary of the good and the bad, the challenges and the joys, filing each sheet away carefully. He wrote that the optimist can then say, "Instead of possibilities, I have realities in my past, not only the reality of work done and of love loved but of sufferings bravely suffered."

In this vein, I wanted to see how people who had passed through illness or were still living with it changed the way they spent their time prior to and following the experience of a life-threatening illness. First, participants was asked how much time they spent on work and work-related travel, time on housework and general chores, time with children, time with their spouse or significant other, time with themselves, time volunteering to help others, and time for sleep before receiving their diagnosis. Then, usually later in the interview, they were asked the same set of questions as to how this related to the way they spent their time now. With few exceptions, the greatest areas of difference of time spent in the post-illness life were in the areas of work and work-related travel and time spent with their family members.

With regard to work, I found that nearly all of those represented in this chapter, 93 percent, who continued to work following their treatment said their work hours were more concentrated but shorter. Some of those interviewed told me that they could now get more done in less time, leaving more time to spend in other areas of their lives;

these individuals worked an average of 44 percent fewer hours than they did prediagnosis. Others felt that time they spent at work was now more directed to pursuits they felt contributed to society in some way, a topic that will be addressed in chapters 7 and 9.

And, invariably, those who spent less time at work devoted those extra hours to their children and their significant others. Although the category of time spent with themselves also grew, those who devoted less time to work told me that they experienced a nearly seismic shift in the amount of time they spent in the company of those to whom they were most closely related. Among those whose relationships remained intact following treatment, the increases ranged from 30 percent to 300 percent more time spent with family.

Peter is one of these people. A former Mr. Universe, Peter made his living writing books about his life and bodybuilding, running several locations of his own nutrition and personal-training business, developing television shows on fitness, filming spots for a local television station as a fitness correspondent, and recording other spots for a local radio show. But there was a big price to pay for this ambitious schedule, namely, less and less time spent with his two young daughters and his wife, as his various gigs required him to work seventeen and eighteen-hour days, seven days a week.

That he was able to win numerous bodybuilding titles and do all of the work he did after being diagnosed with Crohn's disease at age fifteen was nothing short of a miracle, considering he suffered through extensive surgery and difficult treatments while spending months in a New York hospital. His weight had dwindled from 140 to 67 pounds, and he faced almost certain death from life-threatening infections. But he turned to weight lifting in order to regain his strength after leaving the hospital and never looked back. His life had stretched on more than two decades without another exacerbation, and he had become the picture of health and fitness; the feeling of living on the edge of the abyss of death had all but vanished for him.

In March 2001, Peter became unconscious twice during a bowel obstruction, a relatively common but life-threatening complication for Crohn's patients. After tests were performed, his surgeon notified him that he would have to have more than a foot of his small bowel removed; further, the surgeon felt a fist-sized mass in Peter's abdomen that looked suspiciously like small-bowel cancer. Surgery was performed and the mass was found to be benign, but the recovery was difficult, long, and painful, as his picture-perfect abdominal muscles had to be severed in order to extract the intestines and the mass.

The threat of extinction forced a change in Peter's schedule. The man who spent less than an hour with his children and a mere half hour with his wife each day, the man who worked weekends and never took more than a day or two for vacation, now cut his hours at work to eight a day and regularly spent three-day weekends with his family. He increased the time he spent with his children to four or more hours a day and more than quadrupled the time he spent alone with his wife. He now thinks nothing of flying to the Florida Keys to spend a week sail fishing or riding his rare motorcycles, something he has grown passionate about collecting.

"Time is speeding. It is funny that you ask about that. It gives me the chills. I never verbalized this to anyone. The weeks go by so quick and I feel like I am not maximizing what I need to do in a week. I want there to be an extra day. I don't want to sleep. I don't want to miss anything. It is not a business thing. I don't want to miss my daughter's front tooth coming out. I don't want to miss my dog jumping in the lake for the first time. I don't want to miss my other daughter catching her first fish. I don't want to miss that stuff," he said.

James, a professor of literature and an author, felt that way after a life-threatening brush with the same disease. Prior to his diagnosis, he would come home from work following classes but frequently found himself sneaking away from his wife and children to his home office to dedicate more time to work, putting in a total of ten or eleven hours a day on course work, preparation, and office time.

Following a particularly acute episode that culminated in a lengthy hospital stay and severe weight loss, James cut the hours he worked to about six a day. No longer did he slip into his home office, preferring instead to spend the time with his family. When I asked him to consider the change in the quality of his life if he had not been ill, James said, "I used to put myself first and my emotional needs first far more than I do now. For me, I don't think I would behave with my children as I behave now, and that is very important to me. I only have kids this little for so long, and I want to make sure that I am here to enjoy as many minutes as is possible. I don't think I would have been like that before. If I went back [to life before diagnosis], I would have stolen time from them for myself."

Again, this theme is echoed in the existing literature. Quotes from two separate published studies sound as if they could have come from the mouths of those interviewed for this book. In a 1983 study on adjusting to threatening events, Dr. Shelley Taylor interviewed seventy-eight women who had survived breast cancer. She found that slightly over half of those who participated in the study reappraised what was important in their lives following the illness and many others instituted changes accordingly in the way they spent their time after examining the experience of illness. The resulting alteration was revealed when the individuals gave a low ranking of importance to things like housework, petty fights, and other people's problems, while devoting more time and effort to family relationships and personal projects or enjoyments such as hobbies or special pursuits.

As one respondent in the study said, "You take a long look at your life and realize that many things that you thought were important before are totally insignificant. That's probably been the major change in my life. What you do is put things into perspective. You find out that things like relationships are really the most important things you have—the way people you know and your family—everything else is just way down the line. It's very strange that it takes something so serious to make you realize that."

McGrath, in the aforementioned 2004 paper on the subject of survival of hematologic cancer patients, said families as a whole benefited from the illness experience in a renewed sense of togetherness, an affirmation of bonds, and a reinforced importance of time spent with family, in part because of the possible threat of loss for all. As one participant of her study said, illness "made me realize that life is too short and family life is very important to me."

Dr. James Brennan, who studied the psychological adjustment to cancer following diagnosis and published the findings in a 2001 paper, said this change is among many that are common experiences in this population.

"Rarely does a cancer patient describe a sense of continuity with their lives before cancer—there is invariably a shift in the individual's sense of themselves and the world," Brennan wrote.

This is particularly true of family relationships, Brennan found. "Whatever the objective prognosis, cancer confronts patients and those in their social world with the threat of permanent separation from loved ones."

A SHIFT IN THE EXPERIENCE OF BEING

When we are no longer able to change a situation—just think of an incurable disease such as inoperable cancer—we are challenged to change ourselves.

—Dr. Viktor Frankl, *Man's Search for Meaning*

While the shift in the experience of time is more of an unseen and theoretical concept to all, far more palpable for those who go through serious illness is a metamorphosis in the sense of being, the vast difference in the experience of our physical bodies prior to and following diagnosis and treatment.

Most of us are born into the world a whole being without too many physical challenges to consider. As our bodies grow, we develop a sense of mastery over them and their functions. At the same time, we develop a sense of entitlement for continuing health and take for granted normal bodily functions. After all, we never struggled to breathe or move; those things came naturally, easily, expectedly. We and the vast majority of our contemporaries were robust and strong, able to pursue our lives and passions without barriers. If we had ever been attacked by mild bacterial or viral illness, we took at most a two-week course of antibiotics or other medication and were back to normal capacity in no time.

But life doesn't always continue along that desired trajectory. Many, many people who lived healthful lives and thus had a sense of expectation that it would continue have had their time cut short due to seemingly unjust and inexplicable diseases. Nonsmokers with lung cancer, athletes with failing hearts, young people with old people's diseases—it doesn't seem fair, but it happens more often than we like to acknowledge, in part because doing so would force us to confront and accept our own mortality. And when serious illness enters our own lives, there is a feeling of being cheated out of that entitlement to which nearly every other human being seems to have been granted, a deeply felt and inherent injustice.

There is also a sense of loss of control or mastery of this body in which we have lived thus far. Normal functions that we have come to count on from our bodies and have taken for granted in the past—walking, talking, grasping, thinking, eating, defecating, and breathing, to name a few—can become temporarily laborious or change forever due to the disease or its treatment. This "new normal" is nothing we bargained for and nothing we particularly welcome. (In a side note, I have yet to locate someone with a disease who experienced welcome changes such as perkier breasts or whiter teeth as symptoms or the results of treatments.)

Individuals interviewed for this book tended to be angry initially at the loss of their expected physical wholeness following a diagnosis of and treatment for a life-threatening illness. They mourned the temporary or permanent changes that now affected their bodies but they eventually had to incorporate these changes into their lives.

Didi was one who had to cope with lasting physical changes. When she was diagnosed with invasive breast cancer, she dove into denial and developed a sense of self-protection. She decided to have her double mastectomy at Memorial Sloan-Kettering Cancer Center in New York rather than in Detroit, where she lived, in order to avoid the stares and sympathy she was sure to receive and did not desire. The surgery went well, nearly assuring Didi that she would not face the same fate as her mother, who twenty-five years earlier battled the identical form of breast cancer and, sadly, lost. While she was grateful for that positive result, Didi told me that she mourned the loss of a part of her body she so cherished and felt anger toward those who did not have to go through a similar physical trauma.

One day, with fresh wounds where there were once breasts, tubes hanging out of her chest, and other lines protruding from her body, Didi sat in the window well of her Manhattan hospital room, watching the healthy world swirl about on the midday streets below her. "It was so busy down there and you could see tons of people. I almost feel like crying when I remember it because I never felt like that before. I remember thinking to myself, 'Damn all of you. You are going on with your lives. Everything is fine down there and I am up here and I could die and I don't know what is going to happen to me. I am suffering and I don't look so good and I don't feel so good.' Life was going on around me. I was resentful that I felt like there was this whole nice fairyland going on down there while I was going through something."

To cope with the physical changes, Didi, a kindergarten teacher, tried to turn a negative into a positive. Always flat-chested by her own admission, she voted to have reconstruction surgery and grew from an A cup to a C cup nearly overnight. Her new enhanced physique brings her chuckles at times. "There was this time we went to Mexico. My boobs were so big when we went that my kids were saying, 'Don't take off your shirt,' because everyone was looking at me. I looked like Dolly Parton!"

Despite the boost in her bra size, she still suffers eight years later from esteem issues brought about by the breast removal. Didi has gone through numerous further reconstructive measures, including having "nipples" created from the loose skin left on the reconstructed breasts, with areolas tattooed around them. But she is still uncomfortable about them in general—especially with the realization that they are a constant reminder of her brush with death—and she is highly sensitive about their appearance to others. To this day, she is shy about removing her shirt in front of anyone or anywhere, from the locker room at the gym to her own bedroom.

The second chance that was rendered by surviving illness appears to usher in a new responsibility as well. Those interviewed for this book say they became more watchful and hypersensitive to even slight physical changes, always on the lookout for signs and symptoms of a recurrence or flare-up. Probing lymph nodes with their fingers to check for swelling, checking their stool for the presence of blood, obsessively monitoring their blood pressure for the slightest flutter—some said they do this to calm a fear of the disease resurfacing. If it all checks out, they continue with their lives until the fear arises again and the checking and rechecking begins anew.

McGrath found in her study of hematologic cancer patients that they no longer felt a need for approval from others, a shift that freed them up to focus on their own needs. By doing so, the individuals experienced an increased ability to listen to the signals that their bodies were sending them. "I listen to my body, which is what you've got to do. I didn't used to do that. I listen to my body now," one respondent told her.

And others said they have developed a stronger sense of responsibility when it comes to their health, making sure they attend doctor's appointments, being religious about having the right tests at the appropriate times, staying current on the research on their diseases even if they have been declared cured. Nearly all interviewed said they are living more healthful lives following illness than they did prior to diagnosis.

For Didi, that second chance that came with surviving breast cancer brought with it a sense of gratitude that translated to an almost hypervigilance for her health.

"I did not walk away from breast cancer and then not keep track of what is going on here as best I can. I didn't dodge the bullet and walk away to be hit by another one," she said, adding that she has been tested for two of the gene mutations thought to cause breast cancer, BRCA 1 and 2, and has regular mammograms as well as a colonoscopy, bone scans, and other exams. "Whatever it is, I wanted to confront it. I have no tolerance or respect for people who ignore stuff like that. They don't go to the doctor, they don't want to have mammograms, they don't want to know. I don't understand that at all because I would be dead if I did that."

For nearly all of those represented in this chapter, as well as scores of others I interviewed for the book, exercise and meditation became very important for survival. On the surface, the idea of working out while ill seems almost counterintuitive, as the more traditional view is that those who are sick need rest to recover. And yet those interviewed said that exercise brought to them a feeling of continuing with life, of fighting back against the changes that illness wrought, of reduced stress, and of increased peace.

Beverly, a registered dietitian, was a long-distance runner when she was diagnosed with scleroderma fifteen years ago. The disease and its initial treatments of high-dose steroids caused her to bloat and suffer from extreme fatigue. Exercise went out the window during that period. But as she improved, she found that simply walking was helpful, as "it was something that I knew I could do."

Now she is a certified yoga teacher and she finds that this provides more than physical benefits. "I find that just breathing and being in the moment in the practice of yoga gives me a certain kind of strength. It calms me. It keeps me centered, and I need that physically as well as mentally," Beverly said.

And nearly everyone represented in this chapter either continued to work out while undergoing treatment or resumed their routines not long after. Of those who appear in this chapter alone, all volunteered without being asked how certain exercise or meditation helped them to recover. For example, Stewart found solace in walking and later running through his neighborhood following his treatments, Macklin was a long-distance runner before his illness but became dedicated to yoga afterward, Ernest pushed himself to resume running in road races within months of treatment, Heidi lifted weights and swam during and after chemotherapy and radiation, Peter turned to weight lifting after sinking to his fourth-grade weight following diagnosis and became a world-champion bodybuilder, and so on. Many of individuals in this chapter as well as most of the others interviewed for the book also incorporated diet changes or undertook a new regimen of vitamin supplements or Chinese medicine to better their chances of avoiding recurrence and attaining optimum health.

In the 1983 paper on breast cancer survivors, Shelley Taylor wrote that exercise along with dietary changes and stress reduction techniques helps a person regain a sense of mastery over their disease. When a person becomes ill, all of their beliefs and patterns of living can change, leaving the ill person with a sense of loss of control over his or her body and the world in general, she wrote. Many of the seventy-eight breast cancer patients she studied believed that they could prevent recurrence by instituting more healthful practices in their lives. Others felt that they needed to make choices in their care and thus learned as much as they could about their disease and its treatments to achieve this same sense. All of these practices gave them a sense of mastery or control over their illness and thus a greater sense of confidence in dealing with it.

Mastery over the illness led many of those I interviewed for this book to become more assertive in controlling the course of their medical or surgical treatments. This concept is one that also appears in the psychology literature. In a paper mentioned previously that was published in 1996 on the feeling of health within the experience of illness, Dr. Elizabeth Lindsey studied a small group of individuals with a variety of chronic diseases, interviewing these people at length about their experiences. She found that a theme she labeled "Honoring the Self" emerged and said it involved "a self-respect and a self-love. The participants talked of becoming assertive, self-defining and self-protective, with an ability to express their needs, desires and actions."

In Heidi's case, this meant losing a part of the way she was raised and adopting a stiffer spine when it came to the way she was treated medically.

"I had to be my own advocate. I had to really keep after it. Not that I was a pushover, but I was raised as a good Southern girl. You avoid conflict and you don't want to offend anyone. You want to keep the peace, that kind of thing," she said. But after a diagnostic period that was prolonged unnecessarily, Heidi changed. "I had to learn to ask for what I wanted and demand what I needed. You know what it is like. You go into the hospital and you become this sort of cog in the wheel. If you want to buck the routine, you really have to buck the routine. You need to learn how to do that. They knew me. They knew that I would do certain things and that I wouldn't do certain things and that was the status."

LIVING WITH DEATH, A NEW REALITY

When we are faced with illnesses that challenge our very existence, it is hard for us not to consider and reconsider our feelings regarding death, the ultimate end of time and being. During the time of diagnosis and treatment, death moves from the theoretical and distant possibility to the genuine and proximal foe, something very real with which to struggle.

But even as treatment concludes, as the disease is knocked into remission, and as the sense of time and being shift, the fear of returning to that battle and the reality that we might again at an unknown future date continues to settle upon us. And for some interviewed for this book, that fear of death and negative feelings toward it never change. For example, when asked about whether her feelings toward death altered following her treatment for breast cancer, Didi answered, "No. I didn't like the idea before and I certainly don't now. It doesn't sound appealing."

But many others said that the fear of recurrence or a new flare-up, which translated to a fear of another brush with death, loosened over time. Studies bear out that phenomenon. In a 1986 study of sixty male survivors of Hodgkin's disease, researchers found that there existed greater death anxiety among survivors two years following treatment than those with longer survival times, suggesting that this fear lessens with the length of survival.

Twenty years out from her battle, Kathy agrees with that finding.

"Let's just say that the periods of time when I feared death became fewer and farther between, less impactful. The valley of the shadow of death is a real place. We move in and hang curtains. It becomes our place and therefore it can no longer control us," she said.

Yet at the same time, there is less obliviousness about death in the survivors than they experienced before diagnosis. Prior to that seminal moment, many were blissfully unconcerned with their mortality, as it was an issue they had not faced closely, extensively, or personally; after treatment, it was a reality with which they wrestled during their diagnostic and treatment period and continued to do so, sometimes years later.

"The whole notion of undeniable innocence—that innocence that allows you to remain naïve and unaware that you are in a mortal position all of the time—that's gone. That is the one thing that we all share: we are all going to end. That innocence is not a luxury I have anymore. I just don't have it anymore. I don't. I'm sorry. I have seen too much," said Stewart.

"Beforehand, we used to say, joking around, 'Well, if I die . . .' Now, it is like, 'When you die, stupid,'" Stewart continued. "That is just one luxury I don't have. The dog pulled back the curtain. I've seen the shit that is behind the curtain. I know too much."

Still, the proximity of death is something that introduces a feeling of familiarity and, in some, a greater sense of comfort in dealing with it in themselves and in others. Many of the individuals interviewed met others during treatments or through patient organizations who eventually succumbed to the very illness they had in common. Watching someone suffering so similarly but who experienced a bad outcome evoked feelings of compassion in those who survived, especially if the dying were spurned by loved ones and others who remained fearful of death.

While being treated for her cancer, Heidi watched four of the five friends she made through the diagnosis and treatment for her illness die, despite not having a lot of personal life experience with death prior to her diagnosis. She became more acutely aware that society downplays death.

"It is a crime the way that our society covers death up. I see it as a very natural part of life. I think I am much more comfortable in that sense. I am not afraid to talk to someone who is dying. There is a comfort level that wasn't there before," Heidi said.

And like the shifts in time and being that occurred following diagnosis, there appears to be an eventual comfort in the change of feelings for most regarding death. Some of those interviewed for this book found that they came to terms with that fear, which loosened the grip of it on their lives and freed them up to live more at peace.

"I have been a deathophobe all of my life," said James. "But now, my fears are greatly, greatly diminished. I don't fear at all for myself anymore, which I used to. I was afraid of what if there is no afterlife, my personal fear of personal annihilation, essentially. But the only reason I fear now is for my kids, what is going to happen to them and how it would affect them. I have almost no fear for myself anymore. Whatever happens, happens."

REAL STORY—PATTY

A lot can change in the space of five years. Just ask Patty, a forty-five-year-old mother of two teenagers.

Five years ago, Patty was "one hundred twenty pounds of flying terror," says her sister, Janice. Patty and her husband, Sean, were the owners of a rapidly growing heating and cooling shop. Toiling long hours side by side, the couple had just built a new building to house the burgeoning business but still took as much time as they could away to explore the world, racing down steep slopes snow skiing in Colorado or strapping on scuba gear to check out the coral reefs off the coast of Grand Cayman Island in the Caribbean. In Patty's spare time at home, she cultivated numerous friendships among her children's friends' parents; they would spend time working shoulder to shoulder as volunteers at the local elementary school or goofing off at parties in each others' homes.

Patty

"I was on the move," she said. "I never sat still."

It was at one of these parties that Patty's life changed forever. On a sultry summer evening in a friend's garden, Patty's face froze. From across the lawn, Sean saw her and knew something was wrong. He quickly took her to their family doctor, who referred her to a top neurologist. After running numerous tests including an MRI and an angiogram, the neurologist diagnosed an exceedingly rare brain condition, Moyamoya syndrome, which strikes 1 in 2 million Americans.

"I remember that Sean was in the room with me. I was devastated. I cried immediate tears. Time stood still," Patty said of the moment of diagnosis, a memory that survived the greater trauma she would soon face.

Patty was initially crushed but determined that she was going to be among the miniscule number of those afflicted with the disease to live and thrive with it. She researched the treatments but didn't commit herself to any of them, getting by a day at a time.

"I was going to beat this thing. If that isn't denial, I don't know what is. I was going to be the one out of I don't know how many to do so," she said, laughing.

Then, on a cold February day when she was home with her two daughters after they returned from school, Patty developed one of the worst headaches she had ever felt. She told her daughters she was going to lie down.

"And that is all I remember," said Patty, who was seated in her electric wheelchair in her sunny kitchen during our interview.

A massive stroke occurred. Initially, doctors thought she would not survive that event. Knocked into a coma, she recalls a vivid dream about her mother, who had died previously.

"She was telling me to go on, not to give in, to go on with my fight. It made me feel good," she said. "I am now bound and determined to fight everything."

Patty slowly woke from the coma, eventually gaining full consciousness fourteen months after the stroke. She then went through two brain surgeries to reroute the blood supply to her brain, the recovery from which also took several months. The physical toll from the strokes and the surgeries was great, leaving her initially a quadriplegic.

In the months and years since the diagnosis, the experience of time has drastically changed for Patty. Her days, which used fly by with work, volunteering, and general excitement, are now filled with rehabilitation and pass with greater purpose as she looks forward to spending time with her family when they return home at the end of the day.

"Time passes slowly, slowly," Patty said, adding that she doesn't take for granted spending time with her family. Now time has become more palpable to her than she ever noticed in the past. A complicated medication schedule, for example, involves several different doses of many medications throughout the day. The experience of time throughout the year changed more positively, too, as Patty's rehabilitation allowed her to regain the use of one arm and the shoulder of the other; she now stands assisted for longer periods of time.

"I take medication around the clock, so I can see how the day moves. I have to take a certain medication when I wake in the morning, another at noon, and another at two o'clock, and so on. I see how the day moves in that way. I also see it over a year because I keep getting better and better. Things I couldn't do at the beginning of the year, I can do now," Patty said.

Still, the bodily limitations have drastically changed the way that she experiences her physical being. Before, she was extremely active and fully functional, something she admits she took for granted. The paralysis has shattered that state of being, leaving her to rely on aides to feed her, to bathe her, and to move her about.

"I am frustrated all of the time," Patty said. "I am used to doing everything myself and now I have to wait for everything."

Despite this frustration, there are big parts about the shift in her daily time and her new physical state of being that bring joy to her. Several days a week, she spends time at Cross Trainers, a gym that incorporates her hospital's physical therapy program. During the time at the gym, Patty looks forward to talking with others who have faced similar physical hurdles, making new friends who buoy her spirits and lend her courage.

"I love it there," she says. "I work out there for a couple

of hours or stand in my frame. I talk to people as they go by or just put my headphones on and listen to my music—Bruce Springsteen, Peter Frampton, Rod Stewart. I sing along. I have a terrible voice but no one minds. At least they don't tell me they mind."

And, with this shift of time and being, Patty has come to terms with death, something she greatly feared in the past. The potential imminence of death in her life has left her more determined to accomplish her new goals in the time she has left and to focus on enjoying each minute in the process.

"I am not scared of death. But I will walk before then, before I die. I am positive of that," Patty said.

7

GIFT 3: ALTRUISM: THE PURPOSE IN HELPING OTHERS

Do all you can with what you have in the time you have in the place you are.

—Xolani Nkosi Johnson, AIDS activist

XOLANI NKOSI JOHNSON learned a lot about living with illness during his brief life. Born HIV-positive in South Africa, he was considered a longtime survivor of the illness when he succumbed to the disease at the age of twelve in June 2001. During those short years, he was separated from his birth mother when she could no longer look after him due to complications from her own infection, and he subsequently was cared for by a devoted foster mother, Gail Johnson.

Following his mother's death from AIDS, Gail and Nkosi founded Nkosi's Haven, a facility for HIV-positive mothers and their children. The organization provides room and board for the families, funding for the children's education, free over-the-counter medications, and burial fees for either the mother or the children. It is a relatively small effort in a continent ravaged by AIDS but a significant one nonetheless, as it allows mothers and children to remain together throughout the disease, an option Nkosi did not have when his mother was dying.

Like Nkosi, virtually all of those I interviewed for this book were moved to help others through altruistic acts during and after their illness. Some of those I interviewed made huge shifts in their lives in terms of altruism, such as shelving their careers to found charities related to their diseases. Others made smaller but no less significant contributions to society following their diagnosis; these acts could be as seemingly small as writing an e-mail to offer encouragement and support to someone going through treatment or as large as raising millions of dollars to support research.

Many journal articles and studies validated the resulting increase in altruism among those who have suffered chronic or acute life-threatening illnesses. For example, in her 1996 study on finding health within chronic illness, Dr. Elizabeth Lindsey wrote that all of her study subjects engaged in volunteer activities as a result of their experience with illness.

"All of the participants talked of a commitment to helping others with chronic conditions. This help came in different forms," Lindsey wrote. "A respondent with multiple sclerosis talked of wanting to share her knowledge with others: 'For me, part of my vision, my mission, my purpose in life is to share whatever I am learning.' Others spoke of initiating support groups, providing workshops, and acting as resource people for those with chronic conditions; they talked of a heightened awareness and sensitivity to the needs of others. One person explained that 'as one sensation is dulled other sensations are heightened, which leads me to a greater sensitivity to what other people are experiencing.'"

In another 1989 paper, produced by a team of American

researchers on the subject of surviving adult cancers, altruism was seen as a natural by-product of the illness experience. "Helping others represents a kind of end point at which survivors felt lucky and eager to use those painful and helpful parts of their experience to improve the lives of others and get on with living," the researchers wrote.

For this chapter, I selected interviews from individuals who represented the spectrum of volunteer behavior both prediagnosis and post-treatment. Some did no volunteer work prior to being diagnosed, while others were far more active; some made admittedly small contributions following treatment, while others made altruistic acts the focus of their lives. In all, those who appear in this chapter alone increased the amount of time spent per day volunteering to help others from an average of eight minutes per day prior to their diagnosis to an average of five hours per day at the time they were interviewed.

ALTRUISM BEFORE THE DIAGNOSIS

For many who were interviewed for this book, virtually no time was devoted toward volunteerism during their daily lives prior to their diagnosis. And this is not only common but understandable. Young people's lives tend to have a number of time constraints: getting through college, establishing a career, building a social life, starting a family. As years pass, most individuals' daily constraints grow to include time spent maintaining a marriage, taking care of children, and tending to household obligations. Volunteerism is low on the list of priorities in such a busy life until illness and the ensuing focus on survival send those and all other obligations to a screeching halt. During treatment or in the years after are common times for the significance of helping others to be recognized.

Tony worked as a mid-level manager in a large department store, usually putting in nine- to twelve-hour days there before returning home to chores and time spent with his partner. He spent no time volunteering, as his life was full of activities and interests. But at the end of 1985, he became rundown with a flu that seemingly never went away. A blood test revealed that Tony was HIV-positive, a condition that caused a number of serious illnesses and that eventually led him to leave him the work world entirely. He now volunteers eight hours a week.

"I was successful in my job before the illness and I am once again successful after dealing with the illness and incorporating it into my everyday life. I actually get more out of my work now. Before it was just a job. Now I truly enjoy what I do," Tony said.

Others may have volunteered a little in the past but made no significant contribution in terms of time, nor was the volunteerism related to the illness they suffered. Major fundraisers and the like can be fun social events, and some of those interviewed said they were goaded by friends or family members to help out at these activities, leading them to spend hours helping with some aspect of the event but not really dedicating themselves to the cause.

Jeff fit that profile. A community mental health professional, he estimates that he gave an average of ten minutes a day of his time toward community projects prior to his diagnosis of colon cancer. In the eight years since that time, he served as national president of the Colon Cancer Alliance, devoting hundreds of hours each year to raising awareness of the disease and pushing the importance of early detection into the forefront of the nation's conscience. He reorganized parts of his life in order to spend more time with this type of volunteering.

"With my work with the Colon Cancer Alliance, there is a higher level of meaning that I want to make sure that my time takes on," Jeff said.

Both Tony's and Jeff's pre-illness amounts and types of volunteerism are fairly ordinary, a finding supported by research. A study by the United States Department of Labor in 2002 found that 26 percent of individuals over the age of sixteen reported volunteering in the year prior to the study. The most common type of activity was either short-term, or a one-time activity, and the average amount of time spent per week in such volunteer activities was one hour or less.

But there are always a few who stick out as the exception to the rule, and prediagnosis altruism is no exception. For a handful of those interviewed, volunteerism was a way of life and something that just continued when they became sick, though usually shifting focus. Cary offers a good example of this. A high-powered lawyer specializing in international law, he spent an average of an hour a day with a few local charities, serving as an active board member. Additionally, he served as a mentor in a Big Brothers Big Sisters of America program, a role he truly cherished. Cary valued the one-on-one time that he spent with two underprivileged boys, regularly devoting several hours each month with them as he watched them grow through the years. "Volunteering has always been a big part of my life," Cary said.

Then he was diagnosed and treated for metastatic esophageal cancer, first having surgery to remove a portion of his esophagus and stomach and then enduring several rounds of chemotherapy as well as radiation. He shifted his focus from serving on the boards of charities to creating one, a Web site for individuals going through treatment for the same disease. People who came to the site see him as a sign of hope and personally contact him, seeking a mentor.

"Now, what I do is just different," Cary said of the focus on cancer treatment, adding that he has doubled the amount of time he spends volunteering. "Without the cancer, I wouldn't have gone in that direction."

THE REASONS FOR THE INCREASE IN ALTRUISM

From what we get, we can make a living. What we give, however, makes a life.

—Arthur Ashe, professional tennis player

On the surface, this trend in volunteerism following a personal battle with illness appears by nature altruistic, the formal meaning of which is the unselfish regard for the welfare of others. And it truly is. However, that does not mean that these acts did not have a benefit or fulfill a personal need for those committing them. For every altruistic action, there appeared to be a reason driving it, a need it was tending in those who participated in the interview.

One reason people volunteered their time and efforts following illness was to work through accepting the illness as a part of their life, in the past, in the present, and in the future. By helping others, they were able to better integrate the illness into their own lives.

This sense of mastery over the illness and the incorporation of it into life after treatment through helping others was elucidated in a 2002 study by a group of Australian researchers. These social scientists felt that some individuals were successful in their emotional and spiritual recovery from a physical illness in part because they were able to weave this new knowledge into the fabric of their lives, at times through helping others. As an example, they wrote about Bert, a colon cancer patient who was originally devastated by his diagnosis but then became a counselor to other patients undergoing colostomy operations. "He turns his experience into expertise and is quite prepared to insist that experience truly brings its own expertise," they wrote.

Linie understands where Bert was coming from. In the late 1980s and early 1990s, she was a healthy, vibrant, successful real estate agent and single mother, living the good life. She told me about the significant amount of hours she spent closing deals that allowed her the luxury of a nice car and a home with a swimming pool in a desirable suburb. Linie spent the vast majority of her spare time with her son, and from that relationship came her only bit of volunteering in her life, first as a room mother in his school and then helping out with his Little League team.

But then she was diagnosed with primary biliary cirrhosis (PBC), an inflammatory condition that damages and then renders useless the bile ducts that lead from the liver. The fatigue caused by liver damage related to PBC forced her to leave her profession prematurely, sell her house, and move to a more affordable area in a somewhat rural location.

All of these changes took a big toll on her life and were compounded by a sense of isolation that came with having a rare and deadly disease.

To help her work through some of the isolation and become more accepting of her fate, she sought others who shared her condition, but there were no formal organizations to turn to for help or understanding. With the help of her son, Linie founded PBCers, a national group that supports patients with her condition. Largely Internet-based, the organization seeks to educate patients, family members, and the public about the disease.

As PBCers grew, she learned more about the disease and began to teach others about it as well. She helped people who were newly diagnosed and others who had shared the same path for a while. Through the people she met, Linie learned that the changes that she had gone through were really not that unusual for those with the disease and not as difficult as they could have been; for example, some individuals she met have gone through liver transplantation, something Linie has yet to do. All of this helped her to incorporate the disease into her life and gain perspective at the same time.

Now Linie travels to four or five conferences a year to give presentations on life with PBC and dedicates three to four hours a day to the work of running the organization. In reflecting on the change from her former life to her current reality, she says, "I was one of the top producers in Houston, in my area. And, you know, I was making very good money. But I feel like I'm accomplishing more now with the PBCers because it's actually helping people."

While working through feelings of grief is definitely a

draw to altruism, some simply were compelled to seek others who are facing the same set of circumstances during treatment and in life beyond. In sharing some of the same treatments and associated feelings that stem from a health-related struggle, these new relationships helped diminish the feeling of loneliness, created a sense of camaraderie, and fostered a mutual learning relationship. Many of the interviewees said that these new friendships were among the best they had made in their entire lives.

Patty is one who sought others with the condition, though she didn't know it at the time. When she was diagnosed with hepatitis C and for years afterward, she was completely unaware that the disease she was carrying around inside of her could be deadly serious. Then a liver biopsy revealed that her liver was becoming cirrhotic. Patty's doctor prescribed a tough antiviral regimen, something that made her feel sick. Not knowing anyone else who even had the disease, much less another who was on the same medication, she felt lonely and afraid.

One Christmas during this treatment, her family bought a computer. After learning the basics on the Internet, Patty had her daughter type "hepatitis C" into a search engine. Patty was amazed at the lengthy list of sites dedicated to living with her disease. She stumbled into a chat room and forum, where she spent New Year's Eve and New Year's Day communicating with others who understood what she was going through.

"That opened a whole new world to me. It was New Year's Day, and I remember my husband serving dinner at the computer because I was in a chat room with all these people that were on the treatment," she said, adding that she became close friends with two other women, both of whom eventually died of the disease.

Because of the relationships she formed with other hepatitis C patients on the Internet, Patty designed her own Internet site for people with hepatitis C. Never a volunteer at the onset of her illness, she now spends about twelve hours a day online, fine-tuning her site and communicating with the people who visit it, many also seeking the same camaraderie that she sought more than a decade ago in that first forum.

"I have helped so many people with their fears, even through their first injection, someone starting treatment, through their diagnosis," Patty said. "You know, in your late forties, it's very rare that you make a new best friend. I know that sounds corny, 'best friend.' But I've been fortunate to make quite a few of these friendships."

Knowing that others were following in their footsteps also fueled a sense of compassion for some of the interviewees. Dr. Pam McGrath, in her 2004 study of the positive spiritual perspective changes in hematologic cancer survivors, said that those she studied became more open to others' suffering and adjusted their lives accordingly. "The positives from the experience were not just related in terms of benefits to the individual but, rather, the increased desire the individual had to make a difference in the lives of others. The renewed sense of altruism and compassion was invested in community activities and a heightened desire to engage in activities that were a benefit to others, such as volunteer work, committee work or being a blood and transplant donor," she wrote.

One of McGrath's study subjects contributed the following quote regarding the matter: "Because I said to someone I didn't fight my guts out to live and end up sick again. It was to make a difference to this world, whether it be for one person or for a hundred people, I don't know."

Urged on by this growing compassion, those I interviewed for this book often sought ways to make a difference in the lives of those suffering in the same way. Maybe there was a gap in services they saw during their treatment that they felt they could fill, or perhaps there is some way they can create laws to make sure certain procedures are covered by insurance. Whatever the motivator, these individuals then made it their mission to effect change so that others who follow in their path would have an easier time navigating the illness landscape.

When Brenda was diagnosed with early-onset Parkinson's disease, there were few services for people like her. She joined a hospital-sponsored chat room and met a woman who faced the same challenges. The pair decided to create a Web site that connected people with others who have Parkinson's and provide them with social support and understanding. The Web site became a formal organization, the organization became a tool for advocacy, and, in turn, legislative change was made to fund more Parkinson's research.

"I've been able to do my share for improving therapy for Parkinson's as well as improving the research for the cure of Parkinson's. And I've met so many people. It was a blessing," Brenda said.

Still more felt an obligation to help others, especially if they felt that they were spared from death in their struggle through treatment. While he was still being treated for esophageal cancer, Cary began dreaming about creating a Web site with content to help others who had just been diagnosed with the same disease. The site, www.esophagealcancer.org, now contains everything from treatment options to tips on living life after treatment. Daily, he answers e-mails filled with questions about procedures and requests for mentorship.

"I haven't a sense that the site is something I am called upon to do, not necessarily a God thing. But it's on a more human level," Cary said. "I think people in my position have an obligation to do that, and I don't mind doing it at all."

MAKING THE DIFFERENCE

Be the change you wish to see in the world.
—Mohandas K. Gandhi

Whatever the reason for the entrée into active volunteerism for others who share the same disease, the people I interviewed displayed a wide range in the amount of time they volunteered, as well as in the ways in which they gave their time and the levels to which they ascended in volunteer organizations. Most started their altruistic acts in small ways, usually through a larger organization. Writing letters to congressional representatives on behalf of an organization, helping out at fund-raising events, soliciting money for research, and providing personal support to others facing the same situation were all ways in which the participants engaged in altruism. For example, Amy had walked in fund-raisers for the Leukemia and Lymphoma Society in honor of a friend who survived a bone marrow transplant for leukemia. But after she was diagnosed with and survived treatment for lymphoma, she became a team leader in the same walk and raised over ten thousand dollars for the organization.

"I almost feel like it is something I need to do," Amy said.

Sometimes, smaller gestures make a huge difference in the life of someone on the verge of losing hope. That is what Alicia hopes to accomplish, though she didn't work through an organization to help her fellow ovarian cancer survivors. While an organization exists for people with the same condition she was diagnosed with when she was twenty-three, she found that the programs offered were more in line with the needs of the majority of the suffers, those who were in their fifth or sixth decade of life. Because of this, Alicia started an Internet-based diary, detailing her struggles with the disease while offering companionship and support for others in similar situations. Her new friends discuss issues such as dating and fertility after ovarian cancer surgery and treatment, not topics usually covered in typical ovarian cancer forums where the patients tend to be older and not as interested in those subjects.

"The blog created a community for a lot of younger women with ovarian cancer. It makes a difference, if only for a small group," Alicia said, adding that she spends about two hours a week tending to the site.

Others make their altruistic acts more of an active hobby. For them, volunteering to help others came in the form of creating elaborate Web sites to educate and to support others going through similar struggles, starting local support groups for individuals who were newly diagnosed and writing e-mails of encouragement or support to people facing a setback. Typically, these individuals spent at least one to four hours daily solely helping others.

John is one of those people. Diagnosed with liver failure, he went through two transplants before permanently leaving his construction job due to disability. He now spends about four hours a day with pre- and post-transplant patients, visiting with them in hospitals, sending supportive e-mails, or conducting support group meetings. He recently added a partner who went through kidney and pancreas transplant, thus widening his support group offerings to include selections for that population.

Though he loved his construction job and what he felt it gave to the community, John feels so dedicated to helping others facing transplant that if he were given the chance to return to the work world, he said, he would want to shift his profession to more of a social work role rather than returning to the field of construction. "I feel that volunteering with the support groups and everything I do is way overbalanced. It means a lot more to me, and I think it means a lot more to many individuals than what I was doing in the past," John said.

While the vast majority of those interviewed confined their altruism to their free time, a few found a calling in their newfound passion of altruism. It is hardly surprising but no less interesting to note that virtually all patient support organizations are founded, run, and supported by fellow survivors who have made it through diagnosis and treatment for an illness. Almost an obligation of sorts, these altruistic acts benefit not only the recipients as individuals or the larger community but also the survivors who engage in them.

Accordingly, some individuals selected for this chapter shelved their professions and made altruistic pursuits their vocation, often forgoing more lucrative careers for the low pay that often comes with helping others. For these individuals, high salaries and prestigious titles do not hold sway as what was once their affliction becomes their raison d'être, and no one can put a price on the passion and purpose helping others in similar straits brings to their lives.

Virgil was a very successful marketing executive in the textile industry. Working ten to twelve hours a day, he spent the balance of his time with his wife, though he was known to donate an hour or two here and there to community-based activities like Junior Achievement. But in 1995, prostate cancer screening tests indicated that he might have the disease. His doctor recommended a biopsy and an ultra-sound, a very depersonalizing experience that left him feeling highly vulnerable.

"That's what kind of helped push me in my path to becoming an advocate. That we had to take the power to be able to ensure that our needs, our emotions, our expectations are all being considered as part of this whole thing and that we aren't just there to let the doctor do what he wants to do but really to be able to engage in a dialogue and a partnership to achieve what we both want, which is to hopefully cure the cancer and return the quality of life," Virgil recalled.

So he started an organization, Virgil's Prostate On-line (www.prostate-online.com), aimed at educating and supporting prostate cancer patients and their families. He gave up his job selling polyester and now deals in hope for those who visit his site in their time of need. Applying a business-model concept to his charity, he now raises over two hundred thousand dollars a year to support the programs his organization provides.

Sean took essentially the same path after she was diagnosed with ovarian cancer. A well-respected consultant, she had spent her pre-illness time flying around the world, providing her specialized knowledge in strategic planning to a variety of different corporate executives in privately held companies. She typically spent twenty-six weeks a year on the road, at least ten hours at work, and two to three hours a day mountain biking or rock climbing. Volunteering, on average, was relegated to maybe five to ten minutes a day, with sporadic things like offering to translate when the World Cup was in her town.

And Sean's life remained in the same pattern for a while after she was diagnosed. But when one setback nearly ended her days, her focus shifted from helping corporations become more successful to helping fellow ovarian cancer patients fight back. One night while in the hospital, Sean was almost given the wrong blood by mistake in a transfusion, the result of which could have been deadly. That event spurred her into action, first with a phone call to her doctor.

"I said, 'Look, you guys need to let me out of here because you guys are going to kill me. You're not going to mean it, but you're going to kill me,'" Sean recalled. "There were other women on the floor who were a lot older or a lot less proactive than I was. I thought, 'This is really ridiculous. You know, women are dismissed by the system. Women are not empowered in the health care system. Ovarian cancer gets so much less funding than prostate cancer. This sucks.'"

So she chucked her prestigious career in favor of starting an ovarian cancer organization, the Hera Women's Cancer Foundation, which aggressively supports research in the field. The foundation, which raises all of its money through rock-climbing events, has funded seven scientists, two of whom have since published their work in major journals.

"[It was] named after the Greek goddess who gave a voice to women in her earliest incarnation," Sean said. "She was the protector of women, so our goal is to stop the loss of mothers, daughters, wives, sisters, and girlfriends from ovarian cancer. We do that by empowering women to take control of their health and empowering research scientists to find new directions in ovarian cancer. We look for outside-the-box solutions."

"We work at the grassroots level, and it has been really rewarding and really exciting to watch it grow," she added.

REAL STORY—GINA

At twenty-two, Gina led a fairly typical life of a young adult.

Gina

While the vast majority of her daytime hours were spent at her job as a graphic artist or pursuing her art hobby, Gina's real focus in life was family and friends, with whom she spent the remainder of her waking moments. In talking about her life before and after illness, she peppers it with references to her parents, with whom she lives, as well as with her grandmother, aunts, uncles, and cousins. She tells of the early-morning hours dancing in clubs with girlfriends or hanging out with her boyfriend during more sedate evenings. She speaks of dreams of someday having a family of her own.

But right at the beginning of her adult life, trouble came to Gina. It started with an unquenchable thirst and a related increase in urination, the need so urgent that it frequently woke her from a sound sleep several times a night. Gina also began to drop pounds from her 5-foot, 5-inch frame, starting at her normal weight of 150 and ending at a near-skeletal 115. And she felt tired and worn down, so much so that she scheduled a doctor's appointment after the exhaustion left her unable to enjoy her cousin's wedding.

"I remember that week like yesterday," Gina said. "My body felt drained. I'd lost a lot of weight. I thought I had cancer or something. I felt lousy."

The doctor ran some tests, including a screening of her urine and blood. The results pointed to diabetes as well as a potentially life-threatening complication, ketoacidosis. Sometimes putting the patient in a coma, this condition occurs in diabetics when the body burns fat as fuel because inadequate amounts of insulin are being produced and carbohydrates can't be converted to energy. Gina immediately was admitted to the hospital, where doctors worked to stabilize her condition and nurses taught her to administer her own shots of insulin.

Shock and fear were the prevailing feelings Gina experienced in that first month following her diagnosis. Not knowing much about the disease, she relied on others in her life to guide her, taking advice on what to eat and what to avoid, on when and how to take her insulin shot. Afraid to administer the insulin in any setting other than home, Gina stayed out of the bars and dance clubs, thus isolating herself from her friends. When a friend left a box of chocolates on her desk, Gina sobbed over the fact that she thought she could no longer enjoy such a treat and the feeling of injustice over the whole situation. In that moment, she also realized she had to learn more on her own to truly take control of the situation and meet others who knew what she was going through.

"I looked all over the place online for support. For me, I didn't want to go to therapy at that time when everybody told me to. It made me more crazy," Gina said. "So, being online, I didn't have to look at anyone. I could just write whatever I want, make up a fake name if I want, but in a weird way, be totally honest about what I felt."

With the exception of an aunt who also had diabetes, she personally knew no one who shared the disease, much less her concerns and fears about it. Using her computer skills, Gina turned to the Internet and learned as much as she could from others in forums and chat rooms, as well as by reading the latest research. At the same time, she began volunteering for the Diabetes Research Institute, an organization that sponsors cure-focused research. There she joined the young-adult division, Immediate Priority A Cure Today (IMPACT), using her artistic and organizational skills to help plan the group's annual fall fund-raiser.

But Gina seemed to find more camaraderie on the Internet. There she formed fast friendships with people affected by diabetes. She shared her hopes and fears with these individuals, and they responded in turn. Gina shared her design work with some of the Web board posters, and one commented that she should use her creativity to make her own Web site.

The idea quickly took on a life of its own. Gina shared this idea with another fellow poster, Jon, the father of a boy with diabetes. Though they have yet to meet in person even today, the pair agreed to a partnership and began to design a site, an online community for those with diabetes.

"I created the site so that other people with diabetes would have a place to share information and their experiences and to just have somewhere to go where other people would just understand. A place where you can be totally anonymous and not be judged by anyone because we are all going through the same thing, a place you wouldn't have to be afraid to say anything," Gina told me, adding that she used those sentiments to guide her in creating the content. "We would chat online for hours to figure out what we wanted on the site. I designed and redesigned about four times in one month to the point it is at right now. We wanted the site to have a community feel so, the scheduled chats and message board became our niche."

Gina's whole life changed as a result of the board. She began coming home from work, eating dinner, and then holing up in her room sometimes until 2 a.m., fine-tuning the page design, links, and general content of the site. For someone who had never given an hour to volunteer activities in the past, this was a big change and really just the beginning.

Diabetestalkfest.com has grown as a result of the partners and their dedication to helping others. The site currently offers a slew of message boards, a store with items that support other diabetes charities, a clip service of the latest news related to diabetes, reviews of products related to diabetes, a blog that highlights other diabetes sites and other diabetes-related blogs, a regular chat schedule that features experts in the field of diabetes research and treatment, and a list of educational resources. The site currently has 359 registered users who participate in the forums and chats and receives five hundred thousand hits a month on average.

"We get people with type 1, type 2, borderline, parents of children, spouses, girl/boy friends, family members, sometimes people just looking to find out about diabetes-related issues," Gina said.

Though she is not paid for this work monetarily, she is more than compensated by the response to the site from people who rely on it for information and support. "So many people have e-mailed me or my partner to thank us for the site and how they really feel as though they are a part of a camaraderie with others who share the same interest in cure research, raising children with diabetes, parents learning what adults with diabetes go through," Gina said, adding that the people who visit her site are also grateful for "their ability to chat live with researchers and other specialists in the field, and just being able to be a part of something."

Gina hopes that one day she can make running her Web site a full-time job and expand it to include an offline community with support groups and learning events that feature nationally known diabetes educators. But what now propels her to that new goal are the personal benefits she continues to derive from her altruistic act.

"Every day I learn something new from the people from my Web site," Gina said. "I love the feeling of having an online family, and community. The feeling of knowing I have affected at least one person makes it all worth it."

8

GIFT 4: EMOTIONS: LIVING LIFE IN BALANCE

THE EXPERIENCE OF life-threatening illness is by nature a highly charged time, emotionally speaking. As we discussed in chapter 3, the course of mourning the past life and considering the possibility of a shortened future sparks an emotional process that differs from patient to patient, from day to day, from hour to hour. Negative feelings like fear, anxiety, depression, anger, disbelief, and disappointment are ever-present, seemingly from the time something serious is suspected, and are recalled in flashes sometimes years after remission or a cure has been declared.

But while these negative emotions are so apparent and expected during this time, there are positive transformative effects from life-threatening illnesses in the emotional lives of those who experience them. Many of those who were interviewed for this book said that though they experienced negative emotions during the diagnostic and treatment phases, they also gained a perspective on and an appreciation for life that altered the way that they experienced emotions ranging from sadness to joy, from fear to humor.

The evidence gathered and published by social scientists regarding the emotional impact of life-threatening illness on an individual is vast. Researchers have explored nearly every emotional stop on the journey of illness, from the moment when symptoms first appeared to the long-term survival experience and just about everything in between.

Again, the majority of this research has focused on the experience of cancer, but some agree that these feelings can relate to any potentially life-threatening illness. For example, researchers from Ohio and Iowa in one 1989 study on gynecologic cancer survivors found that specific points along an illness journey such as during the initial treatment or while facing a recurrence was more important than the type of illness suffered. In their conclusion, the researchers stated, "We have questioned, for example, whether the emotional crisis is unique to cancer or is characteristic of any traumatic diagnosis. When ill adults (e.g., those with rheumatoid arthritis, diabetes, cancer or renal disease) at varying stages of disability have been studied long after diagnosis, few differences have been found."

FEAR

Fear is probably the most dominant feeling when one is dealing with serious illness. Fear of pain, of nausea, of needles, of bad test results, of medical procedures, of treatment side effects, and of dying are just a few of the frights suffered during the diagnosis and treatment phases.

And fear does not necessarily disappear when the last needle is withdrawn or, the last bandage removed. For example, the experience of cancer left emotional "scars" on patients, said researchers from Arizona and New Jersey in a 1989 paper on surviving adult cancers. Cancer and its emotional effects are rather permanently present to some degree, as the experience of it is "characterized by easy recall of the initial feelings and emotions associated with illness and the recovery period, a continuing concern about one's mortality, along with an enduring sense of vulnerability," they wrote.

But that doesn't mean that the fears and anxieties remain as steadfast as they first were during diagnosis or treatment. These social scientists also found that the initial intensity of death anxiety in survivors peaked within two years after treatment concluded and tapered significantly in those who experienced longer survival times, showing a lessening of these feelings when survival became more of a sure thing.

Among the responses from the interviewees, fear of death and the related anticipatory anxiety occurred in those with acute-onset illness, as well as in those whose chronic illnesses suddenly became life-threatening. And that's not exactly surprising. The idea that life could end in the near future causes tremendous quaking even in the bravest of souls.

But an interesting thing happened to these individuals as time went on. In most, their fear of death changed. For some, this meant a crystallizing of exactly what was scary to them about death, such as not being in control of the process of dying or experiencing uncontrollable pain as death neared. During this process, the individuals' fear of death lessened.

Dave had that happen to him. As his Parkinson's disease worsened, he opted to leave his teaching job at the same time that he experienced an increase in symptoms, slowly robbing him of his physical abilities. This slow approach to death made him realize that he is not afraid of death itself.

"I don't really fear death. I fear, you know, going up to it, the process of being bedridden or whatnot. So, I don't think my sense of fear has been really worse," Dave said.

For others, the proximity to death makes it more real and thus removes the mystique and fear of the unknown that surrounded it before they were sick. The onset of Andrew's leukemia led him to confront the idea of his own mortality for the first time in his life. "Prior to it at age forty-five, I saw death from a distance," he said. "And immediately upon diagnosis, I thought it was not."

But instead of becoming afraid of death, he became comfortable with the notion, taking stock in all he did in his relatively short life up to that point. He counted his two children, his long marriage, his friendships, and his career in the media business as tremendous successes. "I remember clearly at the time of diagnosis that, okay, if this is going to lead to my demise and sooner rather than later, how do I feel about it? Almost instantly, I said, 'You know, I feel okay. I've lived fully. I haven't lived as long as I want to, but I've lived,'" he said.

Some individuals also acquired new fears, usually related to their own mortality or to issues caused by their illnesses. Miles offers a good example of this. Prior to his diagnosis, he truly wasn't afraid of death. In fact, dealing with the dead was his job. As a mortician, he prepared bodies for funerals, putting in ten- to twelve-hour days embalming the dead and readying the corpses for viewing by family and friends.

After he was diagnosed with hepatitis C in 1987, Miles told me that he continued to work in this capacity without much thought, as not much was known about the disease then. But after an acute experience of his disease and a resulting treatment regimen that failed to clear the virus from his system, Miles became more fearful of death, specifically, his own demise.

"After having worked in the funeral business for so long, you get a little bit desensitized," he said, adding that new fears began to arise. "I had fears about different things than I used to.

"I was afraid of getting sick all the time. I became a hypochondriac. I mean, you know, I get a new spot on myself somewhere and I'd go to the doctor," Miles said.

While fear of recurrence or relapse continued to haunt most of those interviewed, somewhat healthier fears arose as well, largely because individuals realized their own mortality through the illness experience and thus became more protective of their own welfare. These people were less likely to take risks with their health or safety than they were before illness came into their lives.

Amy can understand this concept. She and her husband hatched a plan early in their relationship to someday go skydiving. But before that could happen, she was diagnosed with lymphoma and was ushered immediately into treatment.

"In some ways, things scare me more. Like my husband and I—he's very adventurous—we wanted to go skydiving. And I said, 'If we don't get around to doing it before we both turn thirty, then we'll go do it to, you know, celebrate thirty.' Well, unfortunately, when I was turning thirty, I was in chemotherapy. So we didn't do it," she said, adding that the experience of a life-threatening illness installed a governor on her life in that death seems far more real to her. "And now it kind of scares me. I could *die* doing that."

But far from becoming more fearful, the vast majority of those interviewed found that they became braver, particularly about facing down the fears that they had in their lives prior to illness. Once a person faces death, childhood fears, such as thunder, snakes, spiders, heights, and flying, lose their choke hold on the individual.

Just the sight of a snake made Kate recoil in terror her whole life. But then she soldiered through not only two bouts of colon cancer but also primary cancers in her ovaries and a breast, requiring she endure several surgeries, rounds of chemotherapy, and weeks of radiation. While on a trip to an island, she took a hike through a remote region, only to literally encounter her greatest fear on the path ahead. "All of the sudden up ahead, there were snakes on the path and instead of—I mean I would not have *looked* at a picture of a snake before. I still don't like them, but there they were. I can still see that picture in my mind, of little green grass snakes crossing a path and not being terrified. There isn't much that scares me much, that really terrifies me now," Kate said.

Prior to her diagnosis at twenty-three of colon cancer, Molly carried with her a childhood fear of spiders but had also developed a newer fear of speaking in public. Even talking in her college classes triggered feelings of fear. Then she was diagnosed with colon cancer after enduring months of pain and misdiagnoses. She quickly began her treatment, undergoing surgery to remove a large mass and pushing through months of chemotherapy to rid herself of the disease.

Molly began advocating for people like herself, younger-than-usual colon cancer patients. An avid hockey player and coach, she traveled the country recently, playing hockey with semiprofessional teams to raise awareness of the disease and speaking before large audiences in the process. Though she still doesn't care for spiders, she doesn't feel scared standing up to speak to hundreds of people at once. "I used to be afraid of what other people were going to think, and now I don't really care. I'm not as concerned about what other people think. And I really used to have a phobia. Now I go out and I speak in front of eight hundred people at a time," Molly said during our interview. "The first thing that comes to mind is that you're much more willing to try new things when you've been through something like this. So even if I had some fear, I've kind of put them aside so that I can try new things."

Their newly developed skills of staring fear down led to greater ability to withstand higher levels of the emotion, allowing these survivors to enjoy things they never would have tried in the past and living their lives more fully in the process. Tales of taking hot-air balloons when a former fear of heights existed or scheduling far-flung trips when flying in an airplane used to make a person quake with terror were common in individuals who were interviewed for the book.

Ellen found that this development in her was attributable to living through some of her worst episodes with MS. After temporarily losing her vision, then losing feeling on one side of her body and the use of her legs, she finds that it takes a lot more to shake her now than it did in her life before illness.

"I think that the experience of living with a chronic illness and having things like this happen to you that are truly out of your control, losing your legs or your eyesight or whatever, your threshold for fear becomes a lot higher. I am not afraid of things like I used to be. When you have those experiences, things like, oh my gosh, you are being told to leave your job, it doesn't have that same grip on me that it would have had in the past," Ellen said, adding that it surprised her when that exact scenario happened to her and she wasn't at all frightened

SADNESS

If we had no winter, the spring would not be so pleasant: if we did not sometimes taste of adversity, prosperity would not be so welcome.

—Anne Bradstreet

Sadness is another negative emotion that is ever-present in illness. Mostly, this is due to the great losses that a person experiences. A person who is diagnosed with an acute life-threatening illness or who experiences a life-threatening turn of events in their chronic illness is certainly entitled to feel sad that the healthy body they once enjoyed has turned on them.

And as time went on, some developed more sad moments that they didn't necessarily experience before their diagnosis, including unwelcome reminders of traumatic things they went through physically. Driving by the hospital in which treatment was rendered, trying to hide a scar so others won't notice the physical mark illness left behind, having a sensory experience like a taste or smell that recalls the illness experience can all provoke sad feelings about what happened.

For her first twenty-two years, Molly's birthday was always a reason to celebrate, naturally. Usually, the festivities surrounding it went on in big and small ways for days, leaving her to call it her "birthday month." Even when she was still in the hospital recovering from surgery on her twenty-third birthday, she was getting ready to party with family and friends who were expected to arrive. But then the doctor walked in and told her that the mass they removed in her colon was cancerous. And this usual day of celebration became an annual reminder of the day cancer entered her life, as well as all she went through to eliminate it from her body.

"My five-year anniversary was the worst. I think it had something to do with what my doctor said to me, you know, one year out with no recurrence is good, three years is better, five years is great," Molly recalled. "And so when that five-year anniversary approached, I was depressed for three months beforehand. In the beginning, I wanted to celebrate it. I wanted to have a huge party with two hundred people, and the closer to it I got, the more I was like, 'Wait a minute. This is my day to celebrate and I'm going to do it in my own way.' The closer I got, the more I didn't even want other people to acknowledge it.

"Now, I get depressed, sad every year when it comes around. When it comes around to that anniversary, I just get sad," she said.

However, some sad moments are far more welcome. For example, most interviewees who went through a serious illness then developed empathy for others who were also sick, even if they did not share the same illness. While it would seem a burden to others to have this increase in sensitivity, those who were interviewed were grateful for this deeper connection to others, as well as an accompanying greater appreciation of the human condition.

Kate now works with individuals who have colon cancer. Some get better and join her in long-term survival, while others are not as fortunate. She noticed recently that she not only feels for these cancer patients still in treatment but also anyone who is sick, most especially children.

"I have become sad in a little better way," Kate said. "Yesterday in church, we had this little girl that the church has been helping. She was there in her wheelchair and I started to cry. That was just real empathy for this little kid. I mean, I'm an adult. I can cope with what I've been through. But she was a little kid. So, there was sadness for her."

Many had the opposite happen, experiencing less sadness in their lives. With a newfound appreciation for life and perspective on its hardships, many of those interviewed said that their experience of sadness decreased in their lives after their illnesses passed an acute juncture.

Jim can speak to this. After his Parkinson's disease left him unable to work and continued to progress with its devastating effects on his body, he found less to be sad about in his life.

"Honestly, my sense of sadness has decreased a lot since then, since my diagnosis. I think because I've again developed this new appreciation of life and what to be afraid of and what to be happy of," Jim explained to me. "So, in my case, I find myself much less saddened over events than I might have been three or five years ago."

James, who has experienced a few severe flare-ups of Crohn's disease, takes the lessened sadness in his life a step further, saying that the disease also gave him an emotional equilibrium that wasn't there before. Sad events do not bring him as low or shake him as much as they did in his life before diagnosis, allowing him to recover from them more quickly.

He related a story about how his family reacted to his mother while she was dying. James spoke to her often about what she was going through and was able to relate to her wish to die, while his brothers and sisters could not, as they had never been that sick and thus were more confused, afraid, and sad.

"Because of this thing with my mom, I realize that I am much more able to deal with tragedies and generally bad things. My brothers and sisters are much more upset about this now than I am," James said. "It is not that I don't love my mom and everything. I am going to miss her and all of that stuff, but she has been through a lot. She has suffered a lot. In these last couple of years, she has had surgeries and treatments and she has been through a lot of unpleasantness, and I totally can understand the thought that, you know, I just want to get rid of this body. That is fine. I can understand that. She is totally happy. She is the least upset of anyone because she has been through so much."

DISAPPOINTMENT

. . . and taste
The melancholy joy of evils pass'd:
For he who much has suffer'd, much will know . . .
—Homer, *The Odyssey,* Book XV

While fear and sadness are intrinsically linked to illness, disappointment is a more subtle feeling associated with the experience. These new disappointments are different from the disappointments in life before illness and can range from losing the level of health as it was perceived before the onset of symptoms to losing friends during a time of need.

Miles is one who experienced new disappointments. Prior to his hepatitis C exacerbation, he was healthy and productive, working fifty to sixty hours a week. A treatment that at one time looked promising failed to work on lowering his viral load permanently, and Miles was left defeated and fatigued.

"Every time treatment doesn't work or every time I get on the medication that's supposed to improve something that's going wrong with me and I have terrible side effects—I get pretty disappointed pretty easily about things like that. One of my major disappointments has come from chronic pain and that my level of activity is way down, and I can't do the things that I want to do. I can't do a lot of the things that everybody else does," he told me, adding that this includes working. "I used to be the primary breadwinner in the household, and not being that anymore has really very much disappointed me."

Once the critical phase passed and life resumed, the experience of disappointment as well as the focus of it changed in most of the individuals represented in this chapter. For some, there were new, though slight, disappointments. After surviving surgery to remove a section of his colon and going through several rounds of chemotherapy that cured his colon cancer, Jeff began to treasure the fragility of human life. But on the flip side, he became disappointed almost to the point of anger at the pettiness some display, evidence that they did not share his new value.

"There's the petty stuff that gets in the way so often at work or at home. I mean I just want to say, 'Come on.' You know?" Jeff said. "I guess you could say I am a little bit less tolerant of the petty stuff."

Following his experience with leukemia, Andrew realizes that this perspective shift has happened with him as well, but he finds that he is not angry like Jeff but rather feels sorry for people who haven't learned the lessons of what is truly important and of what is not worth the effort.

"I have compassion for them. I see them as just, well, I think they just haven't been enlightened. A diagnosis of a serious illness is extremely enlightening about what life is all about," Andrew said. "I mean, most of the things that people get upset about are not big deals."

This reordering of priorities and perspective shift on the value of certain aspects of life is very common, as will be shown in future chapters. In one 2004 study on young breast cancer survivors, four California researchers found that five years after the experience of cancer diagnosis and treatment, the women found that they became less upset with trivial matters. "A common response to how breast cancer changed their lives was they did 'not sweat the small stuff' and lived more fully each day," the researchers wrote.

Bobby, whose cancer was in his testicles, could totally relate to that sentiment. Minor irritations and annoyances that used to disrupt his day and stoke his ire no longer hold sway in his life, as he has since gained perspective on what is truly important in life and what is not worth his time and energy.

"Little things that used to bug me now are kind of like, 'Oh, that's really not that big of a thing to worry about,'" Bobby said during his interview.

And some of the individuals found that their sense of

disappointment dissipated to nothing following their brush with death. These individuals seemed to be so grateful to be alive that even major annoyances failed to hold sway in their present lives.

Linie, mentioned in the previous chapter, is one of these individuals. Formerly a highly successful real estate agent, she was forced to leave that lifestyle behind when she was diagnosed with primary biliary cirrhosis, a rare autoimmune disease that attacks the biliary system and ruins the liver in the process. She traded her beautiful house, flashy sports car, and designer clothes for a simpler life in the country with her son. She finds that she is simply happy to still be alive, a feeling that carries over into newfound appreciation for all people in her life.

"People don't disappoint me. They used to disappoint me a lot because I felt like they could do more and they weren't doing as much as they could. People don't disappoint me anymore. No, I don't get disappointed that much," Linie said.

ANGER

Another feeling related to disappointment in illness is anger. For example, if an individual is disappointed in his or her limitations, the person can become angry with him- or herself and with the situation that caused it. If a person is disappointed in an individual for his or her shortcomings in friendship, the person may become angry with that individual for not living up to expectations.

As with disappointment, there seemed to be a better perspective on anger among those who appear in this chapter. Though some said that they were never angry people, those who did experience it said that they had a better handle on anger now than they did prior to illness.

Molly offers an excellent example of this. A self-described hockey nut, she played intensely, matching the amount of emotion and physical effort she put into each game. Before her diagnosis of colon cancer, she did not always react well when a referee called her on an infraction of the rules.

"I can remember sitting in the penalty box freaking out, throwing my stick or something like that," Molly said of her actions during games leading up to her diagnosis. "Now, I get into the penalty box and I sit there and laugh, you know. I don't think I've thrown my stick since then. I look back at that and I think, 'God, what was I thinking?'"

Her cancer experience taught her to take a more relaxed approach to life. "It taught me to take things with a grain of salt, for starters. It's easier to be happy. Why be angry? Why be mad at somebody over something trivial when you just never know when the last day is for you or for someone else? And that's important," Molly said.

HUMOR

Not all emotional shifts experienced by those who were interviewed for this book were to negative emotions. In fact, the most common changes came from positive emotions such as a greater capacity for joy, an openness to sentimental feelings, and a growth in humor. Even during the treatment experience, many individuals were able to find moments of humor, some almost gallowslike in quality. Years after treatment ends, the thoughts of these moments still provoke laughter.

THE FIVE GIFTS OF ILLNESS

Sometimes the moments come out of the absurdity of the situation. Medical personnel are used to some of the strange tests and procedures that they order on a daily basis, but patients are often astounded to find out exactly what happens during these tests. Mammograms, for instance, have been the target of many jokes, including one popular "preparation guide" that circulates through e-mail to women of a certain age. Here is a sample that has reached my inbox three times in the past year:

> *Many woman are afraid of their mammogram, but there is no need to worry. By taking a few minutes each day for a week preceding the exam and doing the following practice exercises, you will be totally prepared. And best of all, you can do these simple practice exercises right in the privacy of your own home.*

> ***Exercise No. 1:***
> *Freeze two metal bookends overnight. Strip to the waist. Invite a stranger into the room. Place one bookend on each side of your breast. Press the bookends together as hard as you can. Set an appointment with the stranger to meet again next year and do it again. Repeat all steps on the other breast.*

> ***Exercise No. 2:***
> *Open your refrigerator door and insert one breast between the door and the main box. Have one of your strongest friends (or a stranger) slam the door shut as hard as possible and lean on the door for good measure. Hold that position for five seconds. Don't*

breathe. Repeat in case the first time wasn't effective enough. Repeat all steps on the other breast.

Exercise No. 3:
Visit your garage at 3 a.m. when the temperature of the concrete floor is just perfect (anywhere below 32 degrees). Take off all your warm clothes and lie comfortably on the floor with one breast wedged tightly under the rear tire of the car. Ask a friend to slowly back the car up until the breast is sufficiently flattened and chilled. Turn over and repeat for the other breast.

CONGRATULATIONS! Now you are properly prepared for your mammogram.

Stewart gained his appreciation of the absurd while he was in the hospital being prepared for a stem cell transplant. If the thought that the doctors were going to bring him within an inch of death and then bring him back using his sister's stem cells were not insane enough, a nurse one night told him she had to insert a Foley catheter into his bladder. "It was absurd. 'You are going to do what with what?'" he said, recalling the conversation with Charise, his nurse. "She is this really pretty young black girl with a big hair weave that some black women wear. And I said, 'Really? You're going to do that? And it's going to work?' So, you know, when the water met the beach, I reached for anything I could. And I grabbed her hair piece and pulled it right off.

"God, it is just absurd. It's wild. What can you do but laugh? What, are you going to cry? It doesn't go away,"

Stewart said, laughing at the memory a full five years after the incident occurred.

Being able to appreciate the absurdity in illness is just one aspect of developing a darker sense of humor about illness, as many of the respondents discovered. Violet found this to be true not long after she was diagnosed with type 1 diabetes, a disease in which she had never found humor before her diagnosis or during the first year with it. But during a support group meeting for fellow type 1 diabetics, she discovered that her humor about the situation had turned a few shades darker.

"I remember a person in my support group, she was a teenager and she had had diabetes since she was eight. She came to the support group with her mom and dad. When I first met them, they told me they had just been taking down their Christmas tree so they had to get an awful lot of pump tubing because they used it like tinsel on their tree," Violet said. "You know, that's pretty dark—the tree is decorated with medical equipment. It was hysterical."

Often, being able to see the humor in a life-threatening illness seems to be shared only by those who have had serious illness, as those who have not been as sick lack the insight and appreciation for the funny or absurd things that are related to illness. Sean found this to be true. After surviving numerous surgeries for a rare form of ovarian cancer, she found herself in the middle of a group at a party, sharing what she thought was a humorous story from her treatment experience. "The couple of people who had been through catastrophic illnesses laughed hysterically, and the healthy people were mortified, like, 'Oh, my God,'" Sean said.

In turn, some individuals not only saw the humor in the situation illness pressed upon them but also found more humor in life in general. Some found that their ability to laugh at their predicament translated into an increased ability to laugh at themselves. Linie found this to be true in her case. Always a little hard charging in her life before illness and hard on herself as a result, Linie found that her experience of PBC softened her up.

"I think my sense of humor got a little better because, I mean, I can laugh at things. And even when I get angry at myself, the next thing, I'll be laughing at myself, going, 'Well, why did you do that? I'm such a dummy,'" she said.

Dr. Elizabeth Lindsey verified this increased capacity for humor, further saying it was a part of developing a healthy attitude toward life with illness. In her 1996 paper on finding health within chronic illness, the Canadian researcher said her subjects found the use of humor an integral part of the process of celebrating life. "Humour played an important role in the participant's experience of feeling healthy. One person described, 'a good sense of humour, I think that is God in action' and another commented, 'I think the ability to laugh, that's what pulled me through.' For each of the participants, celebrating life, a passion for living, a joy and a sense of humour were essential elements of their experiences of feeling healthy," she wrote.

In his book *Man's Search for Meaning*, Viktor Frankl also wrote about humor and its use as a personal buoy during dark times. While enduring the oppression of concentration camps, he found that moments of humor added a feeling of sweetness and light to the otherwise heavy situation, making that excruciatingly difficult period easier to bear if only for the moment. "It is well known that humor, more than anything else in the human make-up, can afford an aloofness and an ability to rise above any situation, even if only for a few seconds," he wrote.

JOY

Frankl also wrote that even in concentration camps, where fear and death were the order of the day, there were moments of joy and happiness, moments to live for and in which to find sustenance during darker times. He recalled specifically the joy the prisoners felt while traveling in a cattle car one day. When they entered the car, the prisoners didn't know whether they would be sent to the work camp Dachau or the death camp Mauthausen, where their chances for survival diminished to nearly none. As the train lumbered past the turnoff for Mauthausen, the nearly skeletal fellow travelers whooped with joy.

Similarly, interviewees for this book found that joy seeped into their existence, starting during their bleakest periods of treatment. Celebration over positive test and treatment results even when they physically felt like death was near, happiness in the hospital during time spent with those who came to support them, delight over small moments like watching from the window in their hospital room as the sun broke through after a particularly cloudy day were all joyful times reported by those interviewed, often powerful enough to offset the sadness and fear that they felt because of the illness and treatment.

The effect of finding joy during a sad situation spilled over into their lives after treatment ended, though sometimes it took time for the feeling to return. Similarly, Frankl believed that some positive emotions had to be relearned upon liberation. He recalled that at the end of the war, people didn't find immediate joy with the liberators but rather relief that the physical torture was over. Joy came back to Frankl as he was walking through nature after his release. Strolling through the country past miles and miles of meadows, he noticed the beauty of the open space, punctuated by the beautiful song of larks in trees. He stopped, looked around, and fell to his knees, his eyes on the heavens. Frankl said one sentence over and over again, "I called to the Lord from my narrow prison and He answered me in the freedom of space."

When joy did return to their lives, the interviewees told me that they found it had an almost childlike quality to it. Gone were the jaded connotations to everyday life. In their place was an appreciation for tiny, happy moments and little accomplishments. Joy in these small moments became pervasive in daily existence.

Kate still feels those moments, years after the treatments for her colon, breast, and ovarian cancer ended. Toward the end of her final rounds of chemotherapy, she and her husband moved to a house on a lake, where she takes regular moments to enjoy the beauty and serenity of her surroundings. She mentions her dogs; she plays with the younger one, while the older one lies loyally at her feet. "Right now, I am a very joyful person," Kate said. "I find joy everyplace. And that has probably increased."

James understands this sentiment because he is often surprised by his feelings of joy with the formerly mundane. Before a lengthy hospitalization with a severe Crohn's disease flare-up, he would plough through his work as a professor of literature and trudge through daily chores without so much as a thought. But now he does so with profound happiness, even in the midst of a family crisis involving his mother's decline and eventual death.

"The kids left at eight o'clock. So I sat down, I exercised, I had something to eat, and then I started writing. I had a great morning. I wrote something like eight pages that morning. And the whole time, I was doing laundry and chores and stuff in between, and the whole time, I was thinking, 'Boy, this is great.' I was just really happy," James said of his previous day. "I thought, 'I can't help it. I just feel really happy. I am happy that I am helping out with the household, that I am helping, that I am writing. I am happy that I was able to exercise and I felt great. I was just really happy. It was totally random—a Wednesday morning. I mean, I am expectedly happy at the end of the semester. But this was a random Wednesday morning and it wasn't at the end of the semester and I was in a really good, good mood."

Small victories were also treasured, especially in light of a return to normal function. Like James with his joy from doing housework, Ellen found happiness in learning to ski, something she had always wanted to do but became afraid of in light of balance issues caused by her MS. While on a vacation with her family in Park City, Utah, Ellen decided to take the plunge and hired a ski instructor to give her lessons. Though she cautioned him to stick to the easiest slopes, he took her on hills that were two levels more difficult at the end of the day. "We got to the bottom and he said, 'Turn around. Not bad for a girl with MS.' So I remember that. When I think that I can't do something, I tell myself that it is something I can do," Ellen said. "I definitely feel prouder of smaller accomplishments."

Finally, some found renewed joy in things that had

become a drag before the onset of illness. With the threat of death more in the past, these individuals find that even the things that they loathed doing or things to which they became jaded now possess a newer, happier sheen.

Bobby was a doctoral student in psychology when he received his diagnosis of testicular cancer. He was focused entirely on his goal to graduate, taking virtually no breaks between his bachelor's and master's degrees, his master's degree and the doctoral program. In the process, he lost his passion for his studies, becoming almost an automaton in achieving his goals.

With the break in studies that cancer surgery and chemotherapy necessitated, he realized that he missed the work he was doing and, in the process, rediscovered his joy in psychology. "I was getting kind of burnt out and felt like I was ready to be done with school. And I get joy out of those things again because I had them taken away for a while. I have renewed joy. I also get joy out of the small things that I didn't used to, like seeing my family or friends. I used to take those things for granted," Bobby said.

SENTIMENTALITY

Often this new ability to feel more deeply, coupled with a greater respect for the brevity of time, leads to sentimentality, something the interviewees seemed not to disdain as many do but rather to cherish. Kodak commercials celebrating life's special moments, ESPN stories of overcoming tragedy and achieving triumph in sports, and just about any story line in a chick flick can cause even the most hardened of these survivors to reach for the tissues.

In part, this seems to be due to the greater awareness of the fragility of life and the new emphasis on living it as fully emotionally as possible. Sean, a tough, globe-trotting business consultant who prided herself on being highly competitive in all aspects of life, became softer after enduring several years of surgical treatments for her rare ovarian cancer, the treatment for which nearly killed her on a couple of occasions. She is amazed at her growing capacity to feel emotions as she processes some of the experiences she has gone through to survive, often becoming powerfully affected by sentimental moments in movies.

"I can find myself, you know, little things like a movie, I will just boo hoo. It's like something really sappy and corny that triggers some buried emotion," Sean said, laughing. "I'm a really cerebral person. I've spent a good deal of my life in my head, not so much in the physical emotions. And so I think what I'm finding is that I'm much more in touch with my feelings versus my thoughts. And that has been really good."

Jeff, a big bear of a guy, admits to shedding tears in the darkness of movie theaters far, far more often than he did before his colon cancer diagnosis and treatment. He feels this development is a realization of his good fortune in having survived when others have not. "Oh, geez! I got to be such a baby. It's ridiculous," Jeff said. "Sadness, I don't necessarily cry about. I cry when I see people achieving things that nobody else ever thought that they could. I get sappy about relationships. I get sentimental when I see my girls doing things. I have an awareness, that number one, I better savor these moments because you never know how many you're going to get."

Interestingly, nearly all of the individuals interviewed for the book told me that they had more satisfying emotional lives as a result of living through the diagnosis and treatment of a life-threatening illness. Far from being colored by the powerfully negative emotions in the grieving process, they felt their emotional lives were more balanced and that they lived more freely with expressing and experiencing emotions as a result of surviving.

REAL STORY—SCOTT

The time was 1987, the place, New York City. Scott, a twenty-four-year-old gay man, was a living a life he hadn't exactly counted on.

Scott

Though he had received a bachelor's degree in theater focusing on stage performance, he was working as an assistant stage manager, building scenery and making sure things ran smoothly when the actors were working. "For about fifty bucks a week, literally fifty dollars a week, I was hanging lights and painting the walls of the theater and mopping the stage, dreaming of being on the stage when I had enough talent to be on stage," he said. "So I somehow became submissive."

Emotionally, his life was reflected in this position. Having just broken up with someone he loved, he became fearful of feeling more pain and was willing to accept less in terms of a relationship, having unsafe sex in a transient, unfulfilling relationship. In part to avoid feeling, he also buried himself in work, putting in up to fifteen hours in a day, five to six days a week.

Then this unprotected sexual encounter brought into his life the human immunodeficiency virus (HIV); at that time in history, HIV was seen as a certain precursor to the always fatal autoimmune deficiency syndrome (AIDS). Scott spent more than the next decade mourning the life he used to lead, incorporating the disease into his life, and watching dozens of friends die agonizing deaths from the same thing that coursed through his blood.

And then a funny thing happened. Scott began to see that he was going to live with HIV, not die of it so quickly. He also began to see that in learning to cope with a deadly disease, he had changed emotionally.

Perhaps his biggest shift emotionally was with sadness. Scott found that he no longer ran from it or used diversionary tactics like drugs or alcohol to avoid feeling it. In the week before his interview with me, a friend died of AIDS, and the lessons learned from his new take on sadness resurfaced.

"I remember saying at the time, 'It sucks to be this strong because I know how to get through this and I hate that.' I know that recreational drugs won't work and unsafe sex won't work and alcohol won't work. And I know I have to just deal with this and that sucks so much because I have to face this," Scott said. "In saying that I know how to do this, it doesn't make the sadness any less real. It doesn't take any sadness away. It just shows me that I'm going to have to feel and I've been here before."

Instead, he has learned to turn for support to tried-and-true means like support groups, private therapy, and friends, all individuals who help him deal emotionally with his reality in terms of his disease. In place of avoiding the grief as he would have in the past, Scott now embraces the sad feelings, saying that he plans to make the upcoming weeks a "season of grief" to give him time to process the loss. "I am able to access my feelings much more quickly so that I could get the help I need to feel that pain rather than in the old days when I was isolated and in denial," Scott said, adding that sadness had been somewhat crippling to him in the past. "Now I know that it won't last forever."

After his adjustment to his diagnosis, Scott became more acquainted with fear in his life, allowing the new familiarity to lessen the grip the emotion once had on his life. "I don't think I knew what fear was before my diagnosis. I understood what fear looked like, but I hadn't had the chance to actually get inside of fear," he explained. "If fear is a room, I knew where the room was, but I don't think I actually hung out long enough to become familiar with it. [After the adjustment,] I got a chance to weigh it and hang out with it so that when I still feel fear, it's not unfamiliar to me."

This is especially true with regard to his former fears about death. It was the death of his father two years earlier that helped ease his fears regarding death. After watching dozens of friends succumb slowly and agonizingly to AIDS, he witnessed his father's rapid decline from cancer and the grace with which he handled it in a new light. This experience allowed Scott to believe that when his time to die came, he, too, would be able to face it with the same dignity. "When I was little, my father taught me how to ride a bike, and so I learned how to ride a bike. And so on. And then, when my father died, I watched him. And so he taught me how to die," Scott said. "It's not the same with my friends. It's not the same case. That was kind of frightening to watch. With my dad, it wasn't frightening at all. It was absolutely gorgeous."

Just as his awareness of fear has increased, Scott is exponentially more cognizant of all of the moments of joy in his life. "When I feel joy, I'm aware of the fact that I'm feeling joy. There's such an awareness of, wow, there's room for joy again. Then that adds more joy to it because I am conscious of my joy," Scott said. "Sometimes when I am in synagogue and people are dancing and singing, I am aware and I am happy. I am also aware of the fact that somebody in this room might have lost a parent last week, or a best friend was buried yesterday, and I'm aware of that possibility happening. That awareness helps me cherish a little bit more of the joy that I'm feeling."

Scott has also become better at dealing with disappointment and anger. Take disappointment, for example. When he was first diagnosed, a usual letdown like finding a dent in his car would not phase him, especially in comparison to all of the loss that was happening in his life. As he has adjusted to the life of the survivor, he now allows himself to feel disappointed in such minor annoyances but he works his way quickly past it.

His feelings regarding anger have similarly changed. Scott said that he used to feel bad about getting angry in the first place, adding one layer of negative emotion upon another. Now, he allows the anger to flow in and ebb away, like the tides. "I'm better at getting angry, and I am better at getting past anger," he said.

Because of the challenges that living with HIV has placed in his life, Scott has grown stronger emotionally as an individual. With the help of therapy and support groups, he no longer is subservient, having grown enormously confident. He tours the country now, on stage bravely sharing his story with teenagers in an effort to save lives. Scott is also in a committed relationship, one that is far more emotionally fulfilling and stable than the one that led him to his infection.

9

GIFT 5: GOALS: RESETTING THE FUTURE

~~~~~~~

H UMAN BODIES CHANGE as a result of the illnesses suffered, either directly from the disease or from the
treatment endured. Surgeries leave scars, and radiation may
permanently darken the skin or damage tissue below.
Chemotherapy or antibiotic treatment may forever leave a
tingling sensation in the hands and feet, while ongoing
chronic disease activity may continue to rob the body slowly
but persistently of normal function over months and years of
disease activity.

But modifications caused by illness usually go further
than the corporeal being, leaching into an individual's identity. Who a person is can be deeply affected by the experience of a disease. The experience of emotions changes,
providing more balance and perspective. The sense of time
and being changes, giving an appreciation to the passage of
days and to a greater care for the body. Relationships change,
strengthening some, dropping others, and creating new
ones. Altruism changes, growing in importance and lending
meaning to the survival experience.

Because of those alterations, a new map of the future must be charted, sometimes incorporating small modifications and other times resulting in a whole new life course. What used to work in life before a diagnosis of a chronic or acute life-threatening illness was based on being healthy and having the possibility of living for decades without lingering health woes or hampered abilities. With a new life perspective and appreciation of it as well as a potentially shortened forever after, an individual's future may look completely different before a diagnosis than it does after illness barges into life.

FUTURE MEMORY

Future memory is a term that a group of Australian researchers used to describe a part of identity that is changed following the cancer experience. The term sounds absurd on the surface: How can one have memory of something that has yet to occur? Rather, the researchers, in their book *Surviving Survival: Life After Cancer*, say that future memory refers to life plans an individual has constructed for him- or herself before receiving a diagnosis, projecting what memories will be of a life lived far in the future. So, for example, a young person may dream of developing a fulfilling career, getting married, having children, living in the suburbs, and leading a happy and full social life, lending weight to each area as the goals are ranked in order of importance. As months and years pass, plans continue to develop as more of a future is envisioned and can include issues like retirement and travel.

No healthy young person, however, imagines that serious illness is in that future, by saying, for example, "I'll become a lawyer, ascend the ranks to partner, get married, have a few kids, and then, at age forty, I'll develop degenerative cardio-vascular disease." Again, there is a sense of entitlement to good health and to a long life, especially as adulthood begins. Peers, for the most part, seem to achieve those milestones that are common in future memory. Why shouldn't we live as well, as long, and as fully? It is hardly surprising then to realize that not one of the 102 people I interviewed figured illness into their future plans prior to the diagnosis.

RECONSIDERING THE FUTURE

And yet nearly all felt that these future memories had to be reconsidered in big and small ways due to the diagnosis of the illness, its treatment, and/or the lingering threat of relapse or recurrence thereafter. When an acute illness is diagnosed or a chronic illness becomes life-threatening, the future suddenly contracts, as the immediate threat is pos-sibly fatal, leaving the patient with only the present to con-sider. During this sad and scary time, all future memories are shelved for the time being, as the primary goal becomes staying alive until the threat passes. Only when remission or cure is achieved is it possible to reconsider what the future will hold.

One way in which the future is considered is as a general timeline. Because the average life expectancy in the Western world is inching toward eighty, it is not unusual for people to think in terms of living well beyond retirement age. But when illness is present, that time span shrinks. Once an individual has been close to the chasm between life and its end, death no longer seems theoretical or so far in the future. Instead, its reality and proximity remain, in some people more strongly than in others. Quantity of years shifts focus to quality of years, condensing in some the time in which they have to achieve all they can while still aboveground.

The research into the area of resetting goals as a response to surviving illness is considerable, with much of it showing that it is not only necessary but also healthy to do so. That doesn't mean that a patient doesn't mourn the loss of these original goals. Losing a sense of the future can be and often is devastating. But not moving forward and re-creating plans for the altered life ahead leaves patients mired in feelings and thoughts about what the illness took from them. In fact, researchers found that those who made the healthiest transition to life after illness or life with illness mourned their losses and turned with hope to a new and different idea of the future. Here is a sample of some of the studies:

- In a 2001 paper highlighting adjustment to cancer, Dr. James Brennan said that illnesses such as cancer force an individual to reexamine priorities, including future goals. "Implicit long-standing life goals may suddenly be clear and distinct yet, at the same time, their eventual attainment may seem less likely and even unrealistic," he wrote. "Other goals may be dismissed as trivial and no longer important, while a number of people report that their illness helped them develop entirely new motivational priorities."

  Even after these goals are reconsidered, the patient also has to figure in the changes that the illness presented during treatment or continues to present in their lives, he said. "Pre-existing assumptions about life goals must gradually accommodate limitations imposed by the disease (e.g., shortened life expectancy, disability, etc.)."

- Dr. Elizabeth Lindsey wrote in her 1996 study on health within chronic illness that her study subjects who tended to see such a shift in future goals as a chance for growth fared the best in their transition to incorporating their illness into their future lives.

  "A critical element of feeling healthy was the participant's ability to look at their illness and/or disability as a challenge, an opportunity to make changes in their lives, to learn, and to grow. They talked of a spirit of adventure, a sense of courage, and a willingness to take risks," she wrote. A little further on in the text, she quoted a participant as saying, "The minute I stop growing, the minute I stop learning, the minute I stop changing is the minute I die."

- Five Canadian researchers found that ovarian cancer survivors surveyed for a 2001 paper on the experience of survival had better mental health scores than those still in treatment and those in the general population. "Having survived a life-threatening illness, ovarian cancer survivors appear to have put other life difficulties into perspective, altered their priorities and felt enriched by the experience," they wrote. "In general, these women showed impressive and inspiring resilience and reported good physical health and energy, excellent psychological health and feelings of greater pleasure in life and personal relationships."

SETTING NEW SIGHTS IN THE PRESENT

You must live in the present, launch yourself on every wave, find your eternity in each moment. Fools stand on their island of opportunities and look toward another land. There is no other land; there is no other life but this.

—Henry David Thoreau, philosopher and writer

With a new time line being considered, the interviewees examined one of the biggest areas within their own lives where they had previously spent most of their waking hours: work. According to the United States Bureau of Labor Statistics, a full-time employee spent on an average weekday 9.2 hours working, 1.7 hours more than the next largest category, sleeping. The interviewees in this chapter were not that different, daily working a range of seven to 14 hours, averaging 10 hours per day before their diagnoses.

Most were happy in their jobs in their lives before illness. Their positions and titles carried a certain amount of prestige, or the work itself gave them a sense of worth or accomplishment. Sharon is one of those who took pride and found her identity in what she did. Before lung cancer, this co-owner of a furniture store for twenty-three years worked on average eight hours a day, six days a week and barely ever took vacations. Her time away from the store was further colored by the role that work played in her life, as she regularly devoted spare time to charity work with the local Chamber of Commerce. Even the way that she defined success and failure in her previous life was related to business.

"It was more business success," Sharon said. "That always has been pretty much all-consuming."

When illnesses were diagnosed, some people continued to work through treatments, keeping work in the forefront of their priorities. They scheduled the time for therapies or doctor's appointments around their workweek or took short amounts of time off to recuperate from surgery in order to miss as little work as possible. Others had diseases that required long hospital stays and lengthy recoveries, often forcing them to take a leave of absence from their jobs to tend to their health.

However many weeks or months that treatment and recovery required, the people interviewed for this book said that this time was valuable, as they began to see the personal worth of work in their lives during this period. They analyzed their work life, finding that they alternately loved and hated certain aspects of it. Some saw it as a passionate vocation, some found it was a loathsome way to spend their newly valuable hours, and some saw it as a means to an end to allow them to accomplish other important goals in their life.

This specific focus on work was one area of post-illness life examined by a group of California researchers. Studying 185 individuals diagnosed with breast cancer before the age of fifty, the social scientists found that in the five years after diagnosis, the careers of some were affected by the cancer experience. In their study published in 2004, the researchers said the effects were varied.

"The careers of some were affected; either the boss was not sympathetic, they were too tired to work during treatment, or some actually quit their jobs to do something else with their lives," they wrote.

Emily is one who found new purpose in her chosen career. She was a college student, a year from graduating with a degree in education specializing in teaching children to read, when she was diagnosed with non-Hodgkin's lymphoma that was marked by a seventeen-inch tumor in her belly. Due to the size and location of her tumor, she was forced to drop out of her studies for a year and a half while she underwent surgical and chemotherapy treatments. She returned to school, but all of her friends had graduated. Without the support structure that those relationships lent to her education, Emily just wanted to move on.

"It would have taken three or four years to graduate because I lost all of my education credits I would have had to get back into the education program, and so when I went back to college, I changed my major. I wanted to get out in a year, and I could finish off with Japanese," Emily said.

After graduating, Emily realized that she didn't really want to do anything in terms of a career with Japanese because she had no passion for it, she told me during our interview. During that time, a friend who suffered from a vision impairment suggested that Emily might make a good teacher for blind children. Emily gave it a try, first working as a counselor in a summer camp for blind children and then returning the next year as the camp director. She was accepted into a master's program at a southern university, where she is working toward her certification as a teacher of blind students.

"I would never ever have come down here if not for cancer. And I feel like this is exactly what I was meant to do with my life," Emily said. "I'm still going to be teaching reading. I'm just going to be teaching reading and Braille."

During similar post-diagnosis periods, others lost their enthusiasm for their jobs but discovered new passions in the work world. Virgil offers a perfect example of this outcome. Before being diagnosed with prostate cancer, he worked as a marketing executive in a textile company, often spending ten or eleven hours a day toiling to help build the company with his expertise and abilities in selling polyester to the world. During a six-month recuperation period from surgery to cure the condition, Virgil really looked at what he was doing with his life in terms of work and his goals for the future. While he returned to work during that time, he formulated a plan to chuck his career and follow his new passion, founding a prostate cancer charity.

"It got to the point where I realized that I had been spending my professional life building businesses and successes for other organizations, other people, and I think probably the end game on this is that I was tired of dealing with the political bullshit of that organization I was with, and I just said, 'I can't deal with this anymore,'" Virgil said. "I said, 'It's time for me just to go here and be true to myself. And if I'm as good as I think I am, then I can make a business and a career out of what's in my heart.'"

Wendy, too, lost her passion and desire for her pre-illness job but found new interest in her post-illness career path. Prior to her diagnosis, she was a singer and a songwriter, performing in clubs and concert venues. For her work, she had drawn part of her inspiration from her father, who had died of bladder cancer years before. Wendy also devoted her spare time to building a Web site for bladder cancer patients, providing information and support to patients and their families.

But all of that changed when Wendy was diagnosed with metastatic breast cancer, not long after she had buried a sister who had died of the same disease. During her grueling treatment in the years after the cancer was initially diagnosed, she examined her career and found that it had lost its enchantment for her. The cancer, Wendy found, had colored her vision of her life's work.

"For a while, I was so enamored with the cancer patients I was in contact with every day over the Internet that I found that people who did not have cancer were boring. Musicians especially seemed self-absorbed and shallow to me now. Along with the other people on the fringes of the music scene, including club owners, bookers, groupies, and the audiences, they have ceased to be important to me and aren't a part of my reality anymore," Wendy told me.

So she left her profession and began to devote more time to her Web site, her main focus becoming what she formerly viewed as her side job. Wendy is sad about the silence that filled her life after she lost her desire to sing but finds new purpose in helping others who have survived the cancer that killed her father, saying it provides "a sense of achievement, of doing something valuable to the world, and having it recognized by experts is very fulfilling. It's intellectually fulfilling as opposed to emotionally fulfilling, as singing was."

As tempting as it is to quit working the jobs they had before their illnesses, some found that they simply could not, as leaving the job also meant forgoing vital resources like health insurance, an asset that grows in importance and is harder to replace after a diagnosis and treatment for a life-threatening illness. Instead, the careers with which they found value and identity in the past simply became a means to an end, something they tolerated so that they could afford to follow other passions.

Jen was twenty-six when she was diagnosed with ovarian cancer. She was a school social worker, putting in not only a typical eight-hour day but also frequently overtime to finish work assignments, forgoing personal time essentially to please others.

But something changed when she went through surgery and chemotherapy to rid her of the disease. Jen began to see value in following her own bliss. She took dream vacations and pursued activities that she was always interested in doing. While planning her wedding, she shelved her original plans for a simple honeymoon for a more lavish trip to Europe.

"Whereas at first we thought, 'Let's save our money and go somewhere that's low-key, you know, like an island.' And I said, 'No, I want to do it now. What am I waiting for?'" Jen said. "You never know what could happen."

That ethic translated to her work as well. Though she likes what she does and she still puts in the regular eight hours at the same job, Jen is more guarded about taking time away from her personal pursuits. "The one thing that I would say has changed, though, is I'm less likely to work overtime now than I used to. I used to stay if I needed to. Now, I feel, 'No, I'm done. My hours are over. It will wait until tomorrow,'" Jen said. "I don't feel like the need to get everything done. It doesn't seem as important as my own time, you know?"

Sharon, a full three decades older than Jen when she received her cancer diagnosis, said that following surgery to remove part of a lung to cure her disease, she began to see her job as just that: a job. She dropped her volunteer work with the chamber, opting to spend that time making and selling bracelets to support lung cancer research. Most significantly, she cut back on her work hours to spend time with her children and grandchildren.

"I take a lot more time off than I used to. I mean, that eight hours prediagnosis was eight hours, six days a week. Now, it's probably eight hours, five days a week with lots of vacations," she told me. "I guess I feel like some of the things that I did before maybe aren't as important as taking some time off so I can go down to see my son or something like that."

Sharon is also fairly typical in that she considered not only how work affected her current quality of life but also how it affected her future goals. Because work usually is an ongoing concern affecting daily life as well as future plans, it is important to note that the changes made affected not only the immediate life after illness but also anticipated plans, such as retirement or career changes. Though Sharon continues to work to provide a necessary income, she is also actively plotting her retirement, something she considered lightly in the past despite the fact that she was fifty-six when she was diagnosed.

"I thought about retirement sometime in the future, but I was nowhere near thinking of actually taking hold of it," Sharon said. "I guess I am probably closer to it now because I don't feel like I probably have as long as I assumed I had before."

Interestingly, after diagnosis and treatment, those interviewed for this chapter cut back on work an average of 2.6 hours a day, now spending an average of 7.4 hours a day, with the range being zero hours due to disability to ten hours.

REORDERING OTHER AREAS OF LIFE

Of course, work wasn't the only area of life to be reassessed, as many interviewees also reported to me that they had a corresponding change in the way their free time was spent, reflecting a transformation in the way they valued life's other pursuits. Present and future goals shifted regarding how much time they spent with family and friends, how much time was spent on their health and well-being, and how much time was spent helping others, making less important pursuits seem frivolous and time wasting.

And some of the research bears out this notion of present and future goal resetting. Dr. Barbara Carter published a paper in 1993 on the experience of long-term breast cancer survival, interviewing twenty-five California women who had survived the diagnosis of breast cancer for longer than five years without a recurrence. Among six steps she said long-term survivors went through in the years after the cancer experience was a reprioritizing of just about everything in their lives, both in the present and in the future, as was reflected in alterations in their current lifestyle as well as in their life goals.

"Informants interpreted the demands of treatment, convalescence, and recovery in view of sources of meaning reconsidered after the diagnosis. The focusing and reordering of involvements occurred automatically in the practices and attitudes of newly diagnosed women as they faced the demands of the disease and the effects of the disease on their interpreted meanings," Carter wrote, giving examples of a woman who put herself first for the first time in life, another who sorted out the importance of certain relationships over others, and still another who was merely thankful for more time with her daughter. "For some, the changes in priorities lasted for many years."

In the present, changes made to daily life, such as not sweating the small stuff, reassigning meaning to work, or increasing time spent with loved ones, presented almost immediate gratification in interviewees. In a 2003 study on the spiritual effects found in ovarian cancer survivors, a group of researchers in California and Texas found that the experience of the disease on the participants often left them with a new perspective on their lives, which often led to changes in present and future goals

"Survivors of ovarian cancer demonstrated a profound appreciation for life. The ability to appreciate life's simple pleasures and live 'one day at a time' was of utmost importance to them. Many women dealt with the chronic uncertainty of ovarian cancer with the philosophy to live life to the fullest and appreciate family and friends without dwelling on the cancer that threatened their lives," the researchers wrote.

They also showed that the study subjects weren't as bothered by petty intrusions in daily life, adding the following quote from a participant: "It is amazing to me how much better life is after this past year. I appreciate everything. The little things that used to bother me like a dirty house, bad weather, cranky people, not knowing what to fix for dinner, busy numbers, long lines, bad-hair days, all the little irritations of life don't phase me in the least. I am so grateful for this contentment."

This focus on quality of time was again the theme of another literature review paper published in 1997 by Iowa researchers on the subject of quality of life in gynecologic cancer survivors. The authors here quote another study of health care workers who were well. In that study, the participants were asked to rank in importance fifty abilities or functions. Cognitive, social, and emotional functions rated highest, with highest values on "being able to think clearly, to see, to love and be loved, to make decisions for oneself, to maintain contact with family and friends, to live at home and to walk."

But the authors of this paper theorized that when a major illness is diagnosed, these values shift toward a greater quality of time. "When health begins to deteriorate or when a life-threatening situation occurs, evaluation criteria alter dramatically. Where one lives becomes relatively less important than how one lives or, more particularly, how comfortably and how long one lives," they wrote.

Before she was diagnosed with colon cancer, Marilyn was pretty sure her present life would flow smoothly into her future. For example, she always thought that she would continue to work as a computer programmer for nine hours a day until her retirement and spend her free time teaching a children's religious class and leading a youth group at her church every week. Once retired, she was sure she would spend her time chasing grandchildren around the house that she and her husband had paid off.

But her diagnosis changed all of that, forcing her to opt for quality of time. She spends fewer hours at work and has divorced herself from office politics, preferring to do her work and go home earlier. Her church work with young people has dried up to a trickle, as she now prefers to work with the sick in cancer support groups, encouraging people to accept their own cancer diagnosis. Marilyn now uses the word "if" instead of "when" as she discusses retirement and says that any future moving plans will include consideration of the location of good medical facilities in case she suffers a recurrence.

And yet Marilyn is grateful for all of the present and future changes that cancer has ushered into her life. "Cancer just changed my outlook on so many things. It made me a better person," she said. "I look at things differently. I look for the joy in things. Life is so good. Life is so precious. And before, I took so many things for granted. And now, I look at them as treasures."

Tony offers an interesting example of how the immediate modifications and loss that illness caused in his life led him cherish the adjustments he made in response to it. Diagnosed with HIV in 1985, he was angry at first that the disease and its treatment forced him to leave his job as a mid-level department store manager, where he derived part of his identity and spent from nine to twelve hours a day, not including an hour of commuting time.

"I had to eventually change my life and stop working because it finally started to get the best of me and I was getting really ill. So I was angry that the illness was getting the better of me," he said, adding that he was also losing a larger number of friends, further fueling his anger.

After his beloved partner died of AIDS, Tony stopped feeling angry over the losses and decided to look forward to a new future, one in which he focuses on the quality of his life. He now fills his days with such things like travel, volunteering, and new friendships and relationships, all pursuits that bring him joy.

"After going through the task of taking care of my first partner and watching him die, I decided that it was not going to get the better of me for his memory and for my own sake," Tony said. "I started to live again and not let the disease control my life. Although I was taking treatments and they were a constant reminder, I made it a small part of my life and go on with making the most out of life because I knew how precious each day is/was. I look forward to every birthday and want to get old, as before it wasn't an option and I want it to be."

REDEFINING SUCCESS AND FAILURE

To laugh often and much; to win the respect of intelligent people and the affection of children; to earn the appreciation of honest critics and endure the betrayal of false friends; to appreciate beauty, to find the best in others; to leave the world a bit better, whether by a healthy child, a garden patch or a redeemed social condition; to know even one life has breathed easier because you have lived. This is to have succeeded.

—Ralph Waldo Emerson, essayist and poet

As illness transformed the respondents' present and future goals, it also sharpened their ideas of what was valued and what could be scrapped, what was a success and what was failure. And, really, this makes perfect sense. The prediagnosis past remains, but the post-illness present and future change. What defined success and failure before the doctor uttered his or her conclusion may not apply with new realities and thus new goals in place.

For many, goals prior to diagnosis were laden with the acquisition of material goods and prestigious titles, both denoting professional achievement. Bigger homes, nicer cars, important jobs, and financial glory figured into many respondents' ideas of success. Again, this is understandable. All but four of the individuals interviewed lived within the United States and, as a result, were flush with the American idea that hard work leads to higher positions, which in turn leads to higher salaries and thus material goods purchased with those salaries. Failure, on the other hand, was defined by many prior to their diagnoses as the antithesis of this sentiment, as lacking the ability to achieve or the passion to do or to be better professionally.

Ben is one who saw success in this light. Before his diagnosis of non-Hodgkin's lymphoma, Ben lived a life that he defined as a success. He helped head up an information technology department at a prestigious university, owned a nice house as well as a vacation home, drove a sports car, and treated himself to sleek suits and other natty attire. Even his altruistic acts screamed, "Look at me!"

"I loved getting in the papers. You know, I'd volunteer for something, and they'd write a story about me," Ben said, adding that failure was defined as not being able to make it big in the business world. "It was helping others but, wow, it's helping my career. And that was success."

To be sure, there were a good number of people—though not the majority—who didn't define success and failure in this way. Other definitions of success included the number of friendships an individual had, the quality of an individual's character, the amount of altruistic acts they performed, and the value a person placed in family and home life. Failure was thus defined in an individual as having no family or friends and having major character flaws.

For most of the interviewees, these definitions of success and failure altered following their diagnosis and treatment for a life-threatening illness. As their goals for the future shifted from success in their careers to success in their personal lives, these individuals say they moved away from the materialistically based, quantity-over-quality existence they strived for in the past and toward a more balanced life with regard to spiritual, emotional, and relational issues. Thus, their new goals reflected this adjustment, as did their new definitions of success and failure.

After Ben was diagnosed and treated, his cancer went into remission, only to recur less than two years later. He underwent a stem cell transplant and nearly died in the process, lapsing into a coma for several days and emerging a new person entirely. Ben lost his desire for professional success, preferring to put in the time at work but not to scale the ladder of success at the price of his new goals. As a result, the sports car, the glamorous homes, the fancy threads are all gone, replaced by a simpler lifestyle and accoutrements. His volunteering is quieter and less attention-seeking, more one-on-one; for example, he now helps a paralyzed woman navigate the world with the help of her computer.

Ben also now looks forward to retiring from his job so that he can pursue a life in the ministry. "I live a very monastic type of life now. And that came to me again during the months and months of time in that isolation room [during the stem cell transplant process]. I felt that my life was given back to me as a gift," Ben said. "I really felt that I had been handed a gift and I wasn't going to squander it. That's what got me into this type of thinking. I could really help others, you know. Not just sending a kid to camp but how I could use what I went through in a positive way to work with other people."

"I want to have a life of peace, have some more joy, live through helping others but also do more stuff for myself," Ben said. "I want to live simply."

Ironically, Ben now sees himself in the way that he used to define failure prior to illness, as someone who had no desire for the trappings of success or the willingness to work toward those things. Instead, he sees himself as a success as he now defines it, "someone who came through adversity better." Failure, on the other hand, now is defined by him as "not using your second chance well."

Jen can totally understand the shift in success and failure as she defined them before illness and now, post-treatment for her ovarian cancer. Before, someone she defined as a success was "maybe working their way up the career ladder, you know, maybe working for many years and just being happy with it. It was more career-focused." Failure, she said, was the antithesis of that sentiment.

But now, three years out from her treatment experience, she defines success in more noncareer, nonmaterialistic ways. "Now, it's more, you know, are you happy in a relationship, you know?" she said, adding that failure is "not being happy."

And Marilyn experienced a similar shift, in particular with her definition of success, as a result of her experience with colon cancer. Her current and former definition of failure was of a person who had no friends or family and who was bitter and unkind. But success before illness was defined as having self-confidence.

"They had done something meaningful with their

career and that they had enough money that they didn't need to worry about the necessities of life, that they had friends, that people respected them," Marilyn said.

When asked if her post-illness definition of success included self-confidence, material goods, and career gains, Marilyn said, "No," opting instead for a definition that included "kindness, fairness, appreciation for being alive, and being able to just tell it like it is, being an honest person."

The list could go on and on. It didn't really matter what the diagnosis was. Individuals who suffered through the diagnosis and treatment of a life-threatening illness often mourned for their lost future. Those who were the most successful in adapting to their illness were those who did not stay mired in the loss but rather integrated their disease into their lives, examining and making adjustments to the valued parts of their lives. In the process, they changed their vision of and hope for the future, however long it is. And, in turn, they found the gift of resetting the future through establishing new goals.

REAL STORY—CARY

At forty, Cary had achieved nearly all he had dreamed of in early adulthood. But, at the same time, he felt that something had to give.

He was a lawyer, an equity partner at a prestigious law firm. Every day, Cary handled multimillion-dollar lawsuits and felt he was at the height of his career, putting in long hours a day to handle his burgeoning case load. He was married to another lawyer, Vanessa, and the couple had had a son, Jack, eighteen months before. Cary found fatherhood was everything he thought it would be, and more.

"That was all good news to me," he said.

At least on the surface. But a closer inspection of his life found that Cary spent at most two hours a day with his son, not nearly enough to him, as he felt he was disproportionately devoting five to six times those hours to work, helping corporations battle each other. Additionally, Cary spent three to four hours a day with his wife and less than an hour a day

Cary

doing things he enjoyed, such as reading for pleasure, exercising, or pursuing hobbies. He thought that unless he made a change, his future would include "continuing to practice law, growing ever fatter, probably dying somewhat prematurely of some other malady, having a couple of kids, doing a lot of expensive vacations and having quite a bit of money."

This situation led to a great internal tension between what Cary's life was and what he wanted it to be.

"The bad news was that the stress and the time demands of my job put me in a state of personal crisis," Cary said.

However, the job demanded nothing less than what he was already giving, so cutting back on hours was really not an option. Giving up the lifestyle to take a lesser-paying job was not appealing either.

"You go to college and to law school to do this and then you build up your practice," Cary said. "You kind of get to a certain point in terms of earnings and all that, and then to just chuck it is really rough. And it's not that my identity was that wrapped up in being a lawyer. It really wasn't. But it was just such a shift."

While he was wrestling with this dilemma, something strange was happening nearly every time he ate. After swallowing, Cary began to feel food travel down his esophagus. His alarm at the situation grew when he ate a banana and the physical sensation changed from perceptible movement to pain. He also developed acute upper back pain, and both symptoms brought him to his doctor, a Harvard-trained physician.

The doctor assumed his symptoms were caused by a gastroesophageal-reflux-induced irritation of the lining of the esophagus and was ready to send Cary home with a prescription for heartburn medication. But Cary had a nagging feeling that his diagnosis was more serious than heartburn. A relative recently had been diagnosed with esophageal cancer. Even though Cary didn't have any of the risk factors like smoking and drinking, he wanted to rule this potentially fatal possibility out.

"I said, 'Well, I've got this eighteen-month-old at home, and I really want to at least rule out esophageal cancer,'" Cary recalled. "He said, 'The chances of your having esophageal cancer at age forty, [with] no risk factors is one in ninety million.' When I pressed the point, he told me I sound like a quote, cyberchondriac, and I should get off the goddamn Internet.

"I told him to set up the test. I don't go out recreationally looking for additional pain and so for me to sort of insist on an endoscopy was way out of character," he said.

Another gastroenterologist found a tiny nodule near the point where the esophagus meets the stomach. The biopsy of the nodule showed it was malignant, and further testing found that it was only the tip of the iceberg, as a larger growth pierced the outer wall of the esophagus.

Due to the advanced stage of his disease, the next several months of treatment involved six weeks of intense chemotherapy and radiation, four weeks of recovery, and then very invasive surgery to excise the tumor, reconfigure what was left of the esophagus and the stomach, and check for further traces of cancer. The combination of this medical and surgical attack left him with a cylinder-shaped stomach, the adjustment to which caused him to vomit up to twenty times a day and to lose sixty pounds. In the three years since the surgery, Cary continues to struggle with the aftereffects, which include fatigue, insomnia, chronic coughing, weight loss, and less frequent but still present vomiting.

But the physical effects were small compared with how much the disease altered the course of his life. The treatments and the surgery left him too sick to work for many months after they ended. Regular checkups and scans to check for a recurrence—three months apart at first and then spread out as he moved further from the initial treatment—left him too emotionally spent to consider returning to the grind that work had become.

Without the consuming workload to which he used to devote his time, Cary turned to other areas of life to find fulfillment. One memory in particular that pushed him in this direction was that of a coworker who was also sick with cancer. This man, an attorney and father, came into the office wearing a chemotherapy pump just a few days before he died. While some in the office saw these actions as heroic in terms of serving the clients, Cary did not.

"I was thinking, 'I can't imagine spending your final days at the office when you've got three kids at home, you know?'" Cary said.

Instead, Cary committed himself to living a life that he had only dreamt about before his illness experience. He took an extended leave of absence from work to spend time primarily with his family, something that became more important to do after his daughter, Hope, was born a year ago.

"I'm going to take off a total of probably not less than four years just to spend with my kids until my son goes to kindergarten, and then I'm going back to work," he said. "One of the things I am doing is just saying, 'You know what? Until I am out of the woods, I'm going to spend my time doing what matters.' I know that work isn't one of those things."

Currently, his focus on goals is far more personal in nature than they were before. For example, he has increased the amount of time spent with his family fivefold; he spends about eight hours a day with Jack and Hope, and at least that many with Vanessa. He parcels off more of his day for volunteering, using some of that time to create and to maintain a Web site for others who share his diagnosis. Cary also doubled the time he spends on himself, devoting more hours to exercise and to writing, a hobby he always wanted to pursue.

This alteration of priorities has given him a new definition of success and failure. Before his illness, he found success in what he did and defined failure similarly. "Success was a lot more career-identified. You know, winning cases, making a certain amount of money," he said. "Failure would have meant failing in my job in some way, like losing a trial, more identified with my profession. Very much, success and failure were identified as professional success and failure.

"Success now is being a first-rate father. I think success is trying to deepen a relationship with God. Also being a first-rate husband and son and brother," he said. "Failure for me would be defined mainly by backsliding into my previous life, by not maximizing this chance and by not taking what I've learned and acting on it."

While he still finds it difficult to plan very far in the future, Cary feels he is heading in the right direction. He will not return to the demanding work of a trial lawyer and continues to focus on developing personal relationships.

"Everything is more of a priority than career. Career is about tenth. As long as I have enough money to literally keep the lights on, that's about all I care about at this point," he said. "Relationships are huge, faith is a more important thing, maintaining a healthy lifestyle is an important one, maintaining that sense of active gratitude, continuing to help others, especially in the cancer area."

PART III
Moving Beyond Point B

10

THE BIG QUESTION AND THE UNEXPECTED ANSWERS

I know that without the suffering, the growth that I have achieved would have been impossible.

—Jerry Long, quadriplegic, as quoted in Viktor Frankl's
Man's Search for Meaning

THERE WAS A particular question I asked at the end of each of the 102 patient interviews, one for which I was very eager to learn the others' answers. The essence of the question was this: Was the experience of illness and everything it brought into life so meaningful and valuable that, if given the choice in hindsight, it would be relived? Or was the experience so difficult that it would be avoided entirely, despite the positives that came from it?

I asked the question because I felt that my answer to it was so contrary to the way that most of those I knew thought of disease, as something to be avoided entirely. Instead, I embraced all that was in my life precisely because I suffered through my diagnosis and extensive treatment for the disease in the nearly two decades since my diagnosis. Though I could have done without five surgeries and all of the exhausting and painful disease symptoms and medication side effects I had been through, I grew immensely as a human being—learning about qualities like patience, trust, loyalty, endurance, courage, and bravery—in ways I was sure I would not have otherwise. I attained a certain perspective on life and an appreciation for all things in it that I am sure would not have come until later in life, if at all. If trading my illness for a life of full health also meant trading all of the blessings that came with the disease journey, then forget it. I would rather suffer and have a deeper experience as a result.

Many researchers scoff at this idea as being too Pollyannaish or too delusional to accept. Others often remark about such findings with incredulity. But a handful of researchers support this finding. Dr. Pam McGrath, the Australian psychologist, studied hematologic cancer survivors for a paper published in 2004 on serious illness as a spiritual journey. She found that while illness "heightens [the patient's] sense of the fragility of life and presents them with the challenge of finding a framework for making sense of the experience," it also "provides a different 'lens' with which to evaluate outcomes, which allows [the patient] to see a wide range of positives in what could otherwise be seen as a very negative experience." Other papers either directly or indirectly uncovered this finding as well, often quoting the patients who said they had found profound happiness and peace amidst the physical effects of illness.

However, I wasn't sure if those I was interviewing would understand this concept. Certainly the well individuals in my life didn't seem to get it. Almost none of them had been seriously ill during their lives thus far and, though they watched me struggle, they couldn't comprehend the positive impact Crohn's disease had on me. After explaining my position one night over dinner, I looked across the table at a friend, who stared incredulously at me. Without missing a beat, she said, "I'd rather be shallow and well." Another friend, a former nurse, told me that she would rather die than endure what I had gone through.

I thought that maybe those who had shared similar experiences would understand the concept better. Out of curiosity, I crafted a question that addressed that topic and put it at the very end of the first interview. The question went like this: If God came to you and said, 'You have suffered enough. I am going to take you back to the day you were diagnosed and take all of the suffering away from you. But I am also going to take away all that you have gained from the disease.' Would you do it?

And that individual answered, "I wouldn't do it." This was despite the fact that the respondent had just finished outlining tremendous physical and emotional pain that he and his family had suffered, sometimes occurring years after a cure was rendered. The interviewee, instead, considered the disease a gift.

Spurred by this response, I asked the question over and over, always at the end of the interview. The question changed a little over time, especially as people asked if certain conditions could be placed on their answer. One atheist, for example, asked me to rephrase the question, deleting God from the equation. Another individual asked if she could end up somewhere in the middle, without having to experience lingering fears of recurrence or awful annual tests but with the wisdom and courage illness ushered into her life.

The final form of the final question included choices of both a well path and an illness path. It went like this: Imagine if some higher power were to take you back to the time prior to when you felt your first symptoms. At that point, you would be aware of what you had gone through up to the current point in your life. Now, this higher power would give you two choices. You could go back through your life, never experiencing the illness but also never gaining any of the positive things that you have gained from the experience. You would just continue along the same trajectory that you were on prior to becoming ill. Or you could go through everything that you have gone through, the illness and its treatment, and end up exactly where you are, with the any benefits you may have gained from the experience. Which would you choose?

In total, eighty-seven of the individuals interviewed said they would take the illness path and go through the experience again, with all of the suffering from sometimes extensive and life-threatening medical and surgical treatments. The remaining fifteen individuals said they would take the well path and opt never to have their illness in the first place, even if it meant giving up the gifts that illness had bestowed upon them.

ANSWERING NO

Diseases are painful and physically damaging. Diseases are financially devastating. Diseases have impact beyond the individual, affecting family and friends in different ways. Diseases have no redeeming value in an individual's life. At least these are concepts centuries worth of prevailing wisdom historically taught us through the high value placed on health and the opposite view of illness as weakness. It is surprising to many who have never suffered physically through a serious illness to imagine that anyone—especially anyone who has gone the experience of diagnosis and treatment of a life-threatening disease—would to choose that path if the person had to do it over.

And, indeed, some do not. On the individual level, disease can continue to be seen through a negative lens for years after treatment subsides and relatively normal life continues. Of the individuals who were interviewed for the book, not quite 15 percent, or one in seven, answered the last question in the negative, giving five main reasons for the aversion to the idea of choosing the illness path over the well path.

Fear of the physical pain they went through and continuing worry about the possibility of recurrence or relapse was the most common reason given for choosing the former of the options posed in the question. Again, research bears this idea out. In McGrath's paper, she stated that there were elements of the experience that shook a patient's sense of confidence and robbed the patient of any meaning derived from the illness experience, the foremost being the presence of a painful post–stem cell transplant condition known as graft-versus-host disease, as well as low blood counts and treatment-related anorexia. "If the pain and physical distress is severe enough, it can cause the individual to lose a sense of meaning in life," McGrath said, adding that the failure to address these conditions can lead to the loss of the will to live.

Georgia is one who would not go through her experience of Hodgkin's lymphoma again, thanks for asking. Her disease was discovered not long after she gave birth to her first child. After having her rib surgically removed and undergoing several rounds of chemotherapy and radiation, she was too sick to care for her son and was left feeling as though death was nearer than it ever had been. Though her treatments ended more than three years before her interview took place, Georgia told me that she remains haunted by the pain she went through and fears that she will have a treatment-related cancer in her future.

"I'd take the first one. I would like to have never known this ever. And part of it is because treatment is causing trouble and will cause me trouble down the road. There are long-term effects," she said. When asked what she thinks she would be like without the cancer experience, she continued, "I think I'd be shallower definitely, you know, and I wouldn't have some of the friends I have now, some of the ones I've met recently, you know. So those are things that I would miss out on and maybe my husband and I wouldn't have as solid as a relationship, but I'd give it up.

"Just in the practical matter, it sucked completely," Georgia said. "I hated it."

Graham also went through rough treatment for his advanced case of brain cancer, undergoing surgical and medical therapy. In the process of being treated and recovering, Graham notes that he lost fears and gained a new, more rewarding perspective on life, developments for which he is grateful. But after facing his demise during the diagnostic and treatment phases, he is not eager to return to the chasm that separates life and death. Graham's new fears focus on the possibility that recurrence could and very well may happen again, sooner rather than later.

"There's too much of a downside and it's too random

for me," he said. "I don't feel like living on a time bomb. I don't know when it's going to go off, you know. I don't like surprises."

Another common reason that was given for choosing not to experience the illness again was due to the feelings of sadness and regret for the pain caused to others the first time around. Watching friends and family members worry and anguish over the illness and its treatments inspires feelings of guilt in many individuals.

Dan is one of these people. After being diagnosed with Hodgkin's disease, he underwent extensive treatment, only to relapse twice. Grueling chemotherapy, radiation, and a bone marrow transplant finally knocked the disease from his body. Since that time, Dan completed studies to earn a doctorate in psychology, wrote a well-received memoir about his journey through illness and back to health, married, and fathered two children. His scans remain free and clear of the disease that nearly killed him.

But if given the chance to remove the experience of Hodgkin's from his life as well as any perceived benefits it may have brought to him, Dan would not hesitate to do so.

"Take it away," Dan wrote in an e-mail. "I think one's sense of immortality is a gift that most people take for granted. I'd like to have some of that back. I'd gladly be bookless and ignorant about suffering.

"But more than anything, I'd love to have not watched my wife and father and brother and mother suffer—scared to their core I was going to die. I'd like to not have to explain to my seven-year-old daughter that cancers sometimes come back. I'd skip that in a second," he continued. "Which of these buttons do I push?"

Beth was pleased with the benefits from her experience with a tumor pressing on her brain stem. Her friends and family rallied, showing her how much they loved her and sustaining her while she recovered from surgery to correct the problem. Her faith deepened and continues to be a source of strength for her.

But she would never elect to relive it if given the choice. "Can I say I'm grateful for the tumor? Well, no," Beth said. "I don't think that the tumor changed me that much, and I think I'd probably not go through it. Not so much for myself but really for my family and my friends. I mean, they all went through it, too. And so, if I could save all of us from having to go through that, I think I would. It affected more than just me. I don't think the small things I gained are justification for making everybody go through that suffering."

Pain comes in many forms, the physical sort being just one. Financial pain and suffering caused by illness often presents a barrier during the diagnosis and treatment phases due to loss of income and high medical and surgical bills. And it can continue to prove a hindrance and a disability. Additionally, job discrimination and insurance discrimination can continue to challenge an individual long after survival appears to be a more permanent stage.

Pat provides a good example of this. Though she was diagnosed with hepatitis C years ago, she continued to work and live life with barely a notice of the impact of the disease on her life. But when melanoma was discovered on her leg, she went through surgery and chemotherapy, the physical effects of which led to the loss of her ability to work. Because Pat is currently battling a recurrence and a metastasis in her lungs, thoughts of returning to work have been put away, forcing her family to cut back on their expenses and live off her husband's earnings alone.

So despite the closeness the illness has given her and her family and despite all of the friendships she has made with others who are similarly suffering, Pat would do away with the melanoma in a heartbeat, if given the chance to do it all over again.

"A lot of things wouldn't have happened to me because of my illness as far as financially, which has been rough for us as a family. I could do without that struggle because there are a lot of things I want to do. A lot of things that I want cost money, so I can't do them because I don't have the money to do them," Pat said.

Another reason for taking up the offer for the well path occurred when some of those interviewed discovered that the gifts of illness were not worth the price paid for them. The loss of their health carried too steep a cost to opt to go through it again for the perceived benefits.

Some of Miles's personal relationships suffered as a result of his diabetes and hepatitis C treatments. He also lost his ability to be the primary breadwinner and still fights fatigue, thus limiting his ability to enjoy life. Though he has also made a number of friends online as a result of chronicling his journey through hepatitis C treatment, that gift has not been worth all of the trouble and all of the pain.

"I liked my life before," Miles said, succinctly explaining his final answer to me.

Finally, some of those who replied in the negative felt that they would have arrived at the gifts eventually in the absence of the illness. Violet understands this concept. Diagnosed with type 1 diabetes in her thirties, she struggled with learning about her metabolism, the proper balance of carbo-hydrates, the timing of her insulin shots. She also grappled with coming to terms with her possible future with the disease, such as how her disease may shorten her years or may hamper her ability to attain her life goals.

Though she is pleased with a greater emotional equilib-rium and a newfound sense of strength, Violet is sure that she would have found these or other gifts later in life, simply as a part of the natural maturation process. Because of this, she would reject the illness route if given the chance to do it again.

"To me, that does not undermine the value of what has turned out to be the gifts of it, but I believe I would have found other really cool gifts anyway," Violet said. "There are aspects of this disease that suck and they always will. I think that that can be true and at the same time, I consider what I have gotten out of it and appreciate the fact that I've made some choices that have helped me find the silver lining. I honor that and I honor these gifts. And yet, I would rather not have it."

Also, it is important to note that the negativity of the experience was often affected by the proximity to the illness experience. The closer the diagnosis and treatment, the harder it is to see the positive in the experience, thus col-oring the answer to this question in some. McGrath found the same among the respondents in her hematological cancer study.

This is not to say that Violet, who was a year and half out from diagnosis when she was interviewed, or Pat, who was struggling through a recurrence, would ever agree to go down the illness road again. Rather, it acknowledges that, with time and perspective, some of the negativity dissipates.

ANSWERING YES

While choosing to avoid another journey through illness may be the expected path for some, others found there were big enough benefits to the experience that they would forgo a life without tests, exhausting and difficult medical therapies, and painful surgeries in favor of reliving the illness route. In fact, nearly six times the amount of respondents, more than 85 percent, or six out of seven, chose to relive the experience because it was so valuable to them.

The reasons for taking this path again were as varied as the respondents but generally fell into a few categories, the most common being one or a combination of the five gifts of illness. The newly altered sense of time and being, the changed emotional experience, the growth in altruism, the increased value of relationships, and the resetting of goals were common reasons given for their positive answers.

Emotions
A few individuals, for example, found that the emotional changes they went through during the course of their illness and treatment had changed their experience of life so much that they would endure even some of the harshest treatments again in order to secure this benefit. Peter is one of these individuals. Emotions weren't part of his lexicon when he was growing up as a tough kid on the streets of New York. But after two major surgeries for Crohn's disease, he finds that he is far more emotionally pliable than he ever thought he would be. For this change, he is grateful.

"I know life and I see things in Technicolor because of

what I experienced. In the way that people say in the cliché that you only know the good after you go through the bad, but there is so much truth to appreciating life to its fullest when you may not have it anymore," he said. "Because of what I've been through, I am able to help others. I think that I would be jaded. I think that I would be selfish and not as caring. I wouldn't be passionate. I wouldn't have this zest for life that I do because I got such a gift because I know I may not be here tomorrow. And I know how close it is not to be here tomorrow. Only when a person goes through that do they enjoy today."

Bobby totally understands that concept now but didn't always. Before his diagnosis was rendered, he thought it would be insane to embrace such an illness. After undergoing two surgeries and months of chemotherapy for his testicular cancer, he now sees it is not so crazy to want to keep the experience as a part of his life. He is especially pleased with a renewed sense of joy in his life regarding his work.

"When I'd heard other people talk about it before it happened to me, it made no sense. Like I would have rewritten every chapter. I was like, 'Well, that's ridiculous. Why wouldn't I change it?'" he said. "But when you were saying the question, there was no even waffling in my mind. It's very clear that I would change nothing. That doesn't mean that I would wish cancer on someone else. But for me, now that I've gone through it, I know I wouldn't change it. I think it's made me enjoy life more."

Time and being
Others found that the change in their relationship to time and being was significant enough to send them down the path of illness again, if they had to choose. Mostly, these

people were happy to have been forced from a fast-track existence, where careers ruled their world, material success was their focus, and both took up much of their lives.

Ellen, for example, averaged eighty hours of work a week as an attorney. So absorbed was she in her work that at times she would forget to eat. But that changed after three episodes with MS. "For whatever reason, I was not given a personality to create an internal balance without this external issue of a chronic illness. I believe that it was really as if someone came to me and said, 'You couldn't do it your-self but now you have to.' The lessons I have learned as a result of MS have been significant enough that I don't think I would want to be the person that I would have been without it. I really don't think that I could have made the changes by myself," Ellen said, adding that she now works part time, about a quarter of the amount she used to work. "I don't think having children alone would have changed it. I think it would have helped, but I don't think I would be where I am right now if it wasn't for the MS."

Ben related to me that he also felt his fast-paced life shift into low gear after being diagnosed with lymphoma. Prior to his diagnosis, he held a highly regarded position in information technology with a major university, putting in twelve- to fourteen-hour days on average. He was also into all the trappings of success, like a big house, a vacation home, a nice car, and designer suits.

Following initial treatment, a relapse, and a bone marrow transplant, he holds a less stressful lower-level and lower-paying job at another university, planning to retire soon. Ben now lives in a simple apartment and bikes to work, all while preparing to pursue a life in the ministry.

And he would never trade the illness path he has been on for the other he was on prior to his diagnosis.

"The illness has caused me to slow down, read the maps a little more before heading down a fork in the road. It's been the hardest thing I had to go through, but I think it shaped my life. The success I will be is going to be a lot different and a lot more solid than what [it] might have . . . been if I, you know, were flying high. I think I was heading for a burnout anyway back then," Ben said, adding that many work colleagues and friends from his prediagnosis life have lost everything to bankruptcy or substance abuse. "It kind of kicked me off the fast track and onto the country road, and I've kind of stayed there."

Linie could tell the same story. Huge success as a real estate agent, nice car, nice clothes, big house. Then a diagnosis, in her case primary biliary cirrhosis. The illness and its treatment forced her to give her lifestyle up for a smaller house and a slower life in the country. This milder speed allowed her to spend more time with her son, who recently died in a car accident, and to devote more time to helping others who share her diagnosis, some of which have become her dearest friends. Despite all of her losses, she would take the path with illness rather stay on the same trajectory she was on before her diagnosis, as a self-described workaholic who spent little time helping others or with her family.

"I really, honestly believe that God gave me PBC for a reason, to change me so that I would help others and others could help me. You can be going through life and all you're doing is you're a workaholic and you help a little bit on the weekends, when you can or something like that," Linie said. "PBC changed my whole life to where I was able to spend more time with my son. I could take my son to school if I wanted to. I'd pick him up from football practice. I was here with him. If I had been on that other path, it wouldn't have been like that. I wouldn't have spent time with my son."

Linie feels that this slower pace of time gave her a sense of purpose and makes her focus on making each day full of activities to help others who are sick.

"[PBC] forced me to slow down, but it gave me a whole different outlook on life. I really feel good about that because it makes me feel that I'm accomplishing something in life. Like I'm not just floating on earth, you know, taking up space or something like that. You know how you see people and they go through life, and they don't do anything? I feel like at least I'm here for a reason," she said.

Altruism

The gift of altruism is another recurring theme among the respondents who replied that they would go down the illness path again. As Linie has shown, for some, the meaning that altruism gave to their lives in the wake of illness exponentially increased their overall purpose in life. Mostly, this happened in individuals who did not devote many hours to altruistic actions in the past.

Molly is one who did give her time before, but mostly as a volunteer hockey coach, as the sport is her passion. Following her diagnosis and medical and surgical treatment for colon cancer, she now is the president and cofounder of The Colon Club, an organization devoted to raising awareness about colorectal cancer, especially its occurrence in young people. Molly travels the country giving speeches and skating with semiprofessional hockey teams to further her cause.

If given the chance to go back to that twenty-three-year-old version of herself at diagnosis and have the experience of life-threatening illness wiped from her future, she says she would never do it. "You know, having colon cancer, I think it was like a gift and you'll hear a lot of people say that. It gave me direction. It gave me purpose. I feel like I've helped a lot of people. And that's a little bit selfish on my part because that makes me happy," Molly said. "I can look back and if I decide tomorrow that I never want to do this again, I can still look back and say, 'You know what? For a while there I did some-thing that mattered and it made the world a better place.' That matters so much to me. I don't think a lot of people in the world have that opportunity. I don't think a lot of people can say that. It's pretty amazing."

On a slightly smaller scale, Sandee feels the same way about her ability to help others through a breast cancer crisis. Whereas before her own diagnosis she spent no time helping others in volunteer pursuits, she now spends about three hours a day guiding others one-on-one through diagnosis and treatment by e-mail and phone calls and maintaining her own blog about her treatment experiences. Though she has suffered greatly through sur-geries and more than eight years of rigorous medical therapy as her cancer continues to spread, Sandee said she would choose the illness route if she had to do it again because of the pleasure and purpose that altruistic acts lend to her life.

"I just feel more . . . my heart feels complete and my heart feels full. I feel good. I didn't realize how much one person could do to help somebody else and I do now," Sandee said. "It's very rewarding, very rewarding."

Relationships

The heightened importance of interpersonal relationships is another gift that individuals cited as a reason to choose the illness path again. While some relationships were lost during the period of diagnosis and treatment, those that remained gained in strength, depth, and endurance. Others became friends with individuals they were sure they would not have met but for the experience of the illness, lessening any feelings of loneliness and isolation they may have felt that are inherent in disease and treatment.

Decades after being infected with the hepatitis C virus, Patty battles fatigue daily and faces either death or a liver transplant in the not-so-distant future. She knows this not only because she has learned as much as possible about the disease but also because she has watched two friends with the disease die in recent years. But despite all she has lost, Patty feels she has gained much from the disease, enough for her to choose to go through it again and forgo a path of wellness, if the option was offered to her.

"My life has been so much richer. In the people that I've come to know but mainly with what I've learned within myself, who I am, which is a more compassionate person, much more knowledgeable about life around me, and thankful. Thankful and appreciative," Patty told me in answer to the question. "The people I met are incredible, wonderful people, you know. My family I think has bonded closer together. We're stronger."

September also feels this way. Though she has endured a few extremely painful surgeries and a very difficult chemotherapy regimen to fight her metastatic melanoma, she said she has had "a lot of good and a lot of happiness" mixed in with "a lot of sadness and a lot of pain." But it is the new strength and comfort she draws from her family and friends that would send her down the same path again.

"I have the best friends and family anyone could ever ask for and I don't think I would trade that," September said. "My sister and I are closer, which is very important. My mom and I are closer. And I've made some wonderful new relationships."

Even when family members suffered through fear and grief as their loved one battled life-threatening disease, some found the illness experience to ultimately benefit all involved in their lives. Some of those interviewed said that their children became more compassionate and their spousal relationships deepened, despite all of the pain and suffering to which they had to bear witness.

Linda's family members all had different reactions when she was undergoing treatment for multiple myeloma. One child would pat her bald head while another became more introverted. Her sister passed out shortly after witnessing a bone biopsy and her husband became a great source of strength, even as he watched his wife endure grueling chemotherapy and an agonizing stem cell transplant. They have all further suffered after learning that the disease relapsed.

Still, Linda wouldn't change what she has gone through. "The thought would be to not go through it all again. But to be the person I am right now because I went through that? I would definitely keep it as it was. I think I have learned so much out of it. Even as negative as it was for [my husband] and the kids, I think they learned something out of it, too," Linda said.

Goals

The positive transformative effect that illness had on life goals was another reason to choose the disease path over the well one. Often, the experience of life-threatening illness clarified individuals' priorities and helped them to discover and to pursue what was truly important to them.

Emily had this happen to her. Prior to her diagnosis of lymphoma, she was happily drifting through an elementary education program, hoping to become a reading teacher. But the surgery and chemotherapy required for treatment forced her to put school on hold for a while, which in turn forced her to finish college with a degree in Japanese, as the education degree seemed impossible to attain. Not long after, a friend then suggested that Emily apply to work at a camp for the blind. She discovered new purpose in the pursuit of being a teacher of reading, this time for the blind. She married the boyfriend who saw her through her treatment and moved to Louisiana to work toward her certification as a teacher for the blind, an underserved population as far as reading goes.

"If God gave me a choice, I wouldn't change a thing because I feel like if I never had cancer, I wouldn't be where I am now," Emily said. "I would never have thought to come down to Louisiana. I don't know that I would be with my husband because he's a really shy guy and I was pretty shy back then, too. I don't think we would have connected the way that we did. And I just think that I would be living a completely different life, and I'm very happy with the life I have right now."

Gina agrees with that sentiment. Her diagnosis of type 1 diabetes came in the beginning of her adulthood, just when things were getting fun. Nights filled with clubbing and partying were her main pursuits. Then the diagnosis was rendered and she began to see more purpose in her time, shifting it from being spent in smoky clubs to being holed up in her room, creating a Web site and online community for others with diabetes. Gina's new goal is to bring awareness to diabetes and to make her site grow.

"If you had asked me this question five years ago when I was first diagnosed, I would have said the healthy road because I was desperate to not have it and make it go away," she said. "Diabetes does suck. I won't lie and I do hate it most of the day. But without this road I have been given, where would I be today? I would never want to make an impact on society. I would still be going to bars, smoking cigarettes, and getting drunk every weekend with my friends."

Perspective and appreciation

Beyond the gifts of illness, some individuals found other reasons to take the illness route again. Sometimes it was a general appreciation for life that wasn't there before the illness, while other times it was a general feeling that their perspective shifted for the positive. For others, it was a general sense of happiness as a result of both greater appreciation and a more clarified perspective.

Jim said he would take the path of Parkinson's again even though he is now unable to work and feels as though there have been great losses in his life. "From a materialistic sense, yeah, there's a lot that I lost. But I am happier at this point in my life than I've ever been. I have a much greater appreciation of the things that matter than I ever did," Jim said. "Obviously, nobody wants to be sick, but illness can be a very powerful positive force in one's life. It's all in how you let it control you."

Jim now finds more profound appreciation for simple things and beauty than he ever did before, which adds a rich dimension to his life that was lacking prior to his diagnosis. "A sunrise? What's that? Flowers? Eh, they're just in my lawn," Jim said of his attitude prior to Parkinson's. "And now, when I go outside, sometimes I'll stand and stare at the sky. I know my neighbors think I'm nuts. But I'll stand and stare and watch the clouds or I'll watch the breeze blow through the flower garden and I appreciate it. I feel okay with where I am. And I never would have had that if it hadn't been for being sick."

For decades, Bill worked as a cardiac surgeon, eventually attaining the title of chief of cardiac surgery for a midwestern hospital chain. As such, he was always on the healing side in medicine, never the patient side. But when a bump on his face was determined to be lymphoma and a related infection forced him to retire early, Bill's whole perspective on life changed. He spent more time with his wife and family and became a strong force for other patients with lymphoma. As president of the Lymphoma Research Foundation, he has pushed legislators for more research funding and advocated for better patient support.

"I don't think there's any doubt. Knowing what I know today, I would choose the path that I'm on right now," Bill said. "As rewarding as my career was, I would have spent those ten years basically doing the same thing over and over, helping individual patients but not really having the sense of perspective that I think I have now that I could see as a better sense of perspective."

Dana is just happier as a person who has gone through the experience of illness than she was in her life before it. Even though her breast cancer forced her into some frightening times during surgery, chemotherapy, and radiation treatments, she looks at the experience as a valuable one.

"I'd take the cancer. It is scary. But I just think I'm a different person now than I would have been without the cancer. And I like that person," Dana said. "I can't speak to whether or not I would like the person I would have become without that cancer because I don't know who that person would be. But I like the person I am now and cancer played a big part in that."

Illness necessary for transformation

Whatever the reason for choosing the path of illness, the participants who picked the illness path again said that they would not have arrived at the gifts of illness nor would they have had a shift in appreciation or perspective except for having gone through the experience of life-threatening illness. The illness they suffered forced such upheaval but also brought with it such positive transformations that the participants felt they would not have attained these gains on their own without illness.

Linda believes this to be particularly true, and she sees it in the varying reactions she gets from people who have also suffered serious illness as well as those who have not. In those who have suffered similarly, she often feels a bond of support, while she receives a good dose of pity from those who have not.

"Don't you feel that when you run into somebody who has gone through something similar that there is a mental connection? We know what each other has gone through; there have been some ups and downs. It is not a wonderful thing, but having gotten through a certain amount of it, I feel I have grown enormously as a human being," Linda said. "In retrospect, I remember having known people who had cancer and not knowing what to say to them. I felt stupid. But now, as much as I tried to slap people [who don't understand] across the face and say this is a good thing, they don't get it. I think you have to go through it to get it: there is a positive in this."

Cary totally agrees. After undergoing rigorous medical and surgical therapy to cure him of esophageal cancer, he has spent a few years at home recuperating. Illness, he says, has given him a heightened perspective on and appreciation for life that he simply would not have attained if he had continued along his life trajectory without the illness experience.

"I can fully accept that this is the best thing that's ever—except for the birth of my children—the best thing that's ever happened," Cary said. "In terms of how it's had an effect on my lifestyle and all that kind of thing, it's a great gift. I actually feel badly for people who haven't come nose to nose with death in this way because I don't know how any other experience could absolutely kick one in the pants enough to get them to make these changes. It certainly wouldn't have worked for me. I could have read all the books in the world and gone to all the lectures and watched all of the sentimental movies and I wouldn't have done it."

Again, the research bears this feeling out. In another 2004 paper on reflections on serious illness as a spiritual journey, the participants in McGrath's study discovered that they only way they could have found certain aspects of personal growth was to go through the illness experience. "There was a sense in which the insights and life experience provided by the spiritual journey informed who they are at this point in time and thus would be determinant of their future direction and achievements," McGrath wrote.

While the answers to the final question were interesting, they also show the value of the positive transformative power of the gifts of illness in individuals' lives. Despite the pain and misery that illness ushered into their lives, the majority of those interviewed for this book found redemption that the gifts also presented.

11

SUGGESTIONS FOR INDIVIDUALS AND SOCIETY

‿‿‿‿‿‿‿

TO SAY THAT the five gifts of illness exist is not enough. To say that those who have survived a life-threatening illness find value in the experience is not enough. To say that the learned world needs to study and to more fully recognize the plight of the survivor is not enough. Nor is it enough to say that more services are needed for longer-term survivors.

People involved in survivorship want answers and they want direction. And I am not going to directly provide either. Again, I am a writer, not a doctor or a psychologist. My expertise is in my own experience. Instead, I turn to the experts in the field, both fellow survivors and those who study the experience. Those who have survived provide the illumination of personal knowledge to light the path of those who follow in their footsteps, while those who have extensively studied the survivorship experience lend their credibility and insight to the modifications that society can make in order to ease the experience of surviving a life-threatening condition.

SUGGESTIONS FOR INDIVIDUALS

So how does one go from the devastation and grief during the diagnosis and treatment at point A to the successful adaptation to the disease and the recognition of the gifts at point B? According to those interviewed for this book as well as the established research on the subject, it is a long and highly individual process, one that changes from person to person but doesn't seem to be greatly affected by the type of life-threatening disease suffered. It is a process that involves grieving for the life to which one felt entitled, learning about medicine and the body while suffering through treatments, involving friends and family members in the drama at hand, integrating the physical effects of the disease by adapting to limitations, and coping with facing an uncertain future.

Below are eight different steps that individuals interviewed for the book found they went through during their journey from A to B. These are based on human experience, not the double-blind, placebo-controlled, multicentered scientific methods we so often see in the medical and surgical world. Not every person went through every one of these steps, nor did they go through in any particular order. Even when the diagnosis and treatment was exactly the same, the individuals were not, and so their experiences were different as well. Therefore, don't be surprised if you or an individual you know skips a step or misses a stop or even experiences something not listed. Though they are relatively encompassing, these points are meant to be the most common elements of the journey, not all of them.

1. *Finding support.*

Whether it was locating a therapist to walk them through the grieving process, attending a support group, or finding one-on-one mentoring with the help of a role model, nearly all of the participants looked to others to help them through certain parts of the illness experience, from the point of diagnosis to facing a recurrence. This was in part because no one in their immediate family or in their circle of friends had been through the same experience and they sought to identify with someone who did understand it or who simply had been on the same path.

John is one who did this during his second trip through cancer. In his first experience, he was a soldier, returning from duty during World War II. He noticed blood in his urine, which led doctors to discover bladder cancer. As a young man, he decided to undergo radiation therapy rather than radical surgery to remove his bladder. Because cancer was still very taboo in society at the time he was undergoing therapy, he kept the experience to himself, even leaving work during his lunch hour, taking a series of street cars to the hospital for therapy, and returning the same afternoon to complete his workday.

"I didn't know anyone with the bladder cancer. Given my age at the time, there weren't that many around," said John, now a retired municipal worker.

But when he was diagnosed with another primary cancer decades later, this time in his colon, John reached out to others who had gone through ostomy surgery through a local support group. And this made all the difference to him.

"It's not that I felt I needed support, but I thought there were probably a lot of things that other people learned over time that could be helpful to me and there were probably things that I knew that could help someone else," he said, adding that he still regularly attends the meetings. "They have nine meetings a year and I probably go to six. We just chat with each other and give each other tips, you know, tricks of the trade."

"It makes me feel good to look around and say, 'Hey, I'm not alone. There's a whole bunch of folks out there just like me,'" John told me.

Even those who had rare conditions were able to locate one individual or a string of them to serve as role models during and after treatment. For example, Brenda started her sarcoidosis network after not being able to locate a support group for herself, while Patty's family went online and found others with her exceedingly rare neurological disease, Moy-amoya syndrome.

David considers himself exceptionally lucky to have found a fellow brain cancer patient who, like himself, has outlived all of his doctors' predictions. When David, a musician, was diagnosed, he was given six months to live. But while the doctors didn't give him much hope, a man named Matthew in Kansas did. David stumbled on Matthew's story on the Internet and felt compelled to contact him.

"I wrote to him, and I said, 'I saw this online. Is this a mistake or are you really a nine-year survivor of a glioblastoma?'" David said. "He said, 'Yeah, I am.' And I said, 'Well, I don't understand because what I was led to believe is that that's not possible. That, you know, you have six months, if you're lucky maybe a year. And nobody said anything to me about nine years. What's going on?' He says, 'Well, I don't know. I've had treatment. I'm here. I'm living my life. And it's been nine years.'"

"No one had even said that it was possible. For the first time I thought, 'Well, wait a second. If one guy can do it, why can't two?'" David said, adding that he is currently a decade past that original diagnosis and now helps others who are newly diagnosed.

Locating support can be as easy as calling a disease-based organization and asking for a list of support groups in the area. Hospitals and religious organizations also at times offer support groups for individuals with the same condition. A quick Internet search can also track these groups down.

The meetings themselves vary in style, just as those who lead them vary in training and technique. Some have formal structure whereby a learning session is followed by a discussion led by a psychologist or a social worker; others may have a lay leader that changes from week to week.

The bonus of attending such a group is mutual support, meaning that an individual comes to such a meeting seeking support, company, and guidance from others on the same illness path. In turn, those who provide such support receive a boost in self-confidence from being able to help others. Even those who attend but say nothing benefit from learning from others while building a sense of camaraderie. And these public groups are generally free or carry a nominal cost.

But there are downsides to support groups as well. For example, not everyone is comfortable opening up to a group and talking about intimate details in person. Others need more stability, something that may not be present, as members are not required to attend and thus are able to come and go as they

THE FIVE GIFTS OF ILLNESS

please. And all members may not have the same severity of the disease, a potentially frightening development for the newly diagnosed who may encounter someone worse off.

Another option for many, many diseases is the Internet group or message board. Like the in-person support group, these are almost always free and offer many of the same benefits. Another bonus is that one can participate from the comfort of home or, in some cases, from a hospital bed. Unless a scheduled chat is held, these message boards and groups are open twenty-four hours a day, a plus when steroids or scary emotions are causing insomnia at 2 a.m. And participation can be completely anonymous, allowing shy people to express themselves more freely than they feel at a face-to-face group.

The negatives of such Internet-based support options are essentially the same as a more traditional support group, with a few twists. Internet message boards are famous for attracting snake oil salespeople, as well as those who claim to be miraculously cured by changing (fill in the blank) alone. Equally notorious are those who hog the board not only for illness-related issues but also to air every single personal problem that plagues their lives. And sometimes even urgent questions that are posted can linger for days without an answer. For these reasons, some people choose to use the Internet support in addition to a more personal form of support.

Another option for those who prefer a more private or personal form of support is the psychotherapist. Psychologists, psychiatrists, professional counselors, or clinical social workers provide a good alternative to those who aren't into support groups or are looking to work on other personal issues in a private, clinical setting.

The actual experience with a psychotherapist will vary

from person to person, as everyone has a different emotional makeup as well as different issues to deal with. The session will usually take place in a small office and will last a prede-termined amount of time. There are a number of philoso-phies with which psychotherapists affiliate themselves, and the style of treatment will vary accordingly.

The price of psychotherapy is covered for a set period of time by most insurance plans. Therapy prices vary widely and can easily exceed $100 an hour, usually depending upon the area of the country in which it takes place as well as the experience and education level of the individual. If the insurance coverage is not available, a psychotherapist gener-ally can offer a sliding fee scale or payment plans.

Aside from the cost, psychotherapy can have other downsides. Not all psychotherapists were created equally. Some are better able to handle illness issues, while others are more comfortable dealing with other personal problems. In rural or remote areas, there may be few such professionals available or they may not have as much experience as those in urban areas. For these reasons, it may be helpful to ask for references from other patients or from a doctor.

Role models offer another option in support for the newly diagnosed, as well as for those in more extended or permanent survival phases. People who have been on the same illness journey and are a little further down the path can offer wisdom, insight, tips, and support that few others are able to do so. Often, disease-based organizations offer "buddy" programs that match newly diagnosed individuals with specially selected mentors, some of whom have gone through formal or informal training to serve in such a capacity.

As with any form of support, there can be negatives with the buddy system as well. Some buddies are not well trained or may provide unwise medical advice to an individual. At the same time, not all of the people on the same illness path are going to have pleasant, entirely upbeat experiences. Some will suffer setbacks and some will die, potentially leaving the seeker of support feeling more vulnerable. But that's life, not always pleasant or perfect.

Finally, some people find solace in seeking spiritual support from their religious leaders or prayer groups. A pastor, minister, priest, imam, or rabbi is likely to have other individuals in their spiritual care who have met with similar health issues. They can provide solace through prayer and through sharing of religious text at a time when not only the body is under assault but the spirit is as well.

And unlike other forms of support, there is very little downside as long as the religious leader is not advocating relying on prayer alone. As my mother always says, "A little prayer never hurt anyone."

2. Learning about the disease and its treatment options.

When Bill was first diagnosed with lymphoma, he recovered from shock and went into battle mode. First lesson in warfare: Know your enemy. Though he was a cardiac surgeon and had been a doctor for decades, he knew little about the disease attacking his own body. He plunged into research about the disease and his likely treatment options, quickly becoming an expert on the subject. This new passion led him to eventually hold the title of president in a lymphoma research organization.

While not everyone will go as far as Bill did with his

growth in knowledge, it stands to reason that learning as much as possible about a disease and all of its manifestations as well as all possible medical, surgical, and alternative treatment options is a positive step for anyone afflicted with a life-threatening illness. For one, the knowledge helps individuals acclimate to the reality of having a disease, integrate the care for it in their lives, and move through the emotional stage of denial. Second, taking such positive steps can instill a sense of confidence in people who may have felt fearful and uncertain about their future at the point of diagnosis.

In fact, two Swedish researchers published a paper in 2001 on the experience of brain tumor patients and found that understanding the condition was an essential element of coping and therefore should be encouraged. "It is therefore not surprising that information seeking is a recognized and often used coping mechanism that increases both comprehensibility and manageability," the authors wrote. "Information also constituted an unmet need in this study. To listen to patients and to inform them is therefore of utmost importance."

A great first step in the learning process is to contact a disease-specific organization. These organizations exist for virtually every disease, even the rare ones. Sometimes with more common afflictions, there are several organizations to choose from, such as the American Cancer Society, which serves anyone touched by cancer, as well as more specific organizations, such as the International Myeloma Foundation, which serves those affected only by that type of cancer. Some organizations have a number of chapters, many of which carry their own libraries. However, more and more are relying on virtual libraries filled with downloadable patient publications explaining standard and common therapies as well as current news items featuring research breakthroughs and developments in future treatments.

Usually, patient resources are specifically written for the layperson who has little medical knowledge. That said, these publications still can contain words that are unfamiliar or technical in nature. Because of this, it is wise to invest in a good medical or nursing dictionary to have on hand. These can be purchased through an online bookseller or in most brick-and-mortar bookstores.

Books written for patients by patients or by specialists are also excellent resources for the newly diagnosed as well as those further in the illness journey. Building up a personal library made of these reference materials is a good idea. To find a list of available books, plug the name of the condition into an online bookseller. Then use recommendations by others with the condition or check the selections out of a local library to whittle the list to those best to purchase.

For more advanced learning, an excellent source of knowledge is professional journals. Medical and surgical breakthroughs, comparative therapy studies, case studies, causative theories, and more can be found in the pages of these publications, all of which are available to the public in medical school libraries; a few can be found free online, with more available on a pay-per-use basis.

To locate the studies, a government Web site is the best tool. Pubmed.gov contains hundreds of thousands of study listings and abstracts on every conceivable medical and surgical topic. Use the search tool to narrow the scope of information to the topic at hand, scan the available listings, eliminate the impertinent offerings, and print out the rest. Take the list to the medical school library to read the full versions of the studies or locate them online. Be sure to use the medical dictionary to decipher the contents.

Other helpful sites for advanced learning are eMedicine.com and Medscape.com, services of WebMD.com. These free services offer a number of specialty pages that track developments in research and treatments. For example, with Medscape's gastroenterology specialty page, there is a subdivision for inflammatory bowel disease. The latest journal articles are posted on this page along with other available patient resources and continuing medical education programs for physicians. A bonus with this service is that a regular e-mail is sent to the subscriber's mailbox providing updates to the page.

Finally, not all information comes from a book. Some of the best education comes from seminars and events put on by disease-based organizations, most in-person but others broadcast via the Web. The live events also serve as a way to meet others with the condition, while the Webcasts can be watched at the viewer's convenience; both usually provide access to experts in the treatment field.

3. Finding a great team of doctors, surgeons, and support professionals.
This really should be a no-brainer. If you have work done on your home, you want the best construction professional in your price range. If you need work done on your car, you hire the best mechanic you can afford. If you have a disease and need specialized care for your body, are you really going to take the first person who comes along? Of course not.

To form the team, consider what services will be needed. Usually, the members on the roster will include a primary care physician, a medical specialist and/or subspecialist, a surgeon, a physical therapist, and a nutritionist or dietitian. Some diseases won't require all of these members, so narrow or expand the list as necessary.

To find the members, gather recommendations from friends, family members, and support-group members. Look at the applicable disease-based organization's physician listing, and feel around among the membership for who is the best for a particular need. Narrow the list further by taking into consideration aspects like distance to the team member's office, what types of health insurance is accepted by that office, with which hospitals that individual is affiliated, whether that individual is accepting new patients, and how many days or months it takes for a new patient to be seen. Finally, make sure that the health care professional is licensed and certified to practice; this can be done through state medical boards and through specialty board organizations, with affiliated Web sites that usually host search engines to allow patients to run a quick check on their doctors.

For example, I lucked into a fantastic gastroenterologist when I was assigned to his care during my second hospitalization. In the eighteen years since I met him, he has never let me down and is always looking for the best treatment options for me. My subspecialist, a gastroenterologist who exclusively sees patients with my disease, is considered one of the best in the world but is a five-hour drive away; I see him less regularly and was willing to wait six months to schedule an appointment with him. My surgeon just moved to a hospital I do not care for, so I've decided to look for two new surgeons, one to handle emergencies locally and another if the best in the country is not located in the Detroit area. The nutritionist I see not only has my disease but has vast knowledge in the unusual nutritional needs for it.

Following is some profile information on the specific team members that might be needed:

The primary care physician. This doctor specializes in the care of the whole body, from taking care of eye infections to curing foot fungus, from making sure an individual has all his or her vaccinations to suggesting diets. In the United States, these doctors are educated in an undergraduate college, followed by a four-year trip through medical school, and then three to seven years in training periods known as internships and residencies. Family medical specialists, pediatricians, and internists are all primary care physicians.

Often a primary care physician is the first stop along the way to diagnosing a condition; if the physician is unable to make a diagnosis, he or she usually will refer patients to a specialist or subspecialist who can. However, many patients then begin to see the specialist and stop going to the primary care physician for checkups. This is a mistake, as the primary care doctor can help to coordinate care before, during, and after treatment while still caring for the rest of the body that is not affected by the disease.

The medical specialist and subspecialist. A cardiologist works on hearts. An oncologist specializes in the treatment of cancer. A hepatologist treats liver diseases like hepatitis C or cirrhosis. An endocrinologist can help diabetics. A neurologist can treat brain and nervous-system diseases like Parkinson's disease and MS. And so forth and so on. Sometimes an individual needs one or more different specialists or subspecialists to treat the disease and its symptoms.

Whatever the case, these individuals are also extensively schooled, having attended a four-year university and a four-year medical school before devoting several more years toward internships, residencies, and fellowships in their desired fields of expertise. Like other doctors, they also have to continue to learn more about their chosen specialties, earning continuing medical education credits each year and regularly renewing their board certification in their specialties.

Usually this individual is an excellent source of referrals for the other team members. A cardiologist, for example, likely works regularly with cardiac surgeons, dietitians, and rehabilitation specialists. Because of this, he or she likely knows who does the best work in a given area.

The surgeon. While some diseases do not require the work of a surgeon, others use surgery as a first or second line of therapy. Because of this, it is important to not only have a surgeon if one is required but to have one who specializes in surgical intervention for the disease at hand.

A surgeon also goes through extensive education and training, having to survive not only the usual four-year undergraduate and medical schools but also five years of general surgery residency and a few more years in training in the specialized field. For example, a colorectal surgeon will graduate from medical school and then spend five years in a general surgical residency before embarking on another year of training in gut surgery.

If experience is key anywhere in dealing with an illness, it is especially so in the field of surgery. One may not experience the same level of comfort, say, if their brain tumor is removed by an individual who has five of these surgeries in his past as opposed to another who has performed 150 of that procedure.

The physical therapist. Like the surgeon, this is one of those specialties that may not make the roster, as not every disease requires one. And, again, it helps to have one that is experienced and specializes in the disease at hand; the field of physical therapy offers seven subspecialties such as neurologic, orthopedic, and cardiovascular and pulmonary.

In the past, physical therapists required little more than training. Now, however, a physical therapist is required to attend a four-year undergraduate and a two-year master's program in an accredited physical therapy program; some choose to continue into a doctoral program. After a master's level is achieved, they must pass a national licensure examination.

Primary care physicians, surgeons, and specialists at times work with certain physical therapy programs and can refer a patient to a physical therapist when it is required.

The nutritionist or registered dietitian. Again, not every disease will require the use of a nutritionist or registered dietitian. But there is no debate regarding the importance of having a good nutrition program in place after diagnosis and during and after treatment, if for no other reason than to make sure that the basic nutrients, vitamins, and minerals are in the diet. And a nutrition specialist can advise which foods can help or hurt a disease or boost or hinder the efficaciousness of treatments.

A nutritionist is a person who uses the science of nutrition to improve health. There is no accreditation process for nutritionists. Registered dietitians (RDs), on the other hand, must be accredited through the American Dietetic Association (ADA). To attain accreditation, an RD must have completed a four-year degree program that is approved by the ADA. Try to find one who is cognizant of the disease's special needs. For example, some illnesses require a suppression of the immune system or an avoidance of roughage, the opposite advice that a nutrition specialist would normally give for a healthy diet.

One thing to remember when consulting a dietitian or a nutritionist is that insurance doesn't always cover the cost. It might be wise to see if such a visit is covered before making an appointment.

After the team is assembled and treatment has begun, make sure all of the players are on the same page, keeping each updated with any changes in medication and health as is required. Continue to do so after treatment concludes and survival continues in the years ahead.

One important thing to remember for all chronic and acute life-threatening illness patients and survivors is that health surveillance must continue even when the threat of death has passed. Too often, individuals finish therapy or recover from surgery and are so eager to resume their previous lives that they put off or purposely don't make plans to submit to regular health checks afterward. These appointments and tests are crucial to check for relapse or recurrence, as well as to ensure continuing health. Because of this, the health care team should work together to develop a plan of action *before* the last treatment appointment occurs.

Finally, realize that no team member has a lifetime contract. Differences in personality, professional failure, relocation on either party's part, or insurance issues may prompt a parting of the ways. When this occurs, it is important to be as upfront about it as possible, with kindness and dignity, of course. Explain the situation and request that the necessary records be sent to the next professional. Ask that the two professionals to confer on the treatment.

4. Handling friends and family.

While a disease happens directly to one person, it has a ripple effect on the individuals in their lives as well. The spouses and children suffer, as do brothers, sisters, and parents. Extended family members, friends, coworkers, and acquaintances all can be affected by the illness.

Realize right from the start that not everyone has experience with life-threatening illness and therefore at times is unsure of what to do or how to react. More than likely, they will feel helpless and will want to do or say something to ease the unwieldy burden that illness presents to the individual experiencing it. Capitalize on this by letting them know how they can help, but be firm with boundaries, as sometimes these feelings can spur an individual to impose their thoughts, feelings, and actions in a way that is intrusive and unwelcome.

From the point of diagnosis, illness can be overwhelming for a number of reasons to all of those who know the patient. Because of this, communicating the diagnosis can be too difficult for the individual who has yet to wrap his or her mind around what is happening; explaining the finding to several others becomes an insurmountable task.

For this reason, it may be helpful to designate a trusted friend or relative to call others to relate the news.

As treatments progressed, some found it helpful to send out regular e-mail treatment updates to those closest to them, while others created blogs for just this reason. Beth is one who did the latter. During her diagnostic period, in the time leading up to the surgery to remove the tumor pressing on her brain stem, on the day of the surgery, and during her recovery, a blog space provided by the hospital where she was treated was updated by her and by family members to keep others apprised of developments. This allowed friends and family to be a part of the action without constant telephone contact.

Because some loved ones will want to do something—anything—to help and because possible physical limitation imposed by treatments may make maintaining a normal life difficult, it makes sense to assign tasks to those more than willing to help pick up the slack. Household chores, child care, errands, and other regular tasks can be assigned to willing family members, friends, and neighbors who are eager to help out. Again, be clear and specific about what needs to be done and the time frame in which it should be complete.

As briefly mentioned, be sure to set boundaries as well. Some loved ones will go beyond their roles and seriously intrude in their zeal to help, arguing with doctors or over-stepping logical boundaries in helping out with personal matters. One woman, for example, came home from a hospital stay to find that the furniture had been rearranged—not something she had requested but something that a loved one had done in an effort to help. Realize that loved ones may be acting out of great love and great fear, as a threat to a loved one's life can be as bad or worse as a similarly grave threat to one's own. Be gentle but firm about what is appropriate and move on.

Also realize that the experience of illness cannot be shared. Because of this, some misunderstandings may arise. A common one regards the need to communicate a shared experience with others. For example, a spouse may feel threatened by a partner's new friendship with someone who has suffered similarly, asking why matters regarding the disease cannot be shared with him or her on the same level.

Another misunderstanding involves family members and friends who think that life returns to pre-illness normality after treatment concludes. One 1995 study by Dr. Sarah Auchincloss about life after gynecologic cancer confirmed this finding, saying that sentiment is often expressed to patients by others that the end of treatment should be a time of celebration as "normal" life returns. "In reality, the patient may not be able to return to normal life as she knew it, because the cancer experience is life changing," Auchincloss wrote. Another paper on the subject, this one written in 1992 by Susan Leigh, a nurse, further states that survivorship can be complicated by these feelings, as "survivors are reminded that they are 'so lucky to be alive,' many are hesitant to bring up problems or worries for fear or being viewed as ungrateful or demanding."

If either of these situations occurs, it may be helpful to hand loved ones this book or other material to foster a better understanding of survivorship in them or to suggest that they, too, seek a support group as caregivers.

5. *Adjusting to physical limitations.*

Every disease has them, if even small ones limited to the treatment phase. Physical limitations can be as seemingly insignificant as having to navigate the hospital hallways with an unwieldy IV pole for a short time or as large and permanent as having to navigate the world without sight or with paralysis due to treatment complications or the disease itself. Whatever the case, survivors interviewed for this book found it important for both their mental and physical health to mourn the physical losses but also, and perhaps more importantly, to adapt to the changes as best as possible.

Usually these limitations begin around diagnosis and treatment. Because of this, it creates another reason to seek the company of those who have been through the same illness experience. As John found in his ostomy support group, these individuals can be a sounding board for commiseration of these limitations as well as a source of wisdom and tips regarding confronting the task of navigating the world with them. Where to find a good wig shop before chemo starts, how to find fashionable health alert bracelets or attractive kit covers for blood glucose testing machines, how to create reminders for taking medication, what to take to the hospital for a more comfortable stay—this is all information that experienced patients can share with the newly diagnosed.

Another great source for patients of all diseases looking to surmount physical limitations is the Internet. Sites exist for all of the above concerns. With a few keystrokes on a good search engine, a patient can find everything from a listing of all public rest stops during a highway trip to local sources of fashionable wheelchair accessories.

After treatment concludes, incorporate the more permanent changes in ability into daily life, no matter what the limitation is. This doesn't mean that one ignores the obvious disability, nor does it mean that one remains confined to home. Instead, it means figuring out what is needed to pursue all dreams and to live the remaining days, months, and years as fully as possible. After all, isn't that what living is about?

Tonda has learned this. Traveling for her and her family used to be done without much thought. But then her Parkinson's disease left her shuffling and unsteady on her feet, causing her to rely on a wheelchair to get around during more extensive distances. However, she and her children now simply plan activities in which they know she can participate. Recently, her daughter and daughter-in-law planned a trip to Ecuador. It was a given that Tonda would go with them. They considered wheelchair-accessible accommodations and sightseeing options. As this was being discussed, Tonda told me that she realized in that moment that not only had her children grown in their compassion but that her world had grown in opportunities she thought she had lost.

"They just didn't even think about leaving me out. I had already taken myself out of the picture. They said, 'Oh, no, you're coming. We'll do this. It'll be great,'" Tonda recalled. "And I thought right then and there, 'Oh, my life's not over.'"

6. Adopt new health strategies.
Just as it was important to learn about a disease and its treatments options after diagnosis and during the treatment phase, it is equally essential to adopt new health strategies and drop bad habits to give the body the best chance at

health in all stages of survival. For many people who have been diagnosed with a life-threatening illness, the idea of living the rest of their life in optimum health is a no-brainer, as they don't want to waste their second chance at life.

Sometimes it is simple to figure out what to avoid. Smoking should be eliminated from everyone's life, and alcohol intake should be kept in moderation, if used at all. But it is not always easy to figure out what is best and why it is best. We've all heard, for example, that red meat is "bad," but did you ever stop to ask why that is? Some nutrition experts point to higher levels of animal fats and hormones in most red meat sources. However, there are hormone-free, organically raised animals that produce cuts of red meat with lower levels of animal fat than some breeds of fowl. And with a little moderation and careful selection, this important protein source can be safely consumed by an individual trying to combat anemia while avoiding heart disease, for example.

In the same vein, certain lifestyle factors can help keep a disease in check or cause a flare-up, and it is important to know which is which. To do so, it is important to use those same information-gathering muscles developed in point 2 to find the best health strategies to adopt during treatment and in the months and years after the last bandage is removed. Take this information to your health care team, ask questions, and formulate a plan together to achieve the best possible health. Here are a few suggestions of areas to cover:

- *Exercise.* Everyone agrees that exercise is a component of good health, but sometimes it is difficult to know which exercise is the best to do given specific circumstances.

For example, some treatments such as the use of corti-costeroids can cause osteoporosis, and weight-bearing exercise can help prevent this loss from happening by building bone mass. Other times certain exercises can aggravate a condition. Find out which is best before signing up for a personal trainer.

- *Regular checkups.* Nearly all diseases require follow-up exams, not only to adjust medications but also to check for recurrences. Find out what the optimum schedule is for such meetings, as well as which tests should be performed regularly. Come to these appointments pre-pared with any question about further steps to be taken to prevent recurrence and to bolster health.

- *Nutrition.* Many times people will meet with a nutri-tionist or dietitian before and during treatment but will neglect to revisit this individual after treatment has concluded. Just as important as having a body nutritionally sound to fight the disease is continuing this vigilance after a cure or remission has been achieved.

- *Vitamins and supplements.* While it seems that this is something that is covered during that trip to the nutri-tionist, this may also be a bit of information better covered by the specialist. That's because some vitamins and minerals have been shown to cut the risk of recur-rence of a disease or prevent other related diseases from occurring. For example, colon cancer is a risk for individuals with inflammatory bowel disease. At the same time, calcium, vitamin D, and folic acid have been shown to trim the risk of developing this cancer. It makes sense for an inflammatory bowel disease patient to ask a doctor about taking such supplements on a regular basis, and the same is true for patients with other diseases.

While it is important to take these steps to ensure future health, it is also important to not dwell on them or obsess about them to the point of misery. Develop the sound habits to the point where they become second nature and forget about it. Also be sure to forgive yourself about intentional or unintentional departures from the plan. One flame-grilled burger and basket of greasy onion rings is not going to kill a person any more than missing a few doses of vitamins will. Life is meant to be lived, even with a few screwups every now and then.

7. Facing fear of recurrence or worsening symptoms.

First, it is important to recognize that fear is part and parcel of the illness experience. Fear is often the emotion that drives many to that first doctor's visit when symptoms arise and a diagnosis is in the offing. Conversely, it can be the predominant feeling that keeps some from even going to the doctor in the first place, as such a diagnosis is what they hope to avoid. Fear is also the natural emotional response felt during treatment when one's life hangs in the balance.

Sometimes it continues to haunt a patient in the months and years after active treatment ends. Fear repeats for some as new symptoms suggest recurrence or a worsening of a disease or as regular checkups and ensuing test results are anticipated.

And the research backs up the notion that this fear in illness is a common one. In a paper published in 2001, Dr. James

Brennan sites a study of 600 cancer patients in remission that found that the most commonly identified cancer-related problem they faced was fear or uncertainty about the future. A 2003 study of ovarian cancer survivors also found that a common theme the women faced was fear of recurrence. The researchers wrote, "The nature of the illness and the severity of the treatments create stress and uncertainty of living with chronic life threatening illness. Recurrence is especially diffi-cult as it leaves a cloud over life and a feeling of when, not if."

Because fear can sometimes stop people from making sound health choices, it is important to deal with the cir-cumstances head-on and develop a plan for dealing with the threat of recurrence and the fear surrounding it. Two helpful actions to incorporate can be found in points 1 and 2 above. Revisit that support group or the therapist to discuss the feeling and to learn about what can be done to accomplish health objectives while moving through fear. Also allow room to feel the emotion. It's okay to be a raging bitch or bastard during this time.

8. Making life plans while living with uncertainty.
Life didn't stop because of disease, and neither should you stop living it. Be sure to accommodate the changes in life that the disease has ushered while accomplishing those old dreams and making new ones. Be prepared with a plan B when making plans for the future, and go easy on time lines by which to accomplish goals. You have some living to do.

SUGGESTIONS FOR SOCIETY

Before we get to the specific recommendations for society

regarding moving the state of survivorship forward, it might be important to understand where we have been in terms of the history of survivorship in recent years. Within the past two decades, there has been a slow and subtle awakening of sorts in general society to the importance and the intricacy of the needs of survivors of life-threatening illness. For centuries, the emphasis on disease was the physical devastation left in the wake. But as incident rates remained the same and death tolls dropped, the emotional, spiritual, and social price of illness became known.

The wheels began to turn more rapidly in the mid-1980s, around the time that Dr. Fitzhugh Mullan wrote his landmark paper, "Seasons of Survival: Reflections of a Physician with Cancer." The paper, written movingly and succinctly in just over three pages, described three different phases of survival, as outlined in chapter 3. Among other things, it called attention to the very real concerns of the cancer survivor and called for the formation of a cancer survivorship organization, complete with a newsletter and alumni association. Shortly afterward, the National Coalition for Cancer Survivorship (NCCS) was launched. Almost immediately, the NCCS began the dialogue on cancer's long-standing impact, in part by contributing a section on survivorship in the Americans with Disabilities Act of 1990.

Slowly, more and more people joined the movement. Organizations were formed. The emotional, spiritual, and social needs of the survivor—then formally defined by the NCCS as "from the moment of diagnosis and for the balance of life, an individual diagnosed with cancer is a survivor"—were identified. Organizations like Gilda's Club and the Lance Armstrong Foundation (LAF), for example, were formed independently to help provide those services.

As I mentioned in the second chapter, the LAF paired with the CDC in a joint, groundbreaking, seventy-seven-page document, *A National Action Plan for Cancer Survivorship: Advancing Public Health Strategies*. The document was written in 2004 in response to one line in a huge publication issued by the Office of the Surgeon General, *Healthy People 2010* (the Healthy People campaign began in 1979 and serves to set benchmarks for advancing public health initiatives in disease control and prevention). The mention of survivorship issues—"Increase the proportion of cancer survivors who are living 5 years or longer after diagnosis"—was a first for the Healthy People campaign in that survivors had not before been mentioned for cancer or any disease. This line set off the collaborative efforts to further set new goals to achieve in the growing efforts to advance cancer survivorship.

Proposing the use of both public agencies and private cancer organizations, the plan identified several medical and nonmedical needs of the cancer survivorship community and designated strategies to address these needs in four areas of public health: surveillance and applied research; communication, education, and training; programs, policies, and infrastructure; and access to quality care and services. The plan made several recommendations for specific goals to be accomplished through further collaborative efforts of governmental agencies and private organizations. The following are just a few of the actions that were recommended in the document:

- Develop an infrastructure for a comprehensive database on cancer survivorship.

- Develop and maintain patient navigation systems that can facilitate optimum care for cancer survivors.
- Establish and support clinical practice guidelines for each stage of cancer survivorship.
- Develop and disseminate public education programs that empower cancer survivors to make informed decisions.
- Conduct research on preventative interventions to evaluate their impact on issues related to cancer survivorship.
- Establish and support clinical practice guidelines for each stage of cancer survivorship.
- Educate policy and decision makers about the role and value of long-term follow-up care, quality-of-life issues, legal needs, clinical trials, and ancillary services for cancer survivors.
- Establish and disseminate support for quality and timely service provision to cancer survivors.

The issuance of that excellent report brings us to the current era and highlights the first of five recommendations for the larger community in terms of enhancing and moving forward the cause of survivorship while meeting survivors' needs, as identified by both patients and experts in the field.

1. Recognize that cancer is not the only disease that produces survivors.

While the efforts of the cancer community in advancing the cause of survivors have been trailblazing and noteworthy, there is not nearly the same level of recognition in well individuals or even in some cancer survivors of the challenges faced by the survivors of other life-threatening illness. Of all of the diseases mentioned in *Healthy People 2010* except for cancer, not one had a subsection on issues faced by survivors, much less a large collaborative report advocating major changes in society to meet their needs. Even the number one killer of adults in the United States, heart disease, had no similar attention paid to it, no mention of increasing the proportion of five-year survivors. Nor was there an action plan formulated for survivors of heart disease and stroke, only a 14-page report entitled "A Public Health Action Plan to Prevent Heart Disease and Stroke."

But, as an example, let's look at the impact on the larger population of coronary heart disease and stroke, using the government's own figures. A recent report by the Office of Disease Prevention and Health Promotion stated, "Heart disease and stroke are major causes of illness and disability and are significant contributors to healthcare costs and disease-related economic losses. The burden of heart disease and stroke is projected to cost more than $351 billion in 2003 and to grow in the coming decades." The office further projected that the human toll for heart disease will increase sharply between 2010 and 2030 and that the population of heart disease survivors is expected to grow at a much faster rate than the U.S. population as a whole.

Currently, the picture is relatively bleak. Coronary heart disease, the most common form of cardiovascular disease, strikes 12 million Americans, while another 4 million have cerebrovascular disease such as stroke, the third leading cause of death in the United States. And these conditions generally are not one-time major heart attacks leading to death or single massive, fatal strokes, nor are they one-time minor incidents. Instead, these diseases tend to become chronic, progressive illnesses. In the United States, about 50 percent of all heart attacks and 70 percent of coronary heart disease deaths occur in individuals with prior symptoms of cardiovascular disease. The risk for heart attack and death among persons with established coronary heart disease or other atherosclerotic disease is five to seven times higher than among the general population. In other words, individuals having a heart attack or stroke most likely survive such events only to experience another or more before they are eventually killed by one.

While it is not a huge leap to say that these widely prevalent diseases very likely provoke similar emotional and social concerns that cancer survivors face, the psychological evidence regarding survivorship in heart disease is in the comparatively nascent stages of study, while piles of research regarding the physical, psychological, social, and spiritual issues of cancer survivorship have existed for more than a couple of decades. In fact, the August 2006 issue of the *Harvard Heart Letter* emphasized that 10 percent of survivors of heart disease and heart attacks suffer from post-traumatic stress disorder; the disorder, the article said, has been seen in others who have gone through heart transplant or experienced heart surgery and stroke. A Reuters article quoting the editor of the letter said that the psychological disorder is similar to that felt by cancer patients, a long-known psychological complication of that disease. "There can be some long-term emotional or psychological consequences of having a heart attack," the editor was quoted as saying.

And yet, despite the growing number of heart disease and stroke survivors, there is a noticeable gap in support services and study relative to the emotional complications suffered by this population. Sure, there are the same acute survival services like support groups, cooking classes, education events, and fund-raisers for heart attack and stroke survivors, but the efforts to provide services for those in extended and permanent survival are not as apparent, if existent at all.

Outside of cancer, the same could be said of almost any of the diseases that most commonly kill Americans. This will likely change over time as patient organizations for non-cancerous diseases demand more study on the subject of the emotional, spiritual, and social effects of life-threatening disease, using the findings to create programs that follow in the pioneering footsteps of cancer organizations.

2. Address the greater need for support services in the second and third season of survivorship.

When an individual is diagnosed with just about any illness, there is a support organization or a support group to help the person in dealing with the shock of the diagnosis and in learning about the disease and its treatments. Again, this will depend on where the individual is located and the commonality of the disease, but even with rare diseases in rural areas, the Internet communities are there to greet a person and to help him or her on their way through treatment.

And this has been a big change in the last two decades. When Dr. Fitzhugh Mullan wrote his landmark paper, there was one organization, I Can Cope, that helped with supportive services for the cancer survivor. Since then, he has seen a "flowering" of organizations that help with this aspect of patient care. Dr. Mullan, one of the founders of the National Coalition of Cancer Survivors and an author of several books, including *Charting the Journey: An Almanac of Practical Resources for Cancer Survivors* and *Big Doctoring in America*, stated during an interview for this book, "I think there's been a proliferation of cancer organizations, pretty good cancer support groups and support organizations. Though without attempting to quantify how much better it's being met or what percent is being met, I think I can say very comfortably that this part of the world is much better populated with organizations and programs that take into account the psychological, social, as well as medical needs of cancer patients."

But as treatment concludes and the survivor makes the transition from active care to follow-up, the support that was available during the active phase of the diagnosis and treatment falls away. For example, when an individual has a heart attack and later undergoes multiple bypass surgery, he or she is cared for rather intensively by doctors and nurses and cardiac rehabilitation specialists for several months. After the person heals more and requires less immediate care, the person begins to see the medical care team less frequently. It is not uncommon during this time for the patient to feel depression as the medical and therapeutic support, care, and attention he or she received drops away and the emotional, spiritual, and social needs remain.

As another example, an individual with a chronic condition who has been in remission for years may experience long-term effects from treatment or puzzling symptoms that reawaken the fear of recurrence or relapse. Yet when he or she turns for help, the person finds that the support group he or she once attended is populated by individuals who are newly diagnosed or who are still in treatment and not able to relate to someone so advanced in the experience.

And this, says Dr. Betty Ferrell, a research scientist at the City of Hope National Medical Center and author of several papers on cancer survivorship, is a massive problem that is confronting the health care community and society in general. For years, people just died of diseases from which they are now being saved. There was no issue of survivorship because there were no survivors. But within the last few decades, patients who have survived serious illnesses such as diabetes, heart disease, and cancer want to know how to live the rest of their lives in this relatively uncharted territory.

"We have the burden of our blessings. We have a real challenge as a society and as certainly the medical community of how can we treat and support these lives that are now really very long lives," Ferrell said in an interview for this book. "It's a huge, huge issue."

"What society can do is wake up to this reality that with our aging population and with the advances that have been made in medical science that we now have a society of people living with chronic illness and we have to take that seriously," she said later in the interview. "We have to really prepare health care systems and social systems now."

Though there are notable exceptions, patient organizations for the most part fail to offer programs and specific services for this group of survivors, despite a need that Ferrell says is very real. In the extended and permanent phases of survival, the concerns change from side effects and coping with treatments to physical aftereffects of treatments, posttraumatic stress, and fear of relapse or recurrence. Few patient organizations are equipped to deal with these needs.

Ferrell points to some work that is being done in this area, especially in helping patients make meaning of their illness experience; specifically, she said two psychiatrists at major cancer institutions are studying therapeutic interventions involving meaning making in illness, in part because patients with serious illness often lose their sense of meaning in life even while their bodies are recovering from the trauma of the treatment. "We fix the most important pieces, but people are still left somewhat broken and traumatized from these experiences," Ferrell said.

For this reason, it behooves society at large and patient organizations in particular to foster a greater effort in studying the emotional, spiritual, and social aspects for the extended and permanent phases of survival of all life-threatening diseases. Using the results of the studies, new programs can be formulated to best serve these survivors.

3. Address the greater need for easily accessible clearinghouses of information for patients of all illnesses.
Hope inspires confidence and knowledge inspires both. Never is this truer than with illness. There is no argument to the fact that the well-educated patient is better suited to face the challenges of life with illness than one who is in the dark about everything from treatment options to incorporating lifestyle changes to improve the quality of life. Studies also show that the better informed a patient is about his or her disease and treatment options, the more compliant he or she is with the prescribed therapy.

And yet information for various diseases varies from source to source, potentially leading to an ill-informed patient. Books and pamphlets can rapidly become outdated with advances in treatment options or discoveries about the way a disease occurs. Even the Internet, arguably the most easily updated source for information, can be spotty with regard to consistent information, with some sites offering a plethora of pages devoted to the latest developments and others less meticulously maintained.

Let's take my condition, Crohn's disease, as an example, and look at the government information available for people with it. The National Institutes of Health is divided into a number of smaller offices and divisions, with its home Web site listing all of them. During a search for Crohn's disease, the individual is directed to three smaller offices, including the National Institute for Diabetes and Digestive and Kidney Diseases (NIDDK), National Institute of Arthritis and Musculoskeletal and Skin Diseases (NIAMS), and the National Digestive Disease Information Clearinghouse (NDDIC). Sounds quite formidable, right?

A closer look, however, shows that this is an inaccurate perception with regard to the information related to Crohn's. At this writing, the information that the NIDDK provided was about two years out-of-date, leaving off at least three newly developed medications; in addition, the information on surgery and nutrition was sorely lacking, and there was no information on vitamin and mineral nutritional supplements. The site also provided three links to patient organizations, including one very small organization for children who lived in New York and had the disease, clearly of little use for 90 percent of the patient body who are adults or the vast majority of the pediatric patient body who do not live in New York.

The main NIH site directed the information-seeking user to a link regarding gastrointestinal diseases and bone disease. Though there was no information regarding known skeletal complications on the main information sheet provided through the NIDDK, this link looked promising. However, it was a dead link, and no such information could be found through a search at the NIAMS site. A further link to statistics on gastrointestinal diseases at the NIDDC found that the government was still quoting thirty-year-old statistical incidence rates on some diseases when newer, more reliable sources are available through narrow searches on another governmental Web site, pubmed.gov.

While the government site arguably should be an excellent resource and isn't, patients also rely upon information provided by some patient organizations. Even then, however, the information can be out-of-date or biased in its presentation. For example, a patient organization that supplied grant funding for a certain research project may trumpet the results of that study to bolster the organization's credibility, while more significant findings that were not related to grant funding will receive less attention.

Further, information on all diseases cannot be entirely medically or surgically based. As we have learned in the pages of this book thus far, the experience of serious illness carries with it psychological, social, spiritual, and emotional aspects. People coping with these diseases need to know that what they are experiencing in these areas of their lives is par for the course. They also need to know what to do when they experience it.

Finally, all of the information—medical, surgical, psychological, social, spiritual, and emotional—needs to be portrayed in an accurate light, not just with positive brushstrokes. Dr. Pam McGrath said that people who are experiencing serious illness want to see the entire picture, good and bad.

"It's that balancing. It's about allowing people the

permission to see all the positive and the negative," she said in an interview. "To just paint the positive is really as bad as to just paint the negative."

Dr. Karen Dow Meneses, Pegasus Professor, Beat and Jill Kahli Endowed Chair in Oncology Nursing at the University of Central Florida School of Nursing, and the author of several academic papers on the subject of the experience of cancer, feels that patient education as a whole has been somewhat neglected. Long involved in cancer care, she feels this is a crucial element in patient care and an area that needs to be addressed. "We have a great deal of information available, particularly in the U.S. It is puzzling as to why this info does not get to those who need it most. We have a long way to go in terms of helping those cancer survivors 'lost in transition,'" she wrote in an e-mail for this book. She added that low-tech options like telephone counseling and advocacy groups that really stress the education and support aspects of illnesses as well as more high-tech choices like improving online and electronic support groups and creating online illness-related blogs should be considered as ways to improve educational opportunities for survivors.

Therefore, patient organizations and governmental agencies need to work more closely together on developing accurate, up-to-date, and well-stocked clearinghouse information systems for all life-threatening illnesses. Also, the information provided must be easily accessible and easily understood. Not every individual who is diagnosed today with a chronic or acute life-threatening illness will have the wherewithal to find the information that will guide them to lifesaving therapies or other supportive treatments, nor will they have the same educational background.

Further, all clearinghouses that are developed must include easily located portals, but also the information must be written at a level that is equally easily understood by the majority of the patients. Public education campaigns can help patients find the sites of the clearinghouses, while mentors trained by the patient organizations could help individuals locate and understand the information regarding the illness and current treatment options.

4. Train doctors to refer patients for emotional, spiritual, and social support.

A physician is usually the first and most common contact a patient has while being diagnosed and treated for a life-threatening illness. Logically, patients look to the doctor for answers about a wide range of questions regarding their return to health, from discussing treatment options to conferring about long-term therapy effects. Because of this conversation about the effects of the disease in their lives, it is not unusual for patients to bring up the impact of the illness on their emotional, spiritual, and social being.

However, some doctors are uncomfortable dealing with issues outside of the physical realm. They most likely weren't educated in these aspects of illness, nor were they trained to find solutions for them. Because of this, some doctors will steer conversation away from these very real aspects of the disease experience or are unable to direct the patient to the appropriate supportive services, leaving some patients to flounder in the wake of these effects. Providing the physicians with the tools to refer patients to the appropriate sources for education and support becomes vital for the well-being of the entire patient.

Dow Meneses feels the team approach works best in this area. "In cancer care, the team approach works well. Most of the follow up after treatment are with oncologists and primary care physicians. It seems unrealistic that primary care docs have this information, but they most certainly could use the information," she wrote.

Such training for doctors can come from many sources. Governmental agencies can include these lessons as an aspect of the public awareness campaigns, patient organizations can provide information to specialists who treat the illness, and medical boards can include the information as a part of the required continuing medical education programs they host.

5. Encourage media and entertainment change with the portrayal of the illness experience.

Originally, this wasn't going to be a part of the recommendations, but as I was wrapping up the writing of the book, another example of the media focusing on the gloomier part of the illness experience came across my kitchen table.

In a single Sunday newspaper, the *Detroit Free Press* ran not one but two major stories on individuals who are essentially terminally ill with cancer. The first, a follow-up to a story that ran almost two full pages long in June 2006, documented the recurrence of sarcoma in a child whose mother had died three years earlier of unspecified intestinal and liver disease and whose father was bravely caring for her; the child had been given a less than 10 percent chance of surviving the recurrence. The second story, about a security guard for a local professional sports team who is battling a rare cancer of the pancreas and biliary system, started on the cover of the sports section and continued for a full page inside; his chance of surviving was set at 7 percent. On the very same day, CNN's Web site carried a story of a teenage girl who was terminally ill with cancer and whose wish for a wedding was going to be granted. In none of these news sources nor in other such publications that day were there stories about people who had suffered from cancer or any other major illness and survived, this despite the fact that more and more people do so.

Being a journalist for the past eighteen years and being a medical writer for almost a decade, I can safely say that a balance of stories needs to be a goal for all health and general news editors, whether in the print or broadcast media. People can and do survive life-threatening illnesses every day. Their stories are no less compelling than those who do not survive.

The same can be said of the entertainment industry. Told well, survival stories are just as if not more moving as those where illness wins and the protagonist dies. They also serve a social purpose of providing hope to those who need it.

Obviously, there are more actions to further survivorship that can be done by both the individual and society. Because of this, these lists simply serve as the starting point in the discussion of survivorship in America, a serious situation that the country and the world will likely address in the coming years.

REFERENCES

Following is a list of the papers and books consulted for the research in this book.

Albaugh, Jeffrey A. "Spirituality and Life-Threatening Illness: A Phenomenologic Study." *Oncology Nursing Forum* 30 (4), July–August 2003, pp. 593–598.

Andersen, Barbara L. "Surviving Cancer." *Cancer* 74 (4), August 1994, pp. 1484–1495.

Andersen, Barbara L., Barrie Anderson, and Charles de Prosse. "Controlled Prospective Longitudinal Study of Women with Cancer: II. Psychological Outcomes." *Journal of Consulting and Clinical Psychology* 57 (6), July 1989, pp. 692–697.

Anderson, Barrie, and Susan Lutgendorf. "Quality of Life in Gynecologic Cancer Survivors." *CA—A Cancer Journal for Clinicians*. 47, July–August 1997, pp. 218–225.

Armstrong, Lance, with Sally Jenkins. *It's Not about the Bike: My Journey Back to Life*. New York: G. P. Putnam's and Sons, 2000.

———. *Every Second Counts*. New York: Broadway Books, 2003.

Auchincloss, Sarah S. "After Treatment: Psychological Issues in Gynecologic Cancer Survivorship." *Cancer* 76 (10), November 1995, pp. 2117–2124.

Bernardin, Joseph Cardinal. *The Journey to Peace: Reflections on Faith, Embracing Suffering, and Finding New Life*. New York: Image Books, 2003.

————. *The Gift of Peace: Personal Reflections*. Chicago: Loyola Press, 1997.

Bloom, Joan. "Surviving and Thriving?" *Psycho-Oncology* 11 (2), March–April 2002, pp. 89–92.

Bloom, Joan, Susan L. Stewart, Subo Chang, and Priscilla J. Banks. "Then and Now: Quality of Life of Young Breast Cancer Survivors." *Psycho-Oncology* 13 (3), March 2004, pp. 147–160.

Brennan, James. "Adjustment to Cancer—Coping or Personal Transition?" *Psycho-Oncology* 10, 2001, pp. 1–18.

Broyard, Anatole. *Intoxicated by My Illness and Other Writings on Life and Death*. New York: Fawcett Columbine, 1992.

Bushkin, Ellyn. "Signposts of Survivorship." *Oncology Nursing Forum* 22 (3), April 1995, pp. 537–543.

Carter, Barbara J. "Long-term Survivors of Breast Cancer." *Cancer Nursing* 16 (5), October 1992, pp. 354–361.

Cella, David F., and Susan Tross. "Psychological Adjustment to Survival from Hodgkin's Disease." *Journal of Consulting and Clinical Psychology* 54 (5), October 1986, pp. 616–622.

Centers for Disease Control and Prevention and the Lance Armstrong Foundation, cosponsors. "A National Action Plan for Cancer Survivorship: Advancing Public Health Strategies," April 2004.

Dow, Karen Hassey. "The Enduring Seasons of Survival." *Oncology Nursing Forum* 17 (4), July–August 1990, pp. 511–516.

Dow, Karen Hassey, Betty R. Ferrell, Mel R. Haberman, and Linda Eaton. "The Meaning and Quality of Life in Cancer Survivorship." *Oncology Nursing Forum* 26 (3), April 1999, pp. 519–528.

Ferrell, Betty R., and Karen Hassey Dow. "Portraits of Cancer Survivorship: A Glimpse through the Lens of Survivors' Eyes." *Cancer Practice* 4 (2), March–April 1996, pp. 76–80.

Ferrell, Betty R., Karen Hassey Dow, Susan Leigh, John Ly, and Pratheepan Gulasekaram. "Quality of Life in Long-term Cancer Survivors." *Oncology Nursing Forum* 22 (6), July 1995, pp. 915–922.

Ferrell, Betty R., Stephany L. Smith, Gloria Juarez, and Cindy Melancon. "Meaning of Illness and Spirituality in Ovarian Cancer Survivors." *Oncology Nursing Forum* 30 (2), March–April 2003, pp. 249–257.

Fox, Michael J. *Lucky Man: A Memoir*. New York: Hyperion, 2002.

Frank, Arthur. *At the Will of the Body: Reflections on Illness*. Boston and New York: Mariner Books, 1991.

Frankl, Viktor E. *Man's Search for Meaning*. Boston: Beacon Press, 1959.

Groopman, Jerome. *The Anatomy of Hope: How People Prevail in the Face of Illness*. New York: Random House, 2004.

Handler, Evan. *Time on Fire: My Comedy of Terrors*. Boston and New York: Little, Brown and Company, 1996.

Kleinman, Arthur. *The Illness Narratives: Suffering, Healing and the Human Condition*. New York: Basic Books, 1988.

Kübler-Ross, Elisabeth. *On Death and Dying*. New York: Macmillan, 1969.

Kübler-Ross, Elisabeth, and David Kessler. *Life Lessons.* New York: Touchstone, 2000.

———. *On Grief and Grieving.* New York: Scribner, 2005.

Kushner, Harold S. *When Bad Things Happen to Good People.* New York: Avon Books, 1981.

LaTour, Kathy. *The Breast Cancer Companion.* New York: Avon Books, 1993.

Leigh, Susan. "Myths, Monsters, and Magic: Personal Perspectives and Professional Challenges of Survival." *Oncology Nursing Forum* 19 (10), November–December 1992, pp. 1475–1480.

Lindsey, Elizabeth. "Health within Illness: Experiences of Chronically Ill/Disabled People." *Journal of Advanced Nursing* 24 (3), September 1996, 465–472.

Little, Miles, Christopher Jordens, Kim Paul, and Emma-Jane Sayers. *Surviving Survival: Life after Cancer.* New South Wales, Australia: Choice Books, 2001.

Little, Miles, Kim Paul, Christopher F. C. Jordens, and Emma-Jane Sayers. "Survivorship and Discourses of Identity." *Psycho-Oncology* 11(2), March–April 2002, pp. 170–178.

Little, Miles, and Emma-Jane Sayers. "While There's Life: Hope and the Experience of Cancer." *Social Science & Medicine* 59(6), September 2004, pp. 1329–1337.

Loescher, Lois J., Deborah Welch-McCaffrey, Susan A. Leigh, Barbara Hoffman, and Frank L. Meyskens, Jr. "Surviving Adult Cancers, Part 1: Physiologic Effects." *Annals of Internal Medicine* 111 (5), September 1989, 411–432.

McColl, Mary Ann, Jerome Bickenbach, Jane Johnston, Sharon Nishi-hama, Millard Schumaker, Karen Smith, Marsha Smith, and Brian Yealland. "Changes in Spiritual Beliefs after Traumatic Disability."

Archives of Physical Medicine and Rehabilitation 81 (6), June 200 [AU: Please provide last year in date], pp. 817–823.

McGrath, Pam. "Positive Outcomes for Survivors of Haematological Malignancies from a Spiritual Perspective." *International Journal of Nursing Practice* 10 (6), December 2004, pp. 280–291.

———. "Reflections on Serious Illness as Spiritual Journey by Survivors of Haematological Malignancies." *European Journal of Cancer Care* 13 (3), July 2004, pp. 227–237.

"The Burden of 'RA RA' Positive: Survivors' and Hospice Patients' Reflections on Maintaining a Positive Attitude to Serious Illness." *Supportive Care in Cancer* 12 (1), January 2004, 25–33.

Mullan, Fitzhugh. "Seasons of Survival: Reflections of a Physician with Cancer." *New England Journal of Medicine* 313 (4), July 1985, pp. 270–273.

———. "Re-entry: The Educational Needs of the Cancer Survivor." *Health Education Quarterly* 10 Supplement, Spring 1984, pp. 88–94.

Nilsson, Gunilla, Sylvia Larson, Folke Johnsson, and Britt-Inger Saveman. "Patients' Experiences of Illness, Operation and Outcome with Reference to Gastro-oesophageal Reflux Disease." *Journal of Advanced Nursing* 40 (3), July 2002, pp. 307–315.

Petrie, Keith J., John Weinman, Norman Sharpe, and Judith Buckley. "Role of Patients' View of Their Illness in Predicting Return to Work and Functioning after Myocardial Infarction: Longitudinal Study." *British Medical Journal* 312 (7040), May 1996, pp. 1191–1194.

Ramfelt, Ethel, E. Severinsson, and Kim Lutzen. "Attempting to Find Meaning in Illness to Achieve Emotional Coherence: The Experiences of Patients with Colorectal Cancer." *Cancer Nursing* 25 (2), April 2002, 141–149.

Siegel, Joel. *Lessons for Dylan: From Father to Son*. New York: PublicAffairs, 2003.

Smith, Macklin. *Transplant*. Ann Arbor: Shaman Drum Books, 2002.

Sontag, Susan. *Illness as Metaphor* and *AIDS and Its Metaphors*. New York: Picador, 1978, 1989.

Stewart, D. E., F. Wong, S. Duff, C. H. Melancon, and A. M. Cheung. "'What Doesn't Kill You Makes You Stronger': An Ovarian Cancer Survivor Survey." *Gynecologic Oncology* 83 (3), December 2001, pp. 537–542.

Strang, Susan, and Peter Strang. "Spiritual Thoughts, Coping and 'Sense of Coherence' in Brain Tumour Patients and Their Spouses." *Palliative Medicine* 15 (2), March 2001, pp. 127–134.

Taylor, Shelley E. "Adjustment to Threatening Events: A Theory of Cognitive Adaptation." *American Psychologist*, November 1983, 1161–1173.

United States Department of Health and Human Services and the Centers for Disease Control and Prevention. "A Public Health Action Plan to Prevent Heart Disease and Stroke," July 2003.

Welch-McCaffrey, Deborah, Barbara Hoffman, Susan A. Leigh, Lois J. Loescher, and Frank L. Meyskens, Jr. "Surviving Adult Cancers, Part 2: Psychosocial Implications." *Annals of Internal Medicine* 111 (6), September 1989, pp. 517–524.

Wenzel, Lari B., James P. Donnelly, Jeffrey M. Fowler, Rana Habbal, Thomas H. Taylor, Nreen Aziz, and David Cella. "Resilience, Reflection, and Residual Stress in Ovarian Cancer Survivorship: A Gynecologic Oncology Group Study." *Psycho-Oncology* 11(2), March–April 2002, 142–153.

RESURCES

Below is an alphabetical list of diseases and the Web sites for them. It is not nearly complete but instead was created from the suggestions of the interview participants and intended to help those who are newly diagnosed or in treatment.

AUTOIMMUNE DISEASES
www.aarda.org—American Autoimmune Related Diseases Association's Web site has a number of links and information pages for those with autoimmune diseases.

CANCER
General
www.acor.org—The Association for Cancer Online Resources' Web site is a portal to a slew of other Web sites for those with a cancer diagnosis.

www.planetcancer.org—A Web site for a fantastic organization dedicated to serving the needs of young adult cancer patients.

www.gildasclub.org—An international organization that provides education and patient support to those facing a diagnosis of cancer.

www.curetoday.com—A quarterly magazine that focuses on the human and scientific sides of cancer and is written for patients.

www.cancerandcareers.org—A Web site for women facing cancer while also continuing with their careers.

www.cancer.org—The Web site for the American Cancer Society boasts a huge library as well as support and advocacy information.

www.vive4thecure.org—This site sells cancer awareness bracelets with 100 percent of the profits donated to the American Cancer Society.

www.wikicancer.org—A support site for individuals facing a variety of different cancer diagnoses.

www.indiemusicforlife.org—The is a Web site of an organization of musicians that raises money to support music therapy programs for cancer patients.

Bladder Cancer
www.blcwebcafe.org—Bladder Cancer WebCafe's Web site includes information on treatments as well as patient support for those diagnosed with bladder cancer.

Brain Cancer
http://hope.abta.org—The Web site for the American Brain Tumor Association includes educational and support information.

www.braintumor.org—The National Brain Tumor Foundation's Web site includes education and support information for those with either malignant or benign tumors.

www.davidmbailey.com—This is a personal Web site of an individual who survived glioblastoma.

Breast Cancer
www.youngsurvival.org—The Young Survival Coalition's Web site is dedicated to patient support and education as well as advocacy.

www.y-me.org—A national Web site for the Y-ME National Breast Cancer Organization features patient education, support services, and advocacy information.

www.healthcentral.com/breast-cancer/index.html—This is an

education and support Web site for those facing a breast cancer diagnosis.

www.breastcancer.org—This is a patient education and support Web site for those men or women who have been diagnosed with breast cancer.

www.ibcsupport.org—This is an information and support site for those diagnosed with inflammatory breast cancer.

http://health.groups.yahoo.com/group/sistersinsurvivorship—Sisters in Survivorship's online group provides support to those diagnosed with breast cancer.

www.facingourrisk.org—Facing Our Risk of Cancer Empowered (FORCE) is a site for information and support for women with the hereditary genes for breast and ovarian cancers.

www.lbbc.org—This is the Web site for Living Beyond Breast Cancer, a nonprofit organization dedicated to empowering all women affected by breast cancer to live as long as possible with the best quality of life.

www.think_pink.typepad.com—This is a blog by a young woman with breast cancer.

www.therewasnolump.blogspot.com—This is another blog by a woman with breast cancer.

Colorectal Cancer
www.fightcolorectalcancer.org—The Colorectal Cancer Coalition's Web site promotes the fight of the disease through advocacy.

www.uoaa.org—The United Ostomy Association of America's Web site provides patient support and education.

www.semicolonclub.com—An online Web board's address provides patient support to those with a colorectal cancer diagnosis.

www.thecolonclub.org—This group is dedicated to raising awareness of colon cancer, especially in young people, in outside-the-box ways. The site also contains a lot of links to other colon cancer sites.

www.colorectal-cancer.net—This is the patient support, education, and advocacy site for the Colon Cancer Network.

Esophageal Cancer
www.esophagealcancer.org—This is a site for patient support and education for those with the condition.

www.eccafe.org—Cathy's EC Café is a patient support and education Web site for those with esophageal cancer.

www.ecaware.org—Esophageal Cancer Awareness Association's Web site carries information and helpful links.

Leukemia and Lymphoma
www.lls.org—The Leukemia and Lymphoma Society's Web site features an excellent library as well as information about patient support and research.

www.lightthenight.org—This is the Web site for the Leukemia and Lymphoma Society's walks.

www.lymphoma.org—This is a Web site for the Lymphoma Research Foundation, an organization that provides funding for research and patient education.

www.marrow.org—The National Marrow Donor Program's official Web site provides educational information for those facing bone marrow transplants.

www.nbmtlink.org—This is a Web site for the National Bone Marrow Transplant Link, an organization that provides information and support to individuals undergoing such a procedure.

www.geocities.com/billbujake—This is a blog by a man who survived Hodgkin's disease.

www.stewartfrancke.com—This is a Web site and blog by a man who survived chronic myelogenous leukemia with a stem cell transplant.

Melanoma
www.mpip.org—The Melanoma Patients' Information Page is filled with information and links for those diagnosed with this skin cancer.

Ovarian Cancer
www.ovariancancer.jhmi.edu—This full-service Web site through Johns Hopkins Pathology provides information about the disease and its treatments, patient support, clinical trials and more.

www.herafoundation.org—This is a Web site for a grassroots organization that funds ovarian cancer research as well as patient education and support initiatives.

Prostate Cancer
www.theprostatenet.com—This is a patient site for those with prostate cancer.

www.mansgland.com—This is a Web site that attempts to raise public awareness of prostate cancer through the use of humor.

www.pinata.blogspot.com—This is a blog of an individual with prostate cancer.

Testicular Cancer
http://tcrc.acor.org —The Testicular Cancer Resource Center's Web site provides tons of information and support services for those with this diagnosis.

www.tc-cancer.com —Here is another Web site with information and support for those going through a diagnosis of and treatment for testicular cancer.

DIABETES
www.diabetes.org—This is the official Web site for the American Diabetes Association.

www.childrenwithdiabetes.com—This online organization is for patients and families touched by a diabetes diagnosis.

www.diabetestalkfest.com—Linking diabetics coast to coast, this is an online diabetes support group for young adults through adults who have a diabetes diagnosis.

www.diabetesoc.blogspot.com—This is an online listing of blogs with diabetes as a theme or written by individuals with diabetes.

www.diabetesmine.com—This award-winning online diabetes blog contains information and useful links.

www.diabetties.org—A blog and information site, this is run by a young woman with type 1 diabetes.

www.pumplandia.blogspot.com—This is a blog by a young woman who was diagnosed with type 1 diabetes.

HEART DISEASE AND STROKE

www.AmericanHeart.org—This is the official Web site of the American Heart Association, with pages of patient support and education.

www.heart.healthcentersonline.com—Here is an online source for information on common heart ailments.

www.chfpatients.com—This is a fairly comprehensive patient-driven Web site for individuals experiencing congestive heart failure; it is full of information, patient stories, and links.

www.geocities.com/schtgi—The Second Chance Heart Transplant Group's Web site includes information and support for individuals undergoing a heart transplant or surviving after one.

www.healthyheartmarket.com—Here is an online grocery store with hard-to-find products that cater to those on a low-salt diet.

www.bunrab.blogspot.com—A patient with congestive heart failure details her struggles on this blog.

http://blogs.healthcentral.com/heart-disease/deannes-blog—This is a young woman's blog about her experience with stroke.

Hepatitis C
www.janis7hepc.com—This Web site provides support and information for individuals with a hepatitis C diagnosis.

www.statuscunknown.com—This is a Web site for an informational organization that promotes testing and prevention of the hepatitis C virus.

www.mkandrew.com—This is a blog written by a man with hepatitis C.

HIV/AIDS
www.hivzone.com—This site includes a patient's story as well as links to other resources for those living with the conditions

www.scottfried.com—This is a patient's Web site.

Inflammatory Bowel Disease
www.ccfa.org—The Web site for the Crohn's & Colitis Foundation of America has an extensive library of information for those with the diseases, as well as links to local chapters where support group information is available.

www.peternielsen.com—This is a Web site by a patient with Crohn's disease.

Kidney Disease
www.kidney.org—The National Kidney Foundation's Web site features pages of patient information and support as well as updates on research initiatives.

Lupus
www.lupusalliance.org—This is a patient Web site with information

and advocacy information as well as links to other Lupus-related sites.

MULTIPLE SCLEROSIS

www.nationalmssociety.org—This Web site for the national organization provides fund-raising information as well as patient support links and educational pages.

www.msaa.com—The Multiple Sclerosis Association of America's Web site includes an emphasis on research and patient support.

www.msmoms.com—This is a Web site with practical information on living with MS, with a specific focus on women and mothers.

PARKINSON'S DISEASE

www.parkinsonsaction.org—Here is a Parkinson's disease advocacy group's Web site.

www.pdpipeline.org—Parkinson's Disease Pipeline Project's Web site works to help accelerate drug approval for therapies to target the disease.

www.pdf.org—Parkinson's Disease Foundation's Web site contains information on the disease as well as on research projects and patient support.

www.parkinson.org—The National Parkinson Foundation's Web site features information on the disease and its treatments as well as patient support, care, and research.

www.apdaparkinson.org—American Parkinson's Disease Association's Web site raises money for research while providing education and support to patients.

www.youngparkinsons.org—This is a specific group for people with young-onset Parkinson's disease.

www.parkinsonresearchfoundation.org—The Parkinson Research Foundation's Web site contains a very responsive and thorough "Ask the MD" page as well as the latest information on trials and developments in therapies for PD.

www.michaeljfox.org—This is the Web site for the foundation created by the actor and PD sufferer. The goal of the foundation is to accelerate the pace of research for therapies for the disease.

www.pdcreativity.org—Here is a Web site dedicated to the power of art created by those with Parkinson's disease.

PRIMARY BILIARY CIRRHOSIS
www.PBCers.org—This is a Web site catering to patient support and education for those with this condition.

PRIMARY SCLEROSING CHOLANGITIS
www.PSCpartners.org—Here is a Web site for the PSC Partners Seeking a Cure Foundation, an organization dedicated to patient education and to funding research.

SARCOIDOSIS
www.sarcoidosiscirclefriends.org—This is an organization promoting education and patient support for those with sarcoidosis.

GENERAL
www.ada.gov—This is the official Web site for the Americans with Disabilities Act of 1990.

www.jan.wvu.edu/portals/individuals.htm—This Web site is a service of the Job Accommodation Network and provides tons of information on accommodating those with disabilities in the workplace.

www.patientadvocate.org—This is a site for the Patient Advocate Foundation, with wonderful amount of information on just about all of the areas of patient care.

www.friendsindeed.org—Here is a Web site for a New York organization that provides crisis support to those facing a life-threatening physical illness. The organization runs support groups, workshops, seminars, and bodywork classes.

www.healthtalk.com—Here is an informational site for a variety of conditions.

www.4woman.gov/wwd—This is a government Web site for women with disabilities.

www.transplantsuccess.org—This is a Web site dedicated to sharing stories of those who have gone through organ transplantation.

www.organdonor.gov—This is a government site that provides information about organ donation.

www.freewebs.com/adtas—The Alliance for Donation, Transplantation, Awareness and Support's Web site is for those facing transplantation contains information on patient support and advocacy.

www.shareyourlife.org—This is a Web site promoting organ donation.

www.roadback.org —The Road Back Foundation's Web site is dedicated to information about antibiotic therapy for rheumatic diseases.

ACKNOWLEDGMENTS

THIS BOOK TOOK nearly three years to put together, and I had a lot of help along the way. For this, I owe a great deal of thanks.

To start, my publisher, Matthew Lore, was extremely supportive of the concept of the book from the first time I mentioned the idea in a passing conversation about four years ago. Without his persistent interest and help in moving the research and writing along, this wouldn't be in your hands. My agent, Janis Donnaud, was also extremely instrumental, gently prodding me to "just write already" and then helping me to hone the proposal. I couldn't have hoped for a better advocate. To both of them, I owe much thanks. Courtney Napoles, an editorial assistant with Marlowe & Company, was very helpful in keeping me on task. I appreciate her help as well.

There are 102 people for whom I feel an intense amount of gratitude: the interview participants. Some of them I knew, some of them were referred to me by friends and relatives, and some of them were total strangers I met on the Internet. Whichever way they came into my life, they trusted with me their stories, shared with me their struggles, and celebrated with me their triumphs. I will always be grateful for their unselfish contributions. These individuals include the following: Dan Shapiro, PhD; Robin Taviner; James Lang; Didi Wainess; Ernest Rogers; Peter Nielsen; Patricia O'Hara (with Janice Tedd); Heidi Adams; Macklin Smith; Linda McPherson; Beverly Price; William Hawley, MD; Deb Kirkland; Gina Capone; Violet; Marianne Szeto; September Sucher; Alicia Merchant; Sharon Stansvold; Graham Barton; Dave Wallace; Sherrell Gay; Bobby David Bailey; Jane Catlett Pickett; Cary Johnson; Andrew Schorr; Bill Bujake; Jo Anna Elizabeth Larson; Kim Garretson; Patricia Pavin; Colin Pollard; Jeannette Vagnozzi; Louise Bates; Marc Wolfgram; Leonard Bertin; Kate Murphy; Nancy Arnt; Anne Stamm; Molly McMaster; Ricky; Beth Klein Genetti; Lorna Moorhead; Michele M.; Jeff Brown; Dick Harbourt; Tonda Kuznik; Lynda Wolfe; Peggy Willocks; Shirley Malamud; Elissa D. Giffords, PhD; Jim K. Hale; Debbie Sobel; Georgia McNamara; Chuck Rossier; R. Kelly Wagner; Mark T.; Jennifer Davis; Shelley R. Henderson; Sonja F.; Tony Gardner; Virgil Simons; Mary Paul; Steve Preston; Deanne Stein; Liane R. Curtis, Amy Stockinger; Ann; Wendy Sheridan; Maureen I. Wallace; John F. Mitas Jr.; Jerry Lane; Ellen Cogen; the late Mary Lou Krauseneck (with her sister, Bernie Cooper); Nelda Schultz; Scott Fried; Linie Moore; Amy Tenderich; Dana Portwood; Vicki Blankenship; Ruth Thompson; Patricia VanReenen; Pat Hauldren; Neil Rudin; Brenda Harris; Ben Timmons; Sean Patrick; Emily Gibbs; Miles Keaton; Andrew; Beth Finn; James (Jim) Hagar; John Kanters; Kathy LaTour; Jen Wandy; Sandra Fusco; Marilyn Sperka; Tom Cross; Eliza Livingston; Brenda Tucker; Betty Kanavel; and Liberty Skrypeck. Stewart Francke was also among the interviewees but deserves a special mention of thanks for his help in editing, his willingness to act as a professional sounding board, and his constant encouragement. You are a true friend.

Some noted researchers and professionals in the field of survivorship also gave unselfishly of their time and deserve thanks. These individuals—Dr. Fitzhugh Mullan, Dr. Betty Ferrell, Dr. Pam McGrath, and Dr. Karen Dow Meneses—all took time out of their busy lives to sit for interviews. I was awestruck by the work they had done in the past and so grateful to have them participate in interviews for this work. A million thanks to each of them.

Dr. Diane Blau, a noted professor of psychology, was instrumental in guiding my research methods and constantly encouraging my efforts. Colleen Donley pitched in at a crucial time in the creation of the manuscript with her transcription services. She was a lifesaver.

For personal support, I can always count on my mentor, Doron Levin. He has been a caring, guiding force since the beginning, and I truly thank him for taking me under his wing. My friends also have been wonderful in their willingness and ability to distract me. These include the members of my girls' night out group, the people at the Crohn's & Colitis Foundation of America, and my neighbors. I am afraid of leaving any of you out, so let's just say you know who you are.

Last but by no measure least, there are the people who supported me on a daily basis. My husband, Joel, and my son, Jonah, were fantastic, providing constant nurturing, love, and encouragement, while taking my sporadic but admittedly grouchy behavior in stride and with good spirits. I couldn't exist without you two. Jonah, I also want to thank you for sleeping in until the crack of noon every day during the summer when I wrote this. I know it was a true sacrifice for you, somehow. My mother, Kathryn Davidson, deserves a medal for everything she has gone through for me with regard to this damn illness. No parent should ever have to watch their child suffer, but she did, and with incredible love and grace. Thanks, Mom. I also want to express my appreciation and love for the rest of my family, including Greg and Megan; Marie and Jeff; Michelle and Glen; Paul and Nancy; Patrice, Eric; and Amy; Harriet and Manny; Susan and Marty; Melissa; David and Julie; and my nineteen nieces and nephews. I am a lucky woman.

ABOUT THE AUTHOR

JILL SKLAR is an award-winning writer who specializes in medical writing. Her articles, on subjects ranging from heart transplantation to digestive diseases, have appeared in the *New York Times, Style Magazine, Digestive Health & Nutrition Magazine*, and other newspapers and magazines. She is a board member of the Michigan chapter of the Crohn's and Colitis Foundation of America. A patient-expert on www.RevolutionHealth.com, she is the author of *The First Year(r)-Crohn's Disease and Ulcerative Colitis* and coauthor of *Eating for Acid Reflux* (with Annabel Cohen). Sklar lives in Huntington Woods, Michigan, with her husband and son.